Doing Research to Improve Teaching and Learning

Given the increased accountability at the college and university level, one of the most promising ways for faculty at institutions of higher education to improve their teaching is to capitalize upon their skills as researchers. This book is a step-by-step guide for doing research to inform and improve teaching and learning. With background and instruction about how to engage in these methodologies — including qualitative, quantitative, and mixed methods — *Doing Research to Improve Teaching and Learning* provides examples across disciplines of how to use one's research skills to improve teaching. This valuable resource equips faculty with the skills to collect and use different types of research evidence to improve teaching and learning in any college and university classroom.

Special Features:

- Chapter openers highlight the questions and issues that will be addressed in each chapter.
- Recurring text boxes provide authentic examples from actual research studies, student work, and instructor reflections.
- Coverage of challenges, key successes, and lessons learned from classroom research presents a nuanced and complete understanding of the process.

Kimberly M. Williams is a Teaching Support Specialist in the Center for Teaching Excellence at Cornell University. She is also part-time on the graduate faculty at Plymouth State University and an Independent Educational Consultant.

Doing Research to Improve Teaching and Learning

A Guide for College and University Faculty

Kimberly M. Williams

Routledge
Taylor & Francis Group

NEW YORK AND LONDON

First published 2015
by Routledge
711 Third Avenue, New York, NY 10017

and by Routledge
2 Park Square, Milton Park, Abingdon, Oxon, OX14 4RN

Routledge is an imprint of the Taylor & Francis Group, an informa business

Library of Congress Cataloging in Publication Data
Williams, Kimberly M., 1968–
    Doing research to improve teaching and learning: a guide for college
    and university faculty/Kimberly M. Williams.
    pages cm
    Includes bibliographical references and index.
    1. Education, Higher—Research. 2. College teaching. I. Title.
    LB2326.3.W55 2014
    378.1'25—dc23
    2014017101

ISBN: 978-1-138-02090-0 (hbk)
ISBN: 978-1-138-02091-7 (pbk)
ISBN: 978-1-315-77814-3 (ebk)

Typeset in Perpetua and Bell Gothic
by Florence Production Ltd, Stoodleigh, Devon, UK

To my loving and supportive family and my wonderful students, colleagues and contributors to this book.

Contents

Preface

Improving teaching and student learning in higher education is becoming an increasingly popular and pressing topic as many of our nation's top colleges and universities are investing in centers and experts designed to improve teaching and learning. A growing number of colleges and universities have some kind of "Center for Teaching and Learning" or "Center for Innovative Teaching" (they come under a variety of names typically with "teaching" and/or "learning" in the title). These centers often run workshops and work with faculty to improve their teaching and student learning in their classrooms. One concern I have heard faculty consistently raise is that they feel as though those working in these centers are often imposing their own ideas about best practice upon them and that these strategies sometimes do not feel authentic or fit the particular needs of their classrooms, students, and personal style. I do not mean to suggest that every person working at every such center works this way, but we certainly want to avoid this perception. For innovative practice to catch on, it needs to feel authentic, grounded in a faculty member's strengths and individual styles, and work within particular disciplines.

One of the most promising ways to accomplish these lofty goals is to provide faculty members with specific skills that allow them to capitalize upon their skills as researchers to inform and improve their teaching. This book will give a step-by-step "how to" guide to using research (including qualitative and quantitative methodology, mixed methods, inclusion of students voices and student work) to inform and improve teaching and learning in the college and university classroom. With background and instruction about how to engage in these methodologies, this book will also provide examples of these strategies employed within a variety of academic disciplines in the humanities, and the social and natural sciences—providing actual examples of how to use one's research skills to improve one's teaching skills—discussing the challenges as well as the successes and lessons learned.

Those interested in designing training workshops for teaching assistants and faculty, as well as professors teaching college and university courses such as the one I currently teach called "Teaching as Research in Higher Education," can use this book to help faculty and graduate teaching assistants (future faculty) learn from the examples in this book. This book will blend some background theory, concrete steps and strategies with actual concrete examples from a variety of disciplines. The goal is to equip faculty with the skills to collect and use different types of research evidence to improve teaching and learning in all college and university classrooms.

THE STRUCTURE OF THIS BOOK

This book takes the reader on the same journey that I take my doctoral students in a course I designed and teach called "Teaching as Research in Higher Education." This book is set up to provide a variety of different examples of teaching as research projects from the university and college settings. In these chapters, college and university teachers describe their teaching as research projects that are located within a variety of disciplines, in humanities, physical, natural and social sciences. Within each chapter are examples taken from actual studies performed in college and university classrooms as a special feature entitled "Examples of Research from the Classroom." We start in Chapter 1 with a brief roadmap/overview of the history of classroom research in higher education and the Scholarship of Teaching and Learning, and the notion of "teaching as research."

In Chapter 2, general considerations of how to do "teaching as research"—the possibilities and limitations—are explored. In this chapter, we discuss human participants (the students in our classes), concerns about bias and objectivity/subjectivity and methodological philosophies that may be in conflict. We discuss how to design the study by determining your objectives/outcomes for the project—that is, what do you want to know? We also discuss the importance of considering issues of diversity and diverse perspectives and how to be as inclusive as possible in the process.

Chapter 3 focuses on qualitative research methods in teaching as research—what these specific methods are and how we can use them in teaching as research. Several examples of projects that have employed these methods are provided, including a blogging project introduced in an upper-level Italian class, a first year writing seminar on controversial topics, a class on medieval books in the digital age and ways to reconnect students to ancient texts, and a project examining the impact of a particular teaching technique on a bio-engineering class.

Chapter 4 examines quantitative methodology in teaching as research—what are these methods and how can we use them in teaching as research? There are several examples of projects that have employed these methods including students' perceptions of efficacy in their first year and writing in the majors course; motivation and outcomes of an auto-tutorial course in bio-chemistry when compared to a traditional lecture course; voluntary help sessions in a genetics course; and the views of students on "close reading" in an English course.

Chapter 5 discusses the importance of using classroom assessments as data (exams, papers, student homework, etc.) in a formative way (getting feedback along the way in the project) and in a summative way (getting final feedback about learning and performance of students). I will provide a variety of examples from my course teaching doctoral students in both a classroom setting and a more informal workshop setting. The processes of analyzing one's own comments on student work, designing and using rubrics and traditional texts will be examined.

Chapter 6 examines combining both qualitative and quantitative in a mixed method design. We discuss what these are and how we can use them in teaching as research. Examples of projects that have employed these methods range from an anthropology first year writing course on privilege and positionality to a surgical course for veterinarians, field testing an assessment tool to examine surgical skill development.

Chapter 7 discusses the case study approach, in which the researcher delves deeply within a particular context to better understand it. Small pilot studies are also discussed, as are the advantages of starting small and trying out methodologies and pedagogies. Examples are provided including one from an astronomer examining critical thinking among a small group of students in a voluntary support group, and a music theory class using composition and improvisation, and an experience teaching at a maximum security prison.

Chapter 8 discusses the importance of reflective practice in research on one's teaching and how working collaboratively in reflective research in teaching groups shows promise throughout and at the end of the process. Collaboration also offers the opportunity to bring in outside help when possible to observe and collect data (including graduate student assistants and undergraduate student assistants). Allowing students to take a seminal role in the process of conducing research on teaching and learning can be very fruitful in engaging the next generation of faculty (graduate student teaching assistants) in all aspects of the learning process.

Finally, the book will examine the importance of closing the loop—the critical step of using the evidence to inform and improve teaching and learning, continuing the research, sharing research with others and giving back through critique and support. It is this step that often differentiates teaching as research from teaching without research. The research process is about dissemination and informing practice. This step is crucial.

The main lessons learned from the teaching as research projects are discussed, as are the implications for practice with a special focus on colleges and universities. Teaching as research holds great promise in transforming institutions of higher education into spaces where excellent, purposeful teaching and learning happens. Using research to inform and improve teaching allows us to leverage the research skills of the talented researchers that abound in colleges and universities, and purposefully leveraging these skills can have great power to improve teaching and learning for both teachers and students.

Acknowledgments

I would like to thank the generous support from the Teagle Foundation that provided the grant funding that made most of the research studies presented in this book possible. In addition I would like to thank my colleagues in the Center for Teaching Excellence at Cornell University for their support and ongoing work to improve teaching and learning. I would also like to thank each one of my contributors (students and colleagues past and present): Joel Anderson, Adem Birson, Kevin Carrico, Shoshanna Cole, Adhaar Noor Desai, Lorenzo Fabbri, Carolyn Fisher, John Foo, Diana Garvin, Inga Gruß, Jared Hale, Khuram Hussain, Emily Pollina, Baidura Ray, Luisa Rosas, Jennifer Row, and Lauren Schnabel. And thank you to the journal of *Veterinary Surgery* for allowing us to reprint Dr. Schnabel's article here as an excellent example of a classroom research project: "Use of a Formal Assessment Instrument for Evaluation of Veterinary Student Surgical Skills."

Chapter 1

What are "Teaching as Research" and the "Scholarship of Teaching and Learning" and Why Should Everyone in Higher Education Care?

In this chapter:

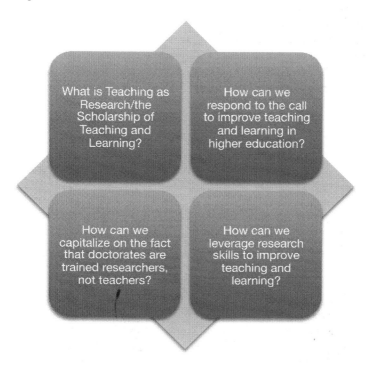

What is Teaching as Research/the Scholarship of Teaching and Learning?

How can we respond to the call to improve teaching and learning in higher education?

How can we capitalize on the fact that doctorates are trained researchers, not teachers?

How can we leverage research skills to improve teaching and learning?

As costs of college and university attendance continue to skyrocket, calls for accountability of student learning have grown louder. Even without outside calls for accountability, as a professor for over two decades at a variety of institutions ranging from my start teaching at a two-year agriculture and technological state institution to a couple of different institutions in the Ivy League, I, like most of my faculty colleagues *want our students to learn what we believe is important enough to be teaching them*. We *want* them to engage with the material in meaningful ways— we *want* them to think critically about it. We *want* to know that learning is taking place, and that what we do as faculty in the classroom matters and makes a difference. We *want* to be good teachers in the classroom. Even beyond the walls of our classrooms and the ever-growing classrooms without walls, such as online courses and Massive Open Online Courses (MOOCs), the best way to improve our society is to build the knowledge-base and critical thinking skills of ourselves and our next generation of the world's citizens. We hope that future generations continue to build upon existing knowledge to make the world a better place. Higher education strives to contribute to the generation of new knowledge. To do so, we must pass along existing knowledge through teaching to the future generations.

BUT HOW DO WE KNOW IF WE ARE EFFECTIVELY ACCOMPLISHING THESE LOFTY GOALS?

We have assessments (papers, exams, reports, etc.). We have final course evaluations that our students complete about our performance. Sometimes we have colleagues observe our teaching. But how do we know if our students are learning anything, or if they are retaining it, or how they are being changed as a result of their time with us? And how can we continue to improve our own practice of the art and science of teaching?

The answers to many of these questions are addressed in this book and involve using what we as faculty know best—research. We can draw upon our skills as researchers and knowledge producers to ask questions about our teaching and student learning. We can systematically collect data. We can analyze data and share it. We can use data to inform new ideas we have about teaching and learning and continue the cycle again. As faculty members, we think like researchers. We received our academic credentials based on our ability to do research— whether we conducted research in the humanities, social or natural sciences— we must demonstrate research skills (or at least the ability to generate new ideas and knowledge) to receive the doctorate.

The use of research to inform teaching seems so elegant in its simplicity, and yet can be so difficult in actual practice without some basic assistance. We have so many students and so little time. We have so much content to cover, and we have so many committees and, of course, our commitment to our own disciplinary research. How can we possibly have time for this additional research that will not necessarily help us in obvious ways toward promotion or tenure? The truth is that by improving teaching, you improve your odds of promotion and tenure. It is possible to do this kind of research within the context of work you are already doing. This book will give you ideas and practical examples to guide you through the process that will make the task manageable as you juggle the many demands of academe.

WHAT IS TEACHING AS RESEARCH AND THE SCHOLARSHIP OF TEACHING AND LEARNING?

Classroom research in higher education settings is not a new idea—it has been around for decades. In fact, the Carnegie Foundation started an initiative in 1998 called the Carnegie Academy for the Scholarship of Teaching and Learning (CASTL) that was based on the scholarly report published in 1990 called *Scholarship Reconsidered* by Ernest Boyer, calling for the use of research to inform and improve teaching in the college and university classroom. More recently, Pat Hutchings, Mary Taylor Huber and Anthony Ciccone have published a book called *The Scholarship of Teaching and Learning Reconsidered: Institutional Integration and Impact* (Jossey-Bass, 2011). And a consortium of several universities nationwide has been working collaboratively under the name of Center for the Integration of Research, Teaching and Learning (CIRTL), funded by the National Science Foundation. The movement is gaining momentum as students, parents, taxpayers, and faculty themselves are clamoring for ways to improve learning in the college classroom.

What exactly do we mean by "Teaching as Research" and "Scholarship of Teaching and Learning?" These terms have become quite popular in higher education. What do they mean exactly? For the past couple of decades, this field of inquiry has been known as "the Scholarship of Teaching and Learning." The notion of "teacher-action research" (a phrase more associated with teacher-conducted classroom research in k-12 education) has been around for decades, as has "the Scholarship of Teaching and Learning." In "teacher-action research" and "teaching as research" the teacher uses research to inform his or her own classroom teaching and student learning in systematic ways. Using qualitative research methods (e.g., interviews, journals, observation, open-ended surveys), quantitative research methods (e.g., numeric surveys, pre and post-tests, control/comparison groups, etc.) and assessment strategies (e.g., formative and summative assessment of student learning) teachers collect data about their own classrooms, as researchers collect data, to inform and improve their teaching and ultimately student learning. The notion is that good research will result in good teaching. The Scholarship of Teaching and Learning (SoTL) typically encompasses teacher-action research and teaching as research, but is broader and beyond just the teacher or professor doing

3

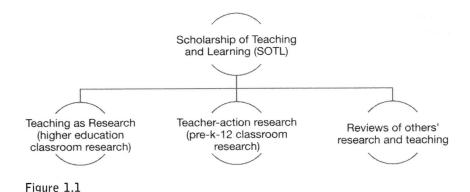

Figure 1.1

research on his or her own classrooms, and includes the whole scholarship of the enterprise of research on teaching and learning—not focused as specifically on one's own classroom research.

Truth is, good teachers use research (or variations of it) to inform their teaching every day, sometimes without knowing it. They are constantly reviewing assessment data, making critical observations of their students and themselves, and collecting qualitative and quantitative data. *Teaching as research* formalizes the process—that is, makes data collection and analysis more purposeful and grounded in specific learning outcomes for students. In addition, it considers deeply the existing research on teaching, as well as considering how their work may contribute to the improvement of teaching in general and in one's own discipline.

Higher education is perfectly positioned to make this shift to a culture of teaching as research and embracing the Scholarship of Teaching and Learning because research is such a major part of the responsibility of the faculty member, and as part of their intellectual preparation for academic work, faculty members have been prepared in research skills. One challenge, however, is that faculty have been trained in discipline-specific research strategies and rarely have been explicitly taught pedagogical/teaching strategies or research strategies outside of the ones they use regularly. Making the leap between a faculty member's discipline-specific research skills and research strategies (ways of producing new knowledge) that can be used to inform and improve teaching is not quite as much of a stretch as one might think, but it does require some background knowledge and effort.

Bridging this gap is the primary goal of this book. In short, this book seeks to provide examples of college and university faculty who have taken their skills from their research worlds, expanded them and learned new strategies outside of their discipline-specific strengths, and applied the tools of research to their teaching to inform and improve learning in their classrooms by using "teaching as research" as a model.

WHAT IS THE "SCHOLARSHIP OF TEACHING AND LEARNING?"

In their article written for the Carnegie Foundation for the Advancement of Teaching, Mary Taylor Huber and Sherwyn Morreale wrote of the Scholarship of Teaching and Learning:

> The Scholarship of Teaching and Learning in higher education currently belongs to no single national association and has no unique campus address. As befits a vigorous, emergent area of intellectual discourse and debate, the Scholarship of Teaching and Learning is springing up in established departments, programs, and centers, and developing new forums and outlets of its own. Yesterday, in every discipline, you could find small cadres of faculty who made education in that field their subject of research. Today, inquiry into college teaching is more than just a specialist's concern. Across the academy, "regular" faculty members are taking systematic interest in curriculum, classroom teaching, and the quality of student learning. Professors in disciplines from anthropology to zoology are beginning to consult pedagogical literature, look critically at education in their field, inquire into teaching and learning in their own classroom, and use what they are discovering to improve their teaching practice. In addition, many are making this work public so that it can be critiqued and built upon.
>
> (Huber and Morreale 2002, para. 1)

This Scholarship of Teaching and Learning is not limited to those in education fields, but includes all of us within the education profession—any faculty member who is dedicated to teaching and learning and uses research systematically to analyze and improve these.

These authors offer a succinct yet purposefully vague definition of the Scholarship of Teaching and Learning that considers the past few decades of work on the topic:

> While it may be unnecessary to attempt too precise a definition for the Scholarship of Teaching and Learning . . ., its distinctive character, for most of our authors, lies in its invitation to mainstream faculty (as well as specialists) to treat teaching as a form of inquiry into student learning, to share results of that inquiry with colleagues, and to critique and build on one anothers' work.
>
> (para. 40).

Keeping the definition broad helps allow all disciplines to engage in the process. The notion that we basically "treat teaching as a form of inquiry into student learning" is the main idea, followed by the sharing of the results and an opportunity to critique and build upon others' work. The Carnegie Foundation has supported the Scholarship of Teaching and Learning for decades and promoted the sharing of materials and opportunities for critique. This organization has promoted this notion for decades, encouraging faculty to engage in the practice.

WHAT IS "TEACHING AS RESEARCH?"

Similarly, and perhaps more specifically, "Teaching as Research" tends to focus more on individual classroom teaching and learning and research within it. For decades, different organizations have come on board, seeing the value of using research to improve teaching and learning. Recently, a consortium of over twenty US institutions have worked together to create a center called the Center for the Integration of Research, Teaching and Learning (CIRTL). This organization uses the term "Teaching as Research" taking the Scholarship of Teaching and Learning perhaps a step farther to argue that, in fact, good teaching is research. According to CIRTL (2005), "Teaching-as-Research involves the deliberate, systematic, and reflective use of research methods to develop and implement teaching practices that advance the learning experiences and outcomes of students and teachers. Participants in Teaching-as-Research apply a variety of research approaches to their teaching practice." They outline the following steps as important in the teaching-as-research process:

1   Learning foundational knowledge. (What is known about the teaching practice? What research has been conducted?)
2   Creating objectives for student learning. (What do we want students to learn?)
3   Developing hypotheses and objectives for practices to achieve the learning objectives. (How can we help students succeed with the learning objectives? What do we observe throughout the process? What are some of the research-based best practices? What does this mean?)
4   Defining measures of success. (What qualitative and quantitative evidence will we need to determine whether students have achieved learning objectives?)
5   Developing and implementing teaching practices within a research design. (What will we do in and out of the classroom to enable students to achieve learning objectives?)
6   Collecting and analyzing data. (How will we collect and analyze information to determine what students have learned? How generalizable is our evidence?)

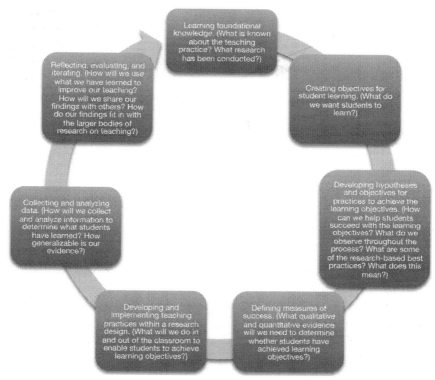

Figure 1.2

7   Reflecting, evaluating, and iterating. (How will we use what we have learned to improve our teaching? How will we share our findings with others? How do our findings fit in with the larger bodies of research on teaching?)

(Adapted from CIRTL 2005)

A shift is happening in higher education toward improved student learning and accountability. To improve student learning, we need improved teaching. College and university professors are skilled researchers. We are trained in research skills in our doctoral programs. We think like researchers. We have knowledge of research methodology within our academic disciplines. Will this alone be sufficient to do teaching as research well? Perhaps. However, learning new strategies *outside* of our academic discipline and merging them with our own research strengths can considerably improve the results we can have engaging in teaching as research.

Some of the philosophical underpinnings of these research methodologies may seem to be in conflict, but I believe these are easily reconciled within the context of improving teaching and learning. However, one must be willing to examine one's own biases, as will be discussed in the next chapter.

Chapter 2

Doing Classroom Research in Higher Education— The Possibilities and Limitations

In this chapter:

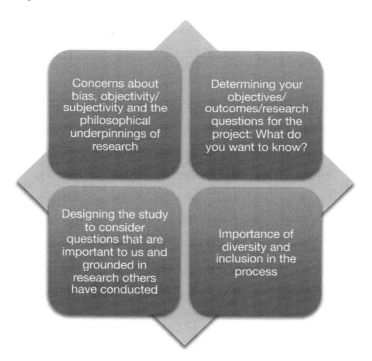

Concerns about bias, objectivity/subjectivity and the philosophical underpinnings of research

Determining your objectives/outcomes/research questions for the project: What do you want to know?

Designing the study to consider questions that are important to us and grounded in research others have conducted

Importance of diversity and inclusion in the process

BELIEFS ABOUT RESEARCH: CONCERNS ABOUT BIAS AND OBJECTIVITY/SUBJECTIVITY

I choose to tackle this topic head on and first. It is perhaps one of the most philosophically challenging topics that researchers face when trying to bridge the divide between qualitative and quantitative research, and how knowledge is considered, examined and created within the different disciplines of the humanities, social sciences and natural sciences.

Both qualitative and quantitative research strategies have much to offer classroom research, but the biases we have about different research paradigms can affect the ways we think about, consider, collect and examine data, so we need to be aware of our beliefs. The philosophical underpinnings of qualitative versus quantitative methodologies influence the ways we think about, approach, defend, conduct, and share our research with others. Our beliefs about research are important to unearth early in the classroom research process.

Maykut and Morehouse (2002) explore the philosophical underpinnings of qualitative versus quantitative research. I will borrow a few select, but important quotes in an attempt to summarize their thorough analysis: "Qualitative research is based on a phenomenological position, while quantitative research is based on a positivist position" (p. 3). They go on to define their terms. Positivism

> has come to mean objective inquiry based on measurable variables and provable propositions. The positivist research orientation holds that science is or should be primarily concerned with the explanation and prediction of observable events. It is the insistence on explanation, prediction and proof that are the hallmarks of positivism.
>
> (p. 4)

Researchers in the natural and some social sciences who tend to focus on these hallmarks also tend to approach research from a positivist perspective. This perspective can be useful in classroom research, as well as when we are concerned with "explanation, prediction, and proof." But we are not always concerned with these in classroom research.

Maykut and Morehouse contrast this positivist view with the phenomenological approach that tends to undergird qualitative research. Included under their "umbrella" of phenomenology are the following: ethnomethodology, symbolic interactionism, hermeneutic inquiry, grounded theory, naturalist inquiry, and ethnography. They summarize the position of phenomenology as seeing "the individual and his or her world as co-constituted. In the truest sense, the person is viewed as having no existence apart from the world, and the world as having no existence apart from the person" (p. 4). Those in humanities and some of the social sciences (particularly anthropology and sociology) have tended to consider research and knowledge production from a phenomenological perspective.

Qualitative researchers typically focus on looking for themes and examining the perspectives of those involved in a particular situation under investigation (in this case, the classroom), closely examining text and text-based evidence (non-

10

numeric) to critically examine meaning to better understand context. They tend not to be searching for a universal truth or generalizable claims.

Quantitative researchers typically focus on hypothesis testing and trying to see if their hypothesis is supported or not. They tend to want to make generalizable claims and seek to be able to "prove" or "predict" behavior. In my experience doing classroom research and working with groups from a variety of disciplines, I have found that this particular issue ends up causing quite a bit of concern and frustration if not directly addressed.

This is an overly simplistic view of the divide between the philosophies of researchers in the natural and social sciences and humanities. Eloquently summed up by Jacob Bronowski in his famous 1973 book *The Ascent of Man*, he wrote: "man is unique not because he does science, and he is unique not because he does art, but because science and art equally are expressions of his marvelous plasticity of mind." I would argue that we can examine phenomenon from a variety of perspectives and philosophical frameworks because of our "plasticity of mind." We can reconcile these different beliefs that underlie qualitative and quantitative methodology. As Lattuca wrote in 2001,

it is no longer safe to assume that faculty within particular disciplines share areas of interest, methods, or even epistemological perspectives . . . the qualitative-quantitative cross currents in the social sciences and the increased use of poststructuralist theories in the humanities and social sciences are two obvious examples of how differences in perspectives can disrupt disciplinary relations.

(p. 3)

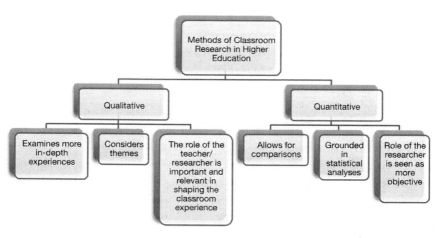

Figure 2.1

Philosophical alignment based on discipline is no longer as cut and dried as it used to be, so we need to consider our own beliefs about teaching and research and how these influence our decisions. For the purposes of your own project, consider your own philosophical beliefs about knowledge, evidence, research, and teaching.

Why does all of this matter for classroom research? The philosophical beliefs that we have about research and teaching influence what we choose to do for our research and what we want to say about our research in fundamental ways. These beliefs affect the ways we think about the nature of evidence and what counts as real evidence; what we think the role of research is; and what we believe the relationship between the participants and the researcher is/can/should be. It can even influence our fundamental beliefs about how we know what we know (how knowledge is constructed) and how we make sense of reality. These beliefs are fundamental and important to examine before engaging in the process of classroom research.

If you have been brought up in a discipline that focuses on objectivity and keeping the researcher as distant from the data and findings as possible (through blind or double-blind trials, for example), then you may have a more difficult time accepting that, within classroom research, the role of the researcher can be quite subjective and even biased. The teacher and researcher are one. We have our own sets of biases when we enter the classroom—not only about our students and their abilities and our expectations, but also of ourselves. We have biases about research and what "true research" is. We have biases about content. We have biases about biases. The bottom line is, in teaching as research, we need to start to identify and recognize the biases we have that affect our teaching and may affect our ability to do research on our teaching. This is not to suggest that we can eliminate our biases, but we may be able to think about how these biases impact our teaching and possibly student learning and our approach to research. We need to acknowledge our fundamental beliefs and consider how they influence what we do in the classroom.

One of the first things I have doctoral students and teaching assistants do when teaching classroom research is to write a short piece called "how I came to this research" or "what brought me to this research." In this piece I ask them to consider their past experiences and thoughts about teaching and learning in the college classroom. What beliefs do they have about themselves and their students? What do they find interesting or baffling or confusing? What are their fundamental beliefs about research? If they have a research question in mind, I ask them consider how they arrived at that question—what experiences led them to develop this question—that is, why is it particularly compelling to them. We need to think about this as we start this journey to gather research evidence to improve our teaching.

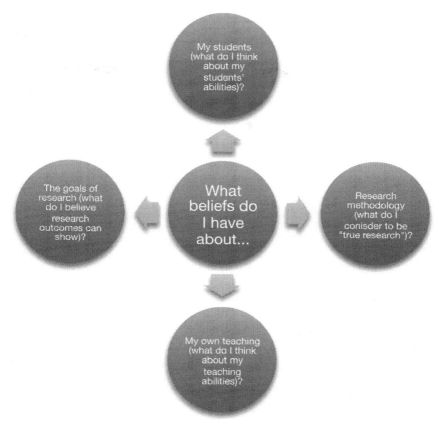

Figure 2.2

BELIEFS ABOUT TEACHING

As we start this journey to conduct research on our classrooms, we must also consider what our fundamental beliefs are about teaching. We may also consider questions such as "what teaching practices might I consider implementing that might improve teaching and learning in my classroom?" As we engage in research to inform and improve our teaching, we may wish to alter some of our teaching practices and use research to determine how effective these changes are. But how do we know what teaching/learning/classroom/educational strategies are likely to yield the most positive impact?

WHAT MIGHT BE CHANGED TO MAKE TEACHING MORE EFFECTIVE: HIGH IMPACT TEACHING PRACTICES IN HIGHER EDUCATION

A question arises as we consider doing research to inform and improve our teaching—"What strategies might I consider using that will help improve teaching and learning in my classroom?" This is an age-old question. What are some of the strategies that have already been supported in the research literature that suggest that their use will improve teaching and learning in various higher education settings?

In an attempt to answer this question, the Association of American Colleges and Universities (AAC&U) has collected evidence from a variety of sources. One such source is George Kuh's (2008) review of the literature entitled *High-Impact Educational Practices: What they are, who has access to them, and why they matter*. Kuh identifies the following strategies that have been shown consistently in the research to have a positive impact on student learning, including their personal and practical gains. Kuh lists these strategies with compelling evidence to support their use:

- First-year seminars and experiences
- Common intellectual experiences
- Learning communities
- Writing-intensive courses
- Collaborative assignments and projects
- Undergraduate research
- Diversity/global learning
- Service learning/community-based learning
- Internships
- Capstone courses and projects.

Not all of these particular programs give specific strategies that may be useful at the classroom level. But some do. The notion of common intellectual experiences is one that we often employ in the college and university classroom. We also have writing-intensive courses (and can employ more writing-intensive opportunities within our classrooms). We can work to create learning communities within the classroom through the use of collaborative assignments, group work in class and out and projects. Students can engage in research and service learning as part of the classroom experience. Classrooms can be made to be more embracing of diversity of learners and the global climate from which our students come. We can allow students more opportunities for internships and other engagement outside of our classrooms that are supported within the classrooms. And finally, we can work to create culminating learning experiences that are capstone courses within a curriculum, and culminating projects at the end of the semester.

Examining the work of Robert Marzano and his colleagues in *Classroom Instruction that Works*, based on his meta-analysis of decades of classroom research, he identified nine broad categories of classroom strategies that have a "high yield" or "high probability of enhancing student achievement" (Marzano *et al.* 2001, p. 31). Marzano's famous "nine" are listed below:

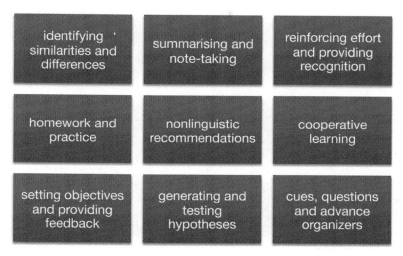

Figure 2.3

However, embedded within each of these nine broad categories are a myriad of possible teaching strategies that may be considered. Marzano also has "a comprehensive list of strategies that relate to effective teaching" that is too detailed for inclusion here, but for more information and a copy of the chart detailing these strategies see Marzano (2009). These specific strategies include such examples as "reflecting on learning (e.g., the teacher asks students to reflect on what they understand or what they are still confused about)" and "elaborating on new information (e.g., the teacher asks questions that require students to make and defend inferences)."

The following questions are important to consider when working to improve your teaching. As you work to address each of these questions, you can then design research to determine their relative effectiveness. Consider the following as you design instruction and research on your instruction:

1. *What are my educational/instructional outcomes/objectives I hope my students will get out of this course?* The answer depends on your course description, content that is essential, and how the course fits in with the rest of the curriculum.

2. *How will I know if students have met the outcomes/objectives I have set forth?* The answer generally is through designing good assessment strategies that are aligned with your outcomes/objectives.

3. *How can I create a positive classroom learning community/environment where all students feel respected and engaged?* The answer depends on the nature of your class—larger classes can create community through engaged, active learners and so can smaller classes, but the logistics of structuring active learning opportunities may be a little different in larger groups. In addition, consider how you as a professor engage with difference in the classroom (aspects of your own identity as well as your students).

4. *How do I get every student engaged in the classroom?* Students vary in their motivation, interest, experience, confidence, and on an endless list of important traits. It is possible to engage all learners. One possible way is through strategies like the "think-pair-share" in which students pair up and discuss problems/questions/issues and then report back to the larger group. It may not be possible to have everyone report, but "random cold calling" (choosing students to respond based on randomly choosing names) can help make the choices fairer and give everyone equal opportunity to share.

5. *How can I use research to determine if the changes I have made have had a positive impact?* Using the different strategies of research outlined in the book it is possible to get a better understanding of how changes implemented in the classroom are influencing student performance. It is important to carefully examine the evidence you have to better understand the implementation of changes and possibly the impact of those changes on students.

EXPLORING OUR BELIEFS ABOUT OURSELVES AS RESEARCHERS AND TEACHERS

To do classroom research, we must first explore our beliefs about research and teaching and try to figure out how these beliefs are shaping what we are interested in examining more deeply for our research project (our research question(s)), as well as how these beliefs are shaping how we approach our research methodologies and our teaching in the classroom.

Fill out the following table, considering what you think are your strengths as a researcher and as a teacher:

Table 2.1

CONSIDER . . .	RESPONSES . . .	WILLING TO EXPLORE OTHER IDEAS . . .
What are the dominant methods used to generate or create new knowledge or do research in my field?		
What are the philosophical beliefs of knowledge generators/researchers in my discipline/field?		
What do I consider to be the goals of research (what do I consider under the umbrella of research)?		
What are my particular strengths as a researcher/knowledge producer?		
What beliefs do I have about teaching (e.g., what is the best way to teach so students can learn? What do I think makes "good teaching")?		
What are my particular strengths as a teacher?		
What beliefs do I have about my students and their abilities?		
What beliefs do I have about my own teaching/teaching abilities?		

After considering your beliefs about research and teaching, think about how strongly held these beliefs are—particularly your fundamental beliefs about teaching and research. Are you willing to explore alternative paradigms/beliefs? If not, this is good to know as you go forward. If you are strongly grounded in particular paradigms or beliefs, then perhaps stay with what you know and about which you feel strongly. If you are open to alternatives, this book will provide opportunities to explore possibilities, as well as building upon your existing beliefs and strengths. It is not absolutely essential to be willing and open to new ideas about research and/or teaching as you can build on your existing skills and ideas. What is essential is trying to be as honest with yourself as possible about your willingness to venture from your dominant beliefs about research and teaching. Considering one's openness to new research and teaching paradigms is important early in the process.

After thinking about your own beliefs and your strengths, think about what additional information you might need to expand your knowledge base. For example, if you feel as though you are strong in doing literature reviews or survey design or statistical analysis then you may need more information and help designing qualitative strategies such as interview protocols. If you have done a bit of qualitative research, you may need more information in the quantitative realm. The exercise above (Table 2.1) is designed to help you identify where you need more information and help.

Figure 2.4

Creating a Research Question

Starting this project, think about the most recent research project you have been conducting in your discipline. Consider:

- How did you come up with the question you are investigating?
- What have others researched about similar questions/hypotheses?
- What evidence/information/data are you collecting?
- What claims will you be able to make as a result of your evidence/data/information?
- How will you share your findings?

All of these questions will have a variety of responses. However, the approach to all is similar for classroom research, as it is for research in your discipline. The answer to the first question, I hope at least in part, is that the research question interests you. For the second, generally we find this out the same way regardless of discipline—we read relevant, related literature. Then there are questions relevant to methodology and the nature of evidence that you will collect.

The same approach is true when coming up with a question to investigate about our teaching. We think about our teaching and come up with a question that interests us. It may be interesting because it is something that troubles or frustrates us. Or it may be interesting because we are not sure what to do about it. Or we have a problem that we want to solve.

Once we have a general question or topic, we may want to see what others have written, published or presented on the topic. We can search scholarly articles to see what has been written. Perhaps you are thinking of implementing a "flipped classroom" and want to see what has been written about it. Or perhaps you are

How will you share your findings?

How did you come up with the question you are investigating?

What have others researched about this question?

What claims will you be able to make as a result of your evidence/ data/information collection/analysis?

What evidence/ information/data are you collecting?

Figure 2.5

struggling to get your students to stay awake in your lecture. Maybe you have recently implemented "clickers" in the classroom and want to see if student learning has improved.

A quick review of the literature will yield many interesting results and may help you shape your research question. You may build on the work of others or you may tweak an existing strategy. Don't rush into a methodology right away. Let the question percolate a bit. What do you want to better understand or figure out? Consider the following possible questions:

Do you want to get *a better or deeper understanding of what is happening* or how things are going in your classroom or course?
OR

Do you want to *test/examine whether or not something has worked or will work* to improve student learning?

Generally the first kind of question (getting a deeper or better understanding about HOW learning experiences are working or what they look like) will lead you down a path toward qualitative research (described in the next chapter).

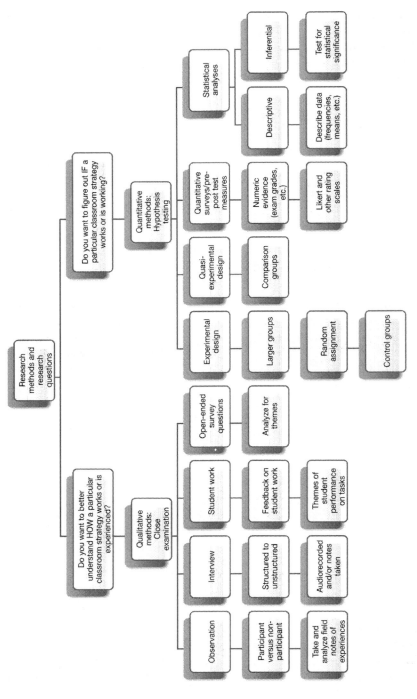

Figure 2.6

Typically the second question will lead you down a path of quantitative research toward hypothesis testing—IF something worked.

Figure 2.6 gives a sneak preview of the different methodological choices. Avoid getting too connected with one side of the diagram or the other. However, this picture may give you an idea of where your methodological biases lie.

What Research Have Others Conducted: Locating Your Project within Existing Studies

Important to the process, and helpful to do as early in the process as possible, is to review the literature. For many academics in disciplines outside of education, this may involve journals and jargon that are unfamiliar. Nonetheless, considering an interdisciplinary approach to your research question and exploration of the existing scholarship may yield fruitful results.

Step 1: See if there is an education-related journal in your field/discipline

Studies of classrooms span across the disciplines and more and more fields are creating journals of teaching or education within their field. For example, one of my former students recently published in the *International Journal of Engineering Education*. There are countless other examples (*International Journal of English and Education*, *Journal of Biological Education*, and so on). Check to see if your discipline has a journal like this.

Table 2.2

Journals that focus on teaching or education within my specific discipline	Journals that deal with teaching or education or learning within my general discipline

Step 2: Search a particular database or set of databases relevant for your topic or area

You could also start a review of the research based on the pedagogical question you may have. For example, if you know you want to research the "flipped classroom" then you might start a broad-based search of that in Google Scholar AND your university's databases. The University of Wisconsin Whitewater has a good resource of "Journal Outlets for the Scholarship of Teaching Articles," which

21

can be found at www.uww.edu/learn/journalsotl.php. There are also more resources that can be found in Appendix A.

Most universities have excellent databases that have greater access to texts than Google Scholar. However, it helps to know what databases might be most useful. The two largest education databases have tended to be ERIC (Education Resources Information Center) and Education Abstracts. JSTOR is a broader database, as are Project MUSE and the Social Science Index database. ProQuest Research Library and PsychINFO also may yield useful searches. Many libraries allow opportunities to search multiple databases at once.

Step 3: Start broad, and narrow and refine as necessary (don't be afraid to "play around" in the literature)

Perhaps start broad and then narrow your topic. For example, a search of "college teaching" and "active learning" in the ERIC database had over 31,000 results, but the first couple of pages of results, and the most recent ones, are quite compelling and give an idea of the kinds of research being published in this area. Perhaps my project is designed for an Anatomy and Physiology classroom so, just out of curiosity, I narrow it further by searching "college teaching" and "active learning" and "anatomy" and limit it by only "peer reviewed" studies. Now I'm down to five really focused studies on anatomy or similarly focused classrooms. Consider completing the table below to help you identify and keep track of relevant journals.

Table 2.3

Good directly related studies	Good tangentially related studies

Step 4: Start an annotated bibliography of your best sources

As you start finding relevant studies, keep a file with them in it (or several if you want to sort them by subtopics). Start to create a formal (or informal) annotated bibliography in which you describe why a particular article seems useful, what the authors did, what they found, and why this might be useful for your project.

Step 5: Use the ongoing literature search to help you find a journal for your own study

If you feel like your research question and design is pretty well articulated and set, you could start writing your literature review. How should you go about writing your literature review? This depends largely on the intended audience of your project. Using the databases and reading existing similar studies can help you find possible journals where you might consider submitting your final written study.

Step 6: Use the guidelines of the journal you are considering to guide the structure of your literature write up and style for other sections

If you find a place to submit your study (or a couple of possibilities), use their guidelines for literature review, style, and so on to structure your write-up of your study as you go. Use their guidelines to help you organize and consider the length, structure, and scope of your own literature review. Of course even if the journal requires only an abridged literature review, this does not preclude going deeper into the literature.

Figure 2.7

Reviewing the literature may also help narrow down the focus of your project, and provide new ideas. Enter into the process with an open mind as you examine and critique what has been conducted in the past and how your project fits in to the academic conversation.

INCLUSION AND DIVERSITY AND PROTECTING PARTICIPANTS

Try to stay open to new ideas and methodological approaches along this journey. All evidence is useful—perhaps not equally useful for all questions and problems we are solving, but useful nonetheless. Let me give an example. I worked with a new faculty member who was consistently getting very poor student evaluations. I would observe her class and students appeared engaged and contributing. The discussion was lively and cognitively demanding and students seemed to like it. I had her informally ask students about midway through the course to write down how they thought the class was going. Many students wrote that they thought the class was going very well and that they were nervous because they had heard she was a bad teacher. They said very positive comments about her as a teacher and the classes and discussions. Still, at the end of the class she received poor evaluations again. It was almost as if students defaulted back to their initial thoughts about her before the class even started. The truth is, we don't really know, so how can we find out? We gather as much evidence as we possibly can to tell the story of what is going on in the class and what students are getting out of the class. We analyze assignments, student work, student participation and engagement. We invite others to observe and we observe and take notes of what we notice after each class period. We construct strategies to test student learning. We use evidence to see what is going on, what is working and what isn't. We rigorously analyze the evidence and report it to others and figure out how to address it to improve instruction.

We need to try to include all student voices, or at least a true representative sample of them. We need to try to gather a diversity of evidence from a variety of people and sources using a variety of strategies. We need to be mindful and protect our human participants by working with Institutional Review Boards (IRBs) to make sure we are taking every precaution to protect the students and others involved in our studies/projects.

If you are planning on sharing your findings outside of your institution (and even if you aren't), it is a good idea to get approval from your institution's IRB, so that at any point if you want to share your findings, you can. The IRB seeks to protect the human participants in the research process. Often in classroom research, this means students. Students need to have their anonymity protected if it would be harmful to them if information got out about their particular performance or comments. Students are also protected by the Family Education Rights and Privacy Act (FERPA), so their academic performance cannot be displayed publicly. The IRB seeks to protect students in the research process to make sure that they are voluntary members of the research process and have the ability to opt out. This can be tricky with classroom research when the "opt out" option is not always readily available. Consult your institution's IRB policies. Many times classroom research ends up being "exempt from review" but typically there is still a form to complete. Often, completing the IRB forms required for your project will help you identify the ethical issues and considerations as well as the engagement of the participants and your specific methodology.

The first steps of our journey are complex and require a bit of soul-searching. It can be very helpful in this process to consider our beliefs about teaching, research, ethics, inclusion, students, participants, the research and so on. Locating yourself in your research project by considering what brought you to do this research can enable you to identify your own biases and beliefs and help you consider additional research questions that are of particular interest to you (or refine the questions you already have). Exploring your ideas and questions in the research literature can help you develop and refine your ideas even further.

Chapter 3

Qualitative Research Methods in Teaching and Learning

In this chapter:

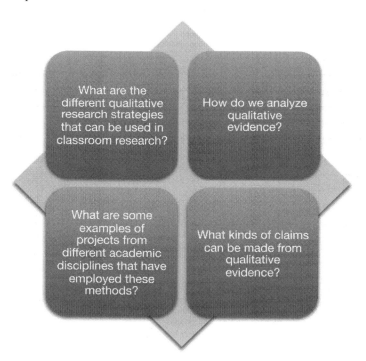

What are the different qualitative research strategies that can be used in classroom research?

How do we analyze qualitative evidence?

What are some examples of projects from different academic disciplines that have employed these methods?

What kinds of claims can be made from qualitative evidence?

This chapter focuses on the left side of Figure 2.6 on page 20—the qualitative methods that allow us to gain a deeper level of understanding about how a particular classroom strategy or strategies are working.

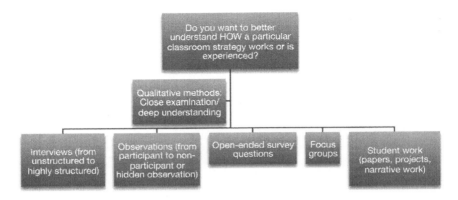

Figure 3.1

QUALITATIVE METHODS

Qualitative evidence is narrative, non-numeric data that can provide a richness and greater depth of understanding of a particular setting, context or culture if analyzed purposefully. Generally, the goals of those conducting qualitative research are to better understand a particular situation, setting, or culture, but without making generalizable claims. The evidence is suited for an examination of a classroom setting, and the findings help us better understand what is happening there, but do not allow us to argue that our findings are replicable or applicable to other settings.

Qualitative research has grown in popularity during the past couple of decades, particularly in classroom research. "Qualitative research is a growing enterprise worldwide" but is still considered as having "minority status" (Maykut and Morehouse 1994, p. 7). Perhaps this is because qualitative research methods are not as well-understood outside of academic disciplines such as anthropology and sociology and education that use them. Perhaps because it is not well understood and has had minority status in academic research it has been considered a "less rigorous and less valued way of doing inquiry" (p. 7). Despite the struggles of qualitative methodologies to gain widespread acceptance as rigorous and important research, the tides are shifting, particularly in education, which has seen the benefits of qualitative inquiry in examining teaching and learning in the classroom because it allows the researcher to delve more deeply into a critical examination of context and lived experience.

In this chapter, we consider those qualitative research methods that are perhaps most useful within the classroom: Observation and ethnography, open-ended questions/surveys, focus groups, video-taping, and interviews. We will save the analysis of student work and course materials (which often has a qualitative component) for the chapter on assessment.

Locating Your Self in Your Research Project: What Brought You to this Research?

When I work with students or faculty doing classroom research, one of the first questions I ask is "what brought you to this research?" Inevitably, each person tells me a very interesting story about their experiences teaching, their experiences as a student, their frustrations, successes, and so on. I am always intrigued by these stories. After listening intently, I encourage these future classroom researchers to "write that down." And to "make it part of the introduction of their write up of their project." Some will look at me with disbelief. I will assure them that it is okay to locate yourself in your research. "You are critical to this research. Without you there is no research, this classroom will not exist as it is . . . who you are is central to the project." This reaction to including one's own voice and position within research is the first place where the philosophical beliefs about research become apparent.

Recently I was speaking with a Chinese American woman who has been a teaching assistant for a few years at a prestigious institution in a very competitive doctoral degree program. She was interested in examining the ways that international students were struggling to understand ambiguous instructions that faculty would give such as "do a project of your choosing—it can be on anything." The professor was a white man and the white male students would go rushing up to him after class posing all kinds of ideas excitedly. The Asian students would timidly approach her (as the teaching assistant of the course) during her office hours and ask: "what does he want from us?" When we discussed her examining this I said: "who you are matters a lot. You should really think about how aspects of your social location matter and influence this project." Coming from a natural science discipline that values objectivity in research I think she struggled a bit initially. She had never done qualitative research nor considered her role in any way as part of her research. I asked, "do you think it matters to those students that you are Asian? Female? Young? A teaching assistant?" She said that she was sure it did. We discussed this more in depth. The long and the short of it—the instructor's as well as the students' social locations matter.

Don't ignore your social location—embrace it and consider the ways it may (or may not) influence the ways that certain things happen in the classroom (and outside the classroom) and affect your classroom research. Consider reflecting meaningfully about your role and your identity and ways these may influence your project—both positively and negatively. Consider what brought you to do your project and what makes this project/research question compelling to you. Don't be afraid to make it personal—most of this work is deeply personal.

A few words about power inherent in the professor role

When I conducted my first classroom research project fairly early in my career (described in *Learning Limits: College Women, Drugs and Relationships*), I considered the issue of power inherent within my role. Taken from the Preface of this book, consider the exploration of coming to terms with this power:

Examples of Research from the Classroom

Within my teacher role, I attempted to downplay my position of power by having students voice their experiences in class and in journals, and by having each student assume the teacher role, teaching part of the course. I showed respect for all ideas presented in the classroom and gave students the choice to write about whatever they felt comfortable in their journals. I thought I had successfully created a safe classroom environment that fostered open and honest discussion among students in the classroom (and outside the classroom), where students felt their opinions and experiences were heard and mattered. I viewed myself as a peer, a colleague, and a fellow researcher of education.

Throughout my project, I was committed to downplaying my power position as much as I could. I did not want to take on a "view from above," which Mies (1983, p. 124) considered popular among researchers. Rather, I wanted to take a view from below where I was seeking help and information from these women. I tried to communicate this perspective throughout the project, and further emphasize it, I did not grade the journals, and conducted interviews after students had completed the course.

I have since realized that I can not deny the power *inherent* in my role. Rather, I must accept it and try to determine how my role as "teacher" may have influenced my relationships with these women, as well as the nature of the information they provided me. I believe that although teachers still initially have the power over their students, they also have the power to decide how to use it, just as the researcher has the power to decide how to gather data from informants.

As professors or instructors in a classroom, we play a significant role within a particular culture at a particular point in time. We create a community of learners in our classrooms. We, as the teacher or professor, as classrooms are typically constructed, are in a position of power over students because we make decisions and judge students in ways that affect them beyond our classrooms. We have the power to create the culture. We develop the syllabus. We choose the readings. We decide on the assessments and grading scheme. We figure out the setup of the classroom and how each class will be run. Important to classroom research in higher education is acknowledging how our role as professor impacts our evidence and analysis. Our role does not negate our evidence or analysis, but it is wise to consider, at least, how our role may influence what we see or find.

Observation and Ethnography

All teachers engage in some form of observation. We observe what is happening with our students. We often reflect on our observations of what we ourselves are doing. Whether we are in a large lecture or a small seminar, we can see what is going on with our students and we make judgments about that. "These students look engaged . . . or bored . . . or like they are checking their email . . . or texting." We are essentially "participant observers" in that we are not outsiders observing an existing culture or phenomenon as anthropologists might do when they study another culture. We are actually an integral part of the culture we are studying. We actually, like most participants in a participant observation, have the power to change or shift the culture. And in fact, we hope to improve it.

While many of us make observations in our teaching, we seldom take notes about what we see and are even less likely to analyze notes from observations in a meaningful and systematic way (as a researcher does). I encourage faculty to keep a journal or to take notes in whatever format is most likely to allow them to get down as many details as possible (laptop, paper, notebook, phone, etc.). You want to write as much down about what you observed as possible—what did your students do, what did you do, what seemed to go well, why did you think that particular plan did not work well? You may reserve judgment until the end or weave it into the field notes in a parenthetical "observer's comment."

For example, consider this example from my own classroom teaching "Teaching as Research in Higher Education":

Examples of research from the classroom

"When I introduced the notion of ethnographic research in class today, a couple of my natural science folks seemed uneasy. Two of them had a sidebar conversation (o.c. I often wonder if this is a sign that students need to talk about it more among themselves or if they are confused or resistant or a bit of both). I asked their thoughts about their use of ethnographic research. As it turned out, Carrie (a doctoral student in the natural sciences) said 'my advisor said this kind of research isn't really research because it isn't testing hypotheses, and it can't be replicated or rigorously tested. He told me a lot of this classroom research is bunk, but he didn't use that term. It made me feel like I was wasting my time.'"

I thought for a moment about what to say because I have come across this conflict between qualitative and quantitative before (o.c. often with natural scientists challenging the authenticity of qualitative research as actual research), but wanted to make sure that my response was not defensive. I said that "ethnography and observation have a different purpose than hypothesis testing. They help us better understand what is going on in a particular culture or context—the nuances and relationships. We may observe something in a lab too that may be fascinating. In the classroom, often we want to better understand what is happening within that context—the relationship of the students with each other and with the professor."

She jumped in "but what about bias? As the professor of course we are biased right?" I agreed that we have biases and these are important to acknowledge and try to just be as honest as possible. I said that the goal is to improve teaching and learning in your classroom and possibly others' classrooms—the more honest you can be about your biases, the better. The more evidence you can collect to inform your understanding of your classroom, the better. But we have different tools for different jobs. Ethnographic observation allows us to analyze more critically what might be happening. She and the other students nodded and then she said "I wish I'd known this sooner when I was talking to him. I think we need to be able to explain our projects to our advisors and colleagues like this" (o.c. this is a constant tension within this work. I wonder if there is a better way to sequence the presentation of information to make it easier for people learning these strategies). I agreed.

The purpose of providing this example is two-fold. First is to see how you can take notes of classroom interactions or observations. The second is to see an example of how the conflict over qualitative research can arise with colleagues, peers, or others who are unfamiliar with the purpose and goal of qualitative research.

Consider the "observer comments" denoted by the "o.c." in the parentheses above. Sometimes these may turn into research questions or themes when you get to your analysis part (discussed in the next section). They are often a preliminary kind of analysis that may ultimately evolve into codes or themes.

Figure 3.2

As demonstrated in the diagram above, the spectrum of observation ranges from the observer being completely absent from the observation (e.g., the "hidden observer" as we see on the left side of the spectrum) to the fully participating participant observer on the right. The hidden observer can be behind a one-way mirror or even observing on a video recording, but the observer is not a part of the classroom environment at any point and is generally unknown to the participants. A non-participant observer is often in the room, but may sit in a discrete part of the classroom (maybe toward the back) and does not participate or engage students or the professor. A partially participating participant observer may engage students—asking questions—and attend class sporadically to observe. The fully participating participant observer would include the professor him or herself—someone who is fully engaged with and an active participant in the classroom/learning process.

Non-participant observation

On the one end of the observation spectrum is non-participant observation. We may want to involve outsiders to engage in non-participant observation of our classes. This strategy can yield some interesting and perhaps more objective findings. However, it is important to recognize that the outside observer comes with his or her own biases about teaching and learning as well.

If the non-participant observer is physically present in the classroom, this may (or may not) influence the dynamic of the class. Professors often feel and act differently when being observed. Students also may feel or act differently when a stranger is present. There are two ways to manage the intrusion of a non-participant observer. One is to acknowledge it and explain to students that this person is observing the class. The other is to ignore the presence of the observer entirely. I have been the observer in both such strategies. I have often found the latter to be much more uncomfortable (at least to me), as students are often looking around and at me trying to figure out why I am there. Typically it is better to acknowledge the presence of the observer. I have had professors whose classes I have observed tell me that they worry that students think that the professor must be "bad" to be observed. I have no evidence that this is the case, but I suspect that if the students already dislike a particular class or professor, the presence of an observer may very well validate their concerns or frustrations. This is speculation, however.

Observing behind a one-way mirror or from a vantage point where students can not see you is a possible (albeit not necessary) way to be a hidden observer. Videotaping may accomplish similar results to being a hidden observer, but has some limitations that will be discussed in the next section. I worked with a faculty member who was very concerned about his students' perceptions of so many people observing his classes and feared that students would use it as evidence of his poor teaching. We settled on videotaping as an alternative, but it was more limiting because the video projector only focused on what he was doing in the front of the room, and not on what students were doing during active learning activities.

You may also want to go and observe others' classrooms as a non-participant or participant observer. Observing others can give us ideas about strategies we might like to employ ourselves (or not), watch how other students respond and react to classroom activities and lectures, and so on. Be sure to take detailed notes about what you notice during these observations and schedule a time to discuss/debrief with the person/people you observed.

Taking Good Field Notes During and/or After Observations

Taking good field notes of your observations is essential. Relying on memory of an observation will likely not yield the depth of detail needed for later analysis. Leave approximately 15–30 minutes after each hour-long observation to take notes of what happened. After each class, if you are observing your own class, be sure to leave time to take detailed notes of what happened. If you can jot down ideas during class to jog your memory when you write more detailed notes after the class, this is often useful. It is challenging to take really detailed field notes during class—but jotting down quick reminders is often possible. However you choose to take notes, be sure to allow enough time to be reflective during these note-taking times. If you are a non-participant observer, you will likely have ample time to take notes during the observation session.

Video Recording

The video recorder doesn't lie. It is technically as objective as can be. However, it is limited in terms of what it can record. If you have a recorder just recording the teacher in the front of the room, this may miss all the rich discussion (or sleeping students) in the classroom. If you have a videographer, this may capture more, but may be distracting and will still miss some things that are happening in the classroom. Despite its limitations, videotaping classes can be really useful. I recommend watching them alone and taking notes and then again if you have a trusted friend or mentor or colleague to watch them with. Undoubtedly you will observe behaviors in yourself you may never have noticed before. We can use videotaping to identify distracting behaviors or speech issues ("um," "er," "uh," "you guys," etc.) or other patterns of behavior that may be useful or problematic. The video recording alone is insufficient for analysis, however. Notes of the observations from the video are necessary and useful for analysis.

Asking Good Open-ended Questions

We can ask open-ended questions in a variety of ways—in surveys, focus groups or interviews, or even informally in class during observations. Open-ended questions are those that yield more than just a numeric or categorical response such as yes/no, agree/disagree, etc. These questions result in a narrative response. When designing open-ended questions consider the following:

1. What types of responses are your questions likely to yield?
2. Is there a wide variety of possible responses and an opportunity for participants/informants to explain what you hope they will explain? Consider asking for specific examples such as "tell me about a time when you felt frustrated in a classroom" or "tell me about one of the most memorable classroom experiences you ever had (both positive and negative)."
3. Consider your research question—what are you trying to learn from your participants? Use your research question(s) to help you design your open-ended questions. For example, if you are trying to find out from students in your class how they feel about a particular active learning strategy you use in the classroom, you could ask something like "when we do the think-pair-share in the classroom, describe what the experience is like for you in the pairings. What typically happens?" Or "can you describe a typical experience for you in a think-pair-share partnership in class?"
4. Make the wording of your questions as authentic for you as possible, particularly if your informants know you and you are engaged in a face-to-face type of methodology (such as interviews, focus groups, observations). Also allow for opportunities for an open flow of discussion. Consider "interviewee-guided" interviews if you feel comfortable with this to allow the questions to flow naturally from the discussion.
5. If respondents are anonymous then consider the relative degree of formality needed and make sure the language choices are clear to respondents.

If you are conducting an interview you have some room to clarify questions. However, in an open-ended survey question, you will not have that opportunity, so you want to make sure that your questions ask exactly what you want to ask and are likely to be interpreted the way you want them to be. Consider the following question: "What makes a lesson successful?" This question is too vague— and depending on your respondents they may have no idea what you're talking about. So you may want to alter it to read, "based on your experiences as a student at _____ University, what do you think makes a classroom lesson successful?" A question like this is tricky to ask students because they cannot always articulate well what exactly may contribute to a lesson's success or failure. So you may want to ask a more concrete question such as "describe an example of a class/lesson that you thought was really successful" and then as a possible follow up "what do you think made it successful?" This might end up producing more fruitful results and more in-depth and varied responses. It is a good idea to ask others from the respondent group to answer the questions to make sure that they are interpreting your questions as you want them to, and the questions encourage them to provide the kind of depth of response that you hope for.

Open-ended surveys

When we use open-ended surveys in the classroom, they can be quite useful because they allow us to gather somewhat anonymous data. We do need to take some steps to make sure we cannot tell which student wrote what and help them to understand that their responses are anonymous—particularly if students think that their responses may influence their grade in any way. This kind of anonymity can be very useful in gathering data throughout a course. Many institutions subscribe to online survey software, but if not, there are free online survey programs such as surveymonkey.com to help you create simple surveys and allow for open-ended questions. Students are perhaps granted a greater degree of feeling more anonymous, but the response rate may be compromised as fewer students may complete the surveys during their own time than when you have them as a captive audience in your class.

A survey may be as simple as a note card or scrap piece of paper where a student is asked to write down their reactions to a particular activity or assignment or discussion. They may be more formal like the open-ended questions in a course evaluation "What did you like best about the course?" or "What do you feel could be changed?" Periodically asking students to respond about aspects of the course anonymously and in writing can be really enlightening and yield some useful data. You may also set up an anonymous survey using survey software. You could use texting, email or blackboard (or other online course tools your institution uses), but with these it is much more difficult to establish anonymity.

Focus Groups

Focus groups can provide useful data in classroom research projects, but given their inherent lack of anonymity may be worrisome for students who fear that an honest but less-than-favorable comment may jeopardize their grade. These can be done with students after a class is over and grades are turned in, but often memories are faulty or reflections are not as fresh. It is also possible at many institutions to seek assistance from people who work at the institution's center or program designed to improve teaching and learning. Often, these people are trained in conducting focus groups with students and can do so without the professor in the room to get more honest feedback. One new faculty member at a small liberal arts college where I worked invited someone from the college's center to improve teaching and learning to do a focus group with her students. This new faculty member was quite surprised with the feedback she received from the focus groups. Students were angry about several aspects of the course design—principally what they felt was too much time spent in small groups without going over content in meaningful ways. Would she have received this same level of negative feedback had she not asked an outsider to do it? Likely not. Would she receive some useful feedback? Perhaps. It is difficult to know—the position of the focus group questioner matters though and, in the analysis, considering the position of the observer or questioner is useful. We do not always know the impact of that position, but we may speculate or consider possible ways in which it might.

Regardless of the challenges and possible limitations, it is possible to get small groups of students together and ask them open-ended questions about aspects of a course. If you explain that you are seeking their feedback to create the best possible course for student learning, students are often quite eager to help. They will typically not be comfortable talking about you with you there (and you may not be either) even if all the feedback is positive. Still, students can give feedback on other aspects of the course or a particular experience or new strategy you have implemented. I have had students in these small focus group settings reveal concerns that I had not noticed. For example, in a somewhat impromptu focus group that developed when I asked a small group if they would be able to stay after class to talk they said they were disturbed about a particular student who was texting through class under the desk. They also said that they did not like having laptops because they were distracting. The next day I polled the class using i-clickers to see how others felt about laptops as a distraction and interestingly the overwhelming majority felt they were, so we agreed to have laptops put away unless they were absolutely necessary for an activity.

Diana Garvin taught an intermediate Italian course at a top research university. Her classroom research project focused on embedding blogging into her class. Among many strategies she used, she engaged her students in focus groups within her small seminar class, asking them specific but open-ended questions about their experiences with blogging. They gave very thoughtful responses about their experiences and how they went about writing their own blogs and searching for Italian blogs of others, and how this process helped them learn the more informal aspects of the Italian language they might otherwise not have learned. Many admitted to looking up words and being motivated to learn more words and different ways of expressing oneself in Italian rather than the more formal ways they had typically learned in the classroom. Were students telling her what they thought she wanted to hear? Perhaps. It is always difficult to know in any self-reported research. In Diana's case, she asked similar questions using a variety of strategies. She asked questions using anonymous surveys and found the same themes emerged as in the focus groups. We can use multiple evidence sources to triangulate our data to determine whether what we are finding is robust (triangulation will be discussed later in the book).

Interviews: Structured versus Unstructured

Another way to gather in-depth, narrative information is through the use of interviews. Interviews can range from very structured (with a set list of questions followed like a script given to every person) to completely unstructured (perhaps starting with a general question or idea such as "tell me your thoughts on the group project . . .") and taking the discussion where the interviewee takes it.

In my own experience interviewing students for a classroom research project, I waited until the course was over and started with very unstructured interview questions such as "how did you feel about the course? The books? The debates? Projects?" As themes started to emerge from participants, I became slightly more structured, honing in on particular issues of interest.

Figure 3.3

Typically I recommend that novice interviewers start with pretty well-structured interviews, but still allowing respondents to answer with somewhat complex responses if possible (not just "yes" or "no" questions). For example, use questions such as "what did you do during that think-pair-share activity?" and "what did your partner do?" "What was challenging?" "What was useful?" and so on. Following a script of well-structured open-ended interview questions (see earlier section on developing good open-ended questions) can be helpful in creating consistency among respondents, but you may also miss out on some unexpected phenomena that might emerge from broader open-ended questions. Whether you choose to create more targeted, specific open-ended structured questions or a more unstructured interview with more general questions or something in between will depend on the phenomenon you are trying to better understand and your research questions.

You may also want to interview colleagues who teach similar courses or have taught similar courses. This kind of information-gathering interview can be incredibly helpful to gain insights into what others have learned and how they have structured their courses and tried to improve student engagement and learning. Consider the purpose of your interview and what you hope to learn about your informants. This may help guide you in determining the structure of your interview questions.

Some considerations about interviews

Audiotaping and transcribing. One of the decisions that interviewers need to consider is whether or not to audiotape an interview, and if it is audiotaped whether or not to engage in a full word-for-word transcription of the interview. Ideally, audiotaping and transcription can help a great deal in the analysis. The full transcript of the word-for-word (including the hesitations, pauses, "likes," "ums," and so on) can really be useful.

Some interviews are less formal and brief, and may not warrant audio recording and transcription. If you are unable to audiotape, and even if you can, taking notes during the session (if you can do it without being distracting) can be useful as well. I do caution against being distracting—interviewees often pay attention to what kinds of comments you may write down, which may influence their further comments. Be aware of your reactions to comments, what you note and what you do not. Try to take notes consistently so you are writing regularly rather than privileging certain ideas over others.

When professors interview their own students, even after the course is over, the power dynamic often remains, so in some cases it may be difficult to get students to talk openly and without deferring to you. Try to encourage the interviewee as he or she speaks to continue speaking—take notes consistently and be careful to avoid interruption. Let the interviewee know through body language and expression that you are genuinely interested in what he or she has to say and you want them to speak as freely and honestly as possible. If you are concerned that your presence as the interviewer might negatively influence the informant, you may want to consider having another person conduct the interview for you.

Interviewing can be a difficult process for many of us because we are so used to thinking about what we are going to say next, rather than truly listening to our respondent. The process of becoming a skilled interviewer takes some practice, building confidence and getting participants to speak openly. If you find that participants are reticent, then be flexible with your questions to see if other questions might prompt more comments. Also, give respondents some time to think about their responses. If they don't respond immediately with a well-formed response, this does not mean that s/he isn't going to respond meaningfully—sometimes it takes time to process the question and come up with a thoughtful response. Pay attention to how much time participants take though, because long wait times may indicate being more guarded in their responses.

Qualitative Analysis

Even though there are very technical and varied ways to analyze qualitative data, this book, for the sake of ease for your teaching as research project will focus on constant comparative narrative analysis. Bernard and Ryan (2010) have a very

37

detailed guide called *Analyzing Qualitative Data: Systematic approaches* that outlines more sophisticated coding strategies, discourse analysis, grounded theory, content analysis, schema analysis, analytic induction, and ethnographic decision models. For our teaching as research projects we will focus on coding and finding categories or themes that emerge from the data.

Constant-comparative analysis: Looking for themes that emerge

Once you have your narrative data/text— field notes from your observations in the classroom or elsewhere, interview or focus group notes or transcripts, and/or responses from open-ended questions—you are ready to start creating coding categories and ultimately analyzing for themes or grounded theory. I recommend reading through everything you have first with an open mind, and then underlining or circling key ideas and writing down what you see as main ideas or themes that seem to emerge. You may want to "code" in the margins ideas or concepts that emerge as interesting, important or recurring. Continue to compare new data to older data or data you've already analyzed to see how the categories or themes hold up—are they consistent? Are there outliers?

One of the possible goals or outcomes of qualitative research is to create what is known as "grounded theory." According to Barney Glasser's (2008) "Grounded Theory Institute" and his many books and articles on the topic:

All research is "grounded" in data, but few studies produce a "grounded theory." Grounded Theory is an inductive methodology. Although many call Grounded Theory a qualitative method, it is not. It is a general method. It is the systematic generation of theory from systematic research. It is a set of rigorous research procedures leading to the emergence of conceptual categories. These concepts/categories are related to each other as a theoretical explanation of the action(s) that continually resolves the main concern of the participants in a substantive area. Grounded Theory can be used with either qualitative or quantitative data.

Notice these fieldnotes from an instructor's own observations of his course. He typically lectured in his course and he was interested in introducing the notion of the "think-pair-share" into the course about halfway through the semester. The "think-pair-share" is a pedagogical technique in which students pair up to discuss an issue/topic/problem together. They are often allowed some time to think about it first—perhaps writing down initial thoughts or ideas. Then they get into a pair (or the teacher pairs them). Then the selected pairs share their discussion points with the class. One of the major themes is student resistance to changing the typical way of doing business in the classroom.

Examples of Research from the Classroom

I had instructed students that we were going to do a "think-pair-share" to discuss the question of language processing in the brain and the brain areas and processes that were activated and how these areas were engaged at this moment. Right when I announced this, there were audible groans. (o.c. resistance to think-pair-share?) A couple of hands went into the air to ask to go to the bathroom. (o.c. another form of resistance?) Most students did split into pairs, but there were a few individuals who did not have a partner, and while I did I noticed that the paired students were talking about other things—not the assigned task. (o.c. another form of resistance?) I partnered them with each other and in a few cases allowed a few groups of three. As I walked around, students were generally focused on the topic and a few stopped to ask me some questions. (o.c. teacher role in addressing resistance). I realized that I had forgotten to give them "think time" to write down their ideas first and put them into pairs too quickly. I also ran out of time and did not have sufficient time to allow for the "sharing" before the end of class. (o.c. timing difficulty of active learning strategies).

In the above example, we see the parenthetical comments in "observer's comments" operating as early codes that may turn into themes. So it may turn out that after a few more times of trying this technique, the resistance wanes (or increases). It may be that the instructor becomes more competent and confident in the technique and students become more familiar with and competent and confident with the technique as well. Certainly more data is needed.

One strategy to consider when engaging in this kind of grounded theory—in which codes get categorized into larger more encompassing themes, is to consider using an inductive kind of structure such as this one:

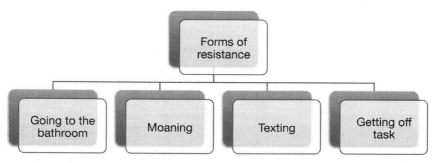

Figure 3.4

The graphic shown above helps articulate how coding the evidence can be categorized or organized around broad themes.

Lessons Learned from Qualitative Projects

Qualitative research was a new experience for many of those who did classroom research included in this book. For example, in Diana Garvin's classroom research project adding blogging to her Italian course, she analyzed her qualitative evidence and found three major themes that emerged. Here are her reflections on her themes that emerged:

Examples of Research from the Classroom

Analyzing quote content pointed to three key themes that students associated with engagement. To characterize what we mean when speaking of "engagement" in writing, let's consider some of the focus group comments on their Blog Project experience: "[Blogging] gave me the chance to write about something I was invested in [and] just practice [what] I'd be looking up in Italy," "I liked reading everybody else's [blogs] . . . I learned a little bit from everybody's," "The assignments made me do it, but then I got into it and discovered it," "This was more about what I found than writing for the sake of writing," "I liked the blog cause you got to choose [the topic and material] you wanted," "I was actually learning, not writing just to prove I can."

In describing engagement, students' comments clustered around these interrelated themes: autonomy, authenticity, and community. Autonomy emerged in terms of student choice of topic, material, tone; having "their own" blog. Many returned to descriptions of authentic voice and its effect. Students reported that writing online made them feel as though their voices mattered more and that they were more engaged. It also motivated them to immerse themselves in the technology as a means to achieve the goal of authentic communication. For students, autonomy linked with authenticity, which they defined as exposure to Italian materials written in slang and dialect and the idea that writing online felt "natural." The connection of autonomy and authenticity with engagement need not evoke the specter of the lonely crowd. In fact, students viewed community, that is learning culture and vocabulary from classmates and contributing to Italian online forums, as an integral factor in online writing's draw.

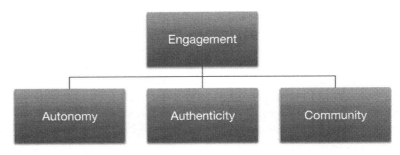

Figure 3.5

The themes that emerged from her multiple sources of qualitative data (including focus groups and observations, and open-ended survey questions) were these major themes of autonomy, authenticity, and community that she felt were best categorized under the theme of student engagement.

Kevin Carrico is an anthropologist, so was comfortable doing an ethnographic study as his first teaching-as-research project. He employed a technique that was most comfortable to him as an anthropologist—ethnography. He observed his students in these class discussions, during uncomfortable video segments, and took field notes of his observations. He also analyzed student writing and work to consider the ways that student thinking shifted. In his small seminar class he had many Asian students—some Asian-American, and some from China. He struggled with this notion of developing good pedagogy that allowed him to tackle such a controversial issue with his students.

Examples of Research from the Classroom

The pedagogy of controversy: Teaching the Cultural Revolution

Kevin Carrico

My project was an ethnographic study of a seminar I designed and taught on the Cultural Revolution (1966–1976). The Cultural Revolution is a decade-long movement in which Chinese Communist Party Chairman Mao Zedong initiated a violent revolt against perceived "counterrevolutionaries" and other so-called "enemies of the people," which led to millions of cases of persecution and death, and which remains a sensitive topic in modern Chinese history to this day. The field of China Studies is replete with such sensitive and often quite contentious historical and political issues, of which the Cultural Revolution is only one example: other cases include the Great Leap Forward (1959–1961), the Tiananmen Massacre (1989), ethnic relations, and human rights issues in general. Largely taboo in a domestic setting beyond vague and falsely reassuring state-defined definitions, the politicization of these issues, and of the field of China Studies as a whole, makes the discussion of these and other topics highly controversial and emotionally charged.

Viewing this controversial topic from a broader pedagogical perspective, it becomes apparent that there is widespread agreement regarding the importance of addressing controversial topics in higher education, but considerably less agreement as to how exactly to go about addressing such topics. Aiming to contribute to the pedagogy of controversy, I asked, how can instructors in China Studies and other fields address sensitive historical topics without promoting demonization, defensiveness, and simplistic oppositions? And how can controversy and contention serve as an object of discussion rather than a hindrance to discussion?

To address these issues, I completed an ethnographic study of a seminar that I taught in the fall of 2011 (and subsequently in the fall of 2012) on the history of the Cultural Revolution and the handling of this history since the movement's conclusion. Students in the course came from: China, where the history of the Cultural Revolution is generally avoided in academic discussion; Chinese families in the United States, some of whom had experienced the Cultural Revolution; and non-Chinese backgrounds, with varying degrees of familiarity with Chinese history. My goal in this course and this ethnography was to create new concepts to generate novel perspectives and approaches for addressing controversial topics.

What I found

As the Merriam-Webster Dictionary states all too accurately, controversy is "a discussion marked especially by the expression of opposing views." This binary structure of controversy produces two opposing and thus mutually reinforcing sides, along with two standard and easily recognizable processes reproducing this structure. The first is *abstraction*, wherein the division of people into opposing sides of "us" and "them" promotes self-reinforcing team-think that is increasingly abstracted or removed from the concrete realities of the controversial topics or events under discussion. The second is *reidentification*, wherein the increasing abstraction from the topic at hand reproduces the initial identification with one's "side," based in presumed stable and unchanging attitudes. Anyone who has ever watched a cable news talk show will immediately recognize these responses, insofar as discussion of controversial topics seems to only reproduce and indeed reinforce people's preconceived opinions, making controversy itself an autopoeitic process without substantive solutions beyond its own perpetuation.

To move beyond these two standards responses, I propose two pedagogically beneficial approaches based upon initial observation and practical application in subsequent years of this course. The first is *humanization*, meaning that the human experience of this event is emphasized against the abstraction inherent within the handling of sensitive or controversial topics. It is far too easy, when reading a conventional history, to feel a comforting distance from the participants: whether victims, or perpetrators, or both. And this leaves far too much room for the type of romanticized projections or distancing denunciations that characterize the discussion of the Cultural Revolution. Against this trend, humanization refers to attention to the detailed realities and particularly the personal experiences of a historical event. By incorporating personal narratives, photographs, and documentary film representations, the topic under discussion is no longer an abstraction, but rather a real event whose intimate effects have been viewed from a variety of conflicting yet also mutually informative perspectives.

The second approach, in response to the dilemma of reidentification, is *deidentification*, by which I mean a destabilization of simplistic national or regional oppositions and identificatory assumptions. The primary oppositions in the field of China

Studies are Chinese/Non-Chinese, as well as Eastern/Western, producing assumptions that there are opinions unique to each side of these binaries, and that one opinion is inherently better than the other due to issues of proximity or openness. Deidentification detaches viewpoints from presumed intrinsic ties to identities, revealing the non-existence of a uniquely "Chinese" or "Western" view of history, and highlighting the debates and diversity of opinions below the surface of such simplistic binary labels. For example, rather than presuming that a "true Chinese" must defend the Cultural Revolution, or that a "Westerner" will have an automatically negative attitude towards the Cultural Revolution, readings and viewings point out that some of the most incisive critics of the Cultural Revolution have come from China, while some of the most passionately misplaced enthusiasts of the Cultural Revolution and its political philosophies have been located in the West. By detaching the analysis of this event from the burden of identity, learners are able to see discussion of this event as a process of growth rather than a process of reinforcing beliefs.

How these findings have informed my practice

Through my research, I have learned that the pedagogy of controversy must do nothing less than teach against our instinctive response to controversy, insofar as the binaries and abstraction surrounding controversial topics promote reidentification and hinder reflection.

In implementing humanization, as mentioned above, I have focused on promoting a diversity of sources to bring the actual experience of this event to life for students. Such media as photographs and documentary film communicate at once the complex political-aesthetic power and human terror of this event far more clearly than detached black and white historical texts.

In implementing deidentification, I have similarly employed a variety of sources from a variety of national and ideological backgrounds, highlighting the need to detach perspectives from identifications to understand the humanity of this event. Perhaps most revealingly in this regard, I have traced the manifold shifts in my own assessment of the Cultural Revolution and Maoism in general for learners, as a demonstration that learning is not a process of reaffirming beliefs but rather of observing and learning from one's mistakes to develop a more refined perspective on an infinitely complex world.

In the description above, we see the ways that the themes Kevin found from his ethnography—that moving beyond the more traditional ways of teaching controversial topics (abstraction and reidentification to humanization to de-identification)—was more useful in getting students from diverse backgrounds entering into the controversy a productive place from which to have discussion and meaningful learning take place. Through his analysis of classroom participant observation and student reflections in student work/writing, he examined the emerging themes of the ways students were engaging or identifying (or not) with the material. And when he made it more human and real, students engagement increased, but they were better able to examine the sides of the controversy when they deidentified from the controversy.

In a humanities course on the medieval book and digital media, Joel Anderson from the department of Medieval Studies brings together qualitative evidence from observations, student discussions, open-ended surveys and also includes an analysis of student work (to be described more fully in Chapter 7). Here he describes his themes that emerged and his key take-away points from the project.

Examples of Research from the Classroom

Reading medieval books in a digital age

In recent years, questions about the future of books, their roles in the classroom, and students' reading habits have occupied educators from a wide variety of fields and disciplines. Prophecies about the "death of the book" and soon-to-be-realized digital utopias have proliferated alongside eulogies for the printed text and complaints about supposed declines in student literacy. While there is little consensus about where we are—or should be—going, the digital age has generated increasing awareness among scholars and teachers that different technologies shape, often quite drastically, how we read, write, and communicate.

As a medievalist teaching in the twenty-first century, I suggest that our present circumstances can help us frame new questions about the books, documents, and media of the distant past. With this perspective in mind, I recently taught a first-year writing seminar at Cornell University titled "Reading in the Middle and Digital Ages" (fall 2012, spring 2013). The course addressed topics related to the production, use, organization, and dissemination of texts in medieval Europe. It also aimed to put medieval texts into dialogue with the information technologies that are in the process of reinventing what it means to read, write, and communicate in our own society. The formats, layouts, and production-modes of medieval manuscripts display a number of features that students raised in an age of web-media can appreciate: for instance, the frequent use of decorative images and borders; an abundance of annotations, glosses, and paratextual commentary; and an embrace of "multiple voices" on one page. The class started from the premise that "reading" and "writing" are practices that occur in modes, manners, places, and communities that are historically specific, yet potentially comparable.

My teaching-as-research project pursued two main questions: first, how might teachers of pre-modern history and literature help students think about "unfamiliar" medieval texts in relation to "familiar" digital ones? Second, what are some of the potentials and pitfalls of these comparisons, and what do students actually make of them? I kept these central questions in mind as I guided my students through a series of essay assignments, mini-lectures, discussions, writing exercises, and field trips to Cornell's Rare and Manuscript Collections (RMC). I accumulated "data" in my classes from a variety of sources. These included: student essays; my handwritten marginalia on these papers; anonymous mid-semester evaluations and final evaluations of the course (both semesters); a short survey after essay five (spring semester only); and my classroom notes and observations.

My primary role in this project was, first and foremost, to be a self-reflective teacher for my first-year seminar. At the end of the spring semester, I drew together the above-mentioned data and then isolated and explored a few "key themes" that emerged from it.

What I found/key themes

In several different forums—final evaluations, in-class surveys, and informal discussions—my students reported, almost uniformly, that they enjoyed the class's two visits to Cornell's RMC. Both semesters, our first visit consisted of a short lecture on how manuscripts were made in the Middle Ages. During the presentation, a curator passed several medieval manuscripts around the table for students to handle. In our second visit, students were organized into groups of four to six. Each group was given a manuscript and 20–30 minutes to inspect it. They then gave short presentations on their findings to the rest of the class.

Reflecting on these experiences, many students remarked that handling medieval manuscripts "in person" helped them make connections between the "real thing" and our in-class activities and lectures: "To actually see manuscripts and feel them backed up everything we talked about in class and I thought the visits were very important for our learning process." Other students were impressed by the physicality of medieval manuscripts: "The visits to the Rare Books Library really help[ed] to give me a direct feeling of how medieval texts were produced. It [was] important for me to actually touch the parchments and see the pigments."

At face value, these reactions are not particularly surprising—who wouldn't be impressed by a 700-year-old book? Still, I think that these experiences were important not only for the "wow, cool" reactions they elicited, but also for the discussions they helped open up. After our first trip to the RMC, students were much more skilled at delineating some of the differences between medieval texts and digital ones. They were impressed by the distinctive materiality, physicality, and craftsmanship of medieval manuscripts, noting that digital screens cannot be "marked," "felt," or "stained" in quite the same way. Moreover, the manuscripts compelled students to "look" and "read" in new ways. In particular, the RMC visits pushed students to think about the relationships between a text's form, its functions, and its historical contexts: how, for example, a small, illustrated book of hours might have facilitated prayer, or how extensive glosses and marginal annotations might indicate that a medieval book was used in a pedagogical setting.

I tried to cultivate these kinds of analysis in my writing assignments, focusing the relations between a text's form, its function, and its historical context. For example, one essay asked students to locate two or three different "versions" of Chaucer's

Canterbury Tales (e.g., a children's book, an academic edition, a medieval manuscript facsimile, an online translation, etc.) and then to explore the ways in which the formal features of each text were connected to their contexts of production, reading, and reception. The newness of this *kind* of thinking was a theme on several student evaluations: "To be honest [before the Chaucer assignment], I had never even thought about these different features of books. Books were just something that I read and [their] marginal spaces and illustrations were of no concern. However, the assignment and all the activities encouraged me to look at [books] from a different perspective."

How these findings have informed my teaching

I was extremely impressed with the results of my class in both semesters. In terms of my project's implications for future practice, I would advance suggestions on at least two fronts. First, I would encourage all instructors to view the special collections libraries at their institutions as active instructional resources. Particularly for historians and literary scholars of the distant past, a visit to the rare books room offers students opportunities for experiential and hands-on learning that are not easily replicated in the classroom.

Second, I think that my project demonstrates the value in finding ways to connect classroom material to students' contemporary present. Students *love* to talk about digital media. Of course, this enthusiasm can lead to strained comparisons and historical distortions. Many of my students' first essays began with sweeping generalizations about "the rise of literacy" and "the progress of technology." However, it seemed to me that the pay-offs of medieval–digital comparisons far outweighed the risks. The more I taught this class, the more I felt that what I was teaching were "modes of analysis" for the critical interrogation of media: students explored how the same "text" can manifest itself in different instantiations; they discovered deep historical continuities and changes in how we read and write; and they recognized texts as objects whose physical features divulge a great deal about their intended audiences and their socio-historical contexts. All of these lessons, I think, equipped students to both embrace and question the media that will confront them in the digital age: to think about the differences between reading the same text on a computer, a tablet, or in a paperback book; to ponder the kinds of communities that online technologies facilitate; or to ask questions about the information that digital screens can, and cannot, represent.

Joel Anderson's participant observations of students as they visited the rare books collection and interacted with the rare books, as well as his observations of class discussions, his notes on student papers and work, allowed him to think differently about teaching students about reading and engaging with printed media in a way that allowed students to still remain within their digital age. He became a more reflective practitioner about students' levels of engagement with text and reading text using different modalities and the nature of communities that can (or cannot) be created using these different formats.

We can see in these examples that qualitative research in the form of observations, interviews, focus groups, and open-ended survey questions analyzed purposefully for themes can yield very helpful results to guide our teaching. Sometimes qualitative data alone can be sufficient to answer a question about your teaching or student learning that you have had, but sometimes more data are needed. Qualitative data gathering can be an excellent place to start doing your research project because you can observe your own classes (or others) and generate questions for exploration. Sometimes our data results in even more questions, which in this process can be an important part of the cycle of teaching as research.

Interestingly, despite their initial discomfort with qualitative methods, many college instructors with whom I worked were willing to try qualitative research alongside quantitative methodologies (described in the next chapter). Their mixed-method designs and outcomes will be described in that chapter.

In conclusion, qualitative research can be a useful starting place for classroom research. Observations, interviews, focus groups, and open-ended surveys can provide a depth of information and improved understanding about a classroom context and culture that may not have been readily apparent before—at least without closer inspection. Sometimes these activities may generate more questions for consideration. Sometimes we may better understand different perspectives of what is happening. Regardless, systematic collection of qualitative data and analysis using coding methods and finding categories or themes can provide important evidence for our journey to utilize research to improve our teaching and our students' learning. Next we consider the role of quantitative research in our journey.

Chapter 4

Quantitative Research Methods in Teaching and Learning

In this chapter:

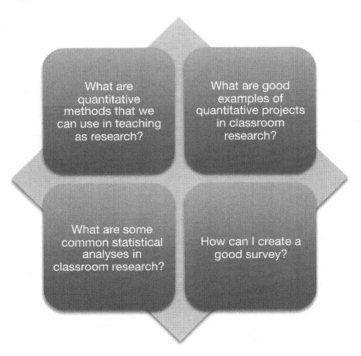

What are quantitative methods that we can use in teaching as research?

What are good examples of quantitative projects in classroom research?

What are some common statistical analyses in classroom research?

How can I create a good survey?

This chapter will focus on the right-hand side of Figure 2.6 on page 20—focusing on quantitative methods.

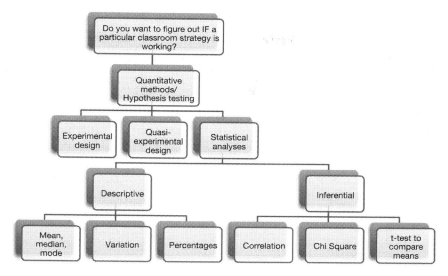

Figure 4.1

DESIGNING THE QUANTITATIVE RESEARCH QUESTION

Generally, classroom research projects that lend themselves well to quantitative methodologies are those that are interested in making statistical and/or generalizable claims and/or interested in testing hypotheses. In classroom research, this typically means those projects interested in determining whether or not a particular classroom strategy (or strategies) works. Perhaps, one would like to implement one of the high impact, active learning practices listed earlier in the book and would like to examine the degree to which student beliefs/attitudes/content learning was changed as a result of this implementation. Or perhaps you want to see if there are statistically significant differences between different groups or classes or pedagogical strategies. So, for example, if one were interested in considering whether that think-pair-share activity worked, one may want to engage in quantitative strategies to see.

True Experimental Design

While an ideal strategy to determine whether or not a particular classroom intervention or technique worked, experimental design can typically be difficult to pull off in educational settings. In experimental design, the experimenter randomly assigns students to either a "control" condition or an "experimental condition." In the "control" condition, students do not receive the intervention. In the "experimental" condition, they do. Students are often measured in both groups both before and after the intervention to determine the impact and the two groups are compared statistically to determine if the difference between the groups can be attributed to the intervention or to chance.

Experimental design using control groups and random assignment is a model that is used in a lot of scientific research. However, in a classroom environment in college and university settings we rarely have the opportunity to control all extraneous variables or randomly assign participants to treatment and non-treatment conditions. Nonetheless, these strategies may be possible with planning and involvement of other collaborators.

On a larger scale, we could examine the impact of a particular curricular decision—that is randomly assign students to first-year writing classes—some taking the course their first semester and some taking their second semester. Then you could assess the writing performance of both groups before and after to determine the degree to which their writing improved with or without the first-year writing course.

On a smaller scale (within the classroom) students within a classroom could be randomly assigned to do two different writing activities—one in which they have a choice of topic and reading and one in which the reading and writing is highly prescriptive. You could assess students' attitudes using a survey about writing before and after and compare the groups. You could have students in a particularly randomly assigned laboratory group engage in a particular active learning task and a different group engage in a more typical help-session lecture and compare the performance of these two groups in a class exam.

Quasi-experimental Design

When conducting quantitative classroom research projects, more often than using experimental design, researchers tend to rely on more quasi-experimental designs. There are a few different ways to do this.

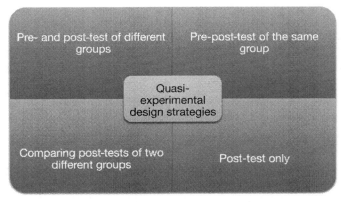

Figure 4.2

As the diagram shows, there are different ways to collect quantitative data using quasi-experimental design. Each of these strategies shows us different pieces of evidence and can be used depending on the research question.

Pre-test and post-test of different groups

This includes giving an assessment or some other measure to two different groups—could be two different laboratory sections, two different sections of the same class, different groups within a class, and so on. If you wanted to compare two different groups, this strategy is helpful. Because the groups are not randomly assigned, there may be another factor at work contributing to differences you may see, however, so just be careful not to over-generalize your findings to suggest that they are generalizable in the same way you might be able to do with experimental design.

Consider the following example from Biomedical Engineer John Foo. He was working within a course on immunology that was exclusively a lecture course and decided to try to add a think-pair-share activity. He was skeptical that it would work, but wanted to see if student performance on assessment measures would be better using the activity. He admitted his bias to me: "I don't think the think-pair-share activity will show any positive impact and I expect that students will not want to do it." He did find quite a bit of student resistance to the activity but despite this he compared the groups before and after the TPS activity and he also compared the males and the females to see if there was a gender difference.

He started with the following research question: *Does "think-pair-share" help students retain information better?* Consider his quasi-experimental design below.

Examples of Research from the Classroom

Does "think-pair-share" help students retain information better?

John Foo

I was interested to know if active learning in the classroom has long-term benefits beyond students being more interactive. In particular, I wanted to investigate if think-pair-share could improve the retention of information by students in my medical physiology class.

Before I began my lecture on immunology, I gave my students a survey with the following two questions:

Q1: How does the innate immune system respond to foreign pathogens?
Q2: What 3 mechanisms do antibodies use against foreign substances/pathogens?

This allowed me to determine the ability of my students to answer these questions prior to my lecture. I then posed these two questions again at the appropriate segments of my lecture. After posing Q1, I proceeded to explain the answer immediately. After posing Q2 I implemented think-pair-share before explaining the answer. I observed student engagement during my lecture, including the think-pair-share session.

At the beginning of the next lecture (nineteen days later due to a week of labs, and spring break), I gave my students the same survey. I determined student scores based on the following grading rubric (each question has three key ideas, and each idea is worth one point):

A1: Tissue-residing macrophages:
■   Phagocytose pathogens
■   Release cytokines that cause vasodilation and increase vascular permeability
■   Release chemokines that recruit neutrophils and more macrophages to the site

A2: The 3 mechanisms are:
■   Neutralization—antibodies bind to pathogen, blocking its access to cells
■   Opsonization—antibodies coat pathogen, increasing its susceptibility to phagocytosis
■   Complement Activation—opsonizes pathogen with complement proteins, or recruits more macrophages, or forms pores in the membrane of the pathogen via the membrane-attack complex

Both male and female students scored significantly better only on the think-pair-share question in the post-survey.

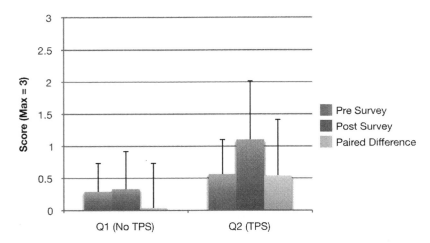

Figure 4.3 The mean student scores for Q1 and Q2 in the pre-survey and post-survey, as well as the paired differences (n = 24). There is a significant difference between the pre-survey and post-survey scores for Q2 as determined using a paired t-test with significance set at $p \leq .05$.

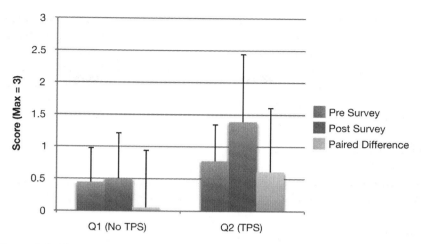

Figure 4.4 The mean scores for male students for Q1 and Q2 in the pre-survey and post-survey, as well as the paired differences (n = 9). There is a significant difference between the pre-survey and post-survey scores for Q2 as determined using a paired t-test with significance set at $p \leq .1$.

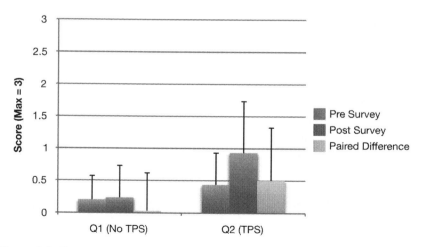

Figure 4.5 The mean scores for female students for Q1 and Q2 in the pre-survey and post-survey, as well as the paired differences (n = 15). There is a significant difference between the pre-survey and post-survey scores for Q2 as determined using a paired t-test with significance set at $p \leq .05$.

Using think-pair-share in my medical physiology class may help me better engage my students, and help them retain information better.

To successfully implement think-pair-share, I need to create *positive learning experiences* by carefully designing questions that spur *discussion and problem solving*, and highlighting the importance of the material through the use of *grades* and *personal accountability*.

In John Foo's example, we notice that he is comparing two groups—males and females—and he is also comparing the same group both before and after the intervention of the think-pair-share on their ability to answer complex questions on a graded assessment. We see that, despite his biases to the contrary, students did better after engaging in the TPS activity than they did after the activity without TPS. Can we make absolute causal claims from this evidence? Not really, but we have more evidence about the possible impact of this process than we otherwise might have. Notice the careful wording of his conclusion as to not over-generalize or make causal claims that may not be the case: *Using think-pair-share in my medical physiology class may help me better engage my students, and help them retain information better.*

John Foo provides a good example of *pre-test post-test of the same group* from the diagram above. This is a popular strategy used in classroom research—providing some kind of pre-assessment measure or pre-test survey and then engaging in an intervention or series of interventions, and then conducting a post-test assessment or survey.

Post-test of two groups

Sometimes we may want to compare two groups at the end of two different learning experiences to compare their experiences. In the example below, Carolyn Fisher from a Biochemistry course wanted to compare students who opted to take a biochemistry course as an "auto-tutorial" course (meaning they taught themselves from a book and lessons on the computer with a weekly meeting that consisted of assessments and opportunities for questions) with students who took biochemistry in the more traditional lecture-based format. She wanted to determine whether there were differences in these groups in their perceptions of what they learned, how difficult the course was, and their level of interest in the material. She also wanted to see what influenced students to choose either of the two options. In her own words below are her research questions and her reasons for examining this.

Examples of Research from the Classroom

I was interested in investigating the different motivations, experiences, and outcomes between students who take an auto-tutorial versus a lecture-based biochemistry course.

■ What motivates students to take an auto-tutorial course or a lecture-based course?

■ What do students feel they get out of an auto-tutorial course compared to previous lecture-based courses they have taken?

■ Was the learning experience within an auto-tutorial course worth the extra effort that is required of them?

■ Is there only a certain kind of student that can be successful in an auto-tutorial or lecture-based course or can any student of any learning style and study habit be successful in either learning environment?

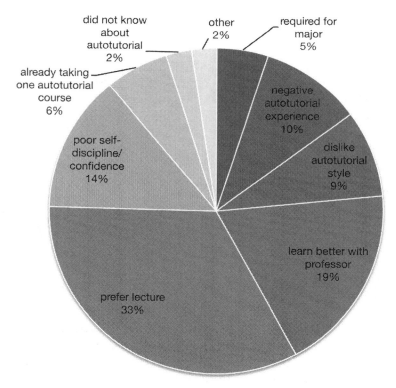

Figure 4.6 Motivation for taking the traditional course.

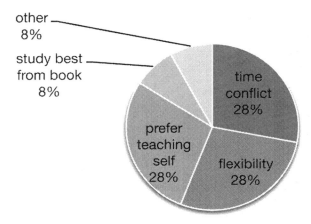

Figure 4.7 Motivation for taking the auto-tutorial course.

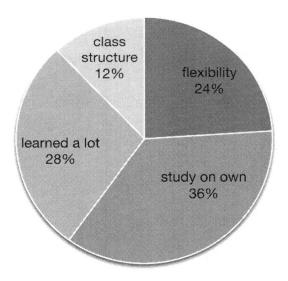

Figure 4.8 The most beneficial aspect of the course, according to students.

Conclusions and summary

■ Most auto-tutorial students chose the course for the flexible structure, because they had a time conflict with the lecture-based course, or because they were confident in their ability to teach themselves.

■ Most lecture students chose the course because they admitted that they lacked self-discipline to teach themselves or had a distinct preference for learning via lecture from a knowledgeable and enthusiastic professor.

- Auto-tutorial students seemed to generally feel that they were learning the information more thoroughly because of the design of the course. They also gained confidence in their ability to teach themselves a rigorous subject.
- Most of the comments (ten out of twelve) from the auto-tutorial students suggested that, despite the extra effort, they did feel like they were learning and remembering more of the course content.
- Most of the students in the lecture course reported they would likely never take an auto-tutorial course.
- The auto-tutorial students seemed to have more of an interest in biochemistry, were more likely to take another biochemistry course, and saw more improvements in their study habits than the lecture students.

Carolyn's project had many more examples of these kinds of descriptive analyses. It is not always necessary to look for statistical significance or engage in sophisticated statistical analyses to analyze quantitative data. Sometimes, in a project like hers, it is interesting enough to examine general differences between the groups and determine what students reported. In the first example, these are pie charts of each group at the conclusion of the courses. In Figure 4.7, we can see the motivations students had for taking the auto-tutorial class. In Figure 4.6, we see the motivations students had for taking the traditional lecture-based course. We can tell by eyeballing the data in this format that the students either had a strong preference for teaching themselves and liked the flexibility (to choose the auto-tutorial course) or they prefered learning from a professor and lecture (to choose the lecture-based course). There were some other interesting responses as well.

Carolyn also compared the two groups on a number of variables—time spent studying, how much they felt they had worked, learned, etc. When comparing the two groups on the question of how easy/difficult they felt their biochemistry course was, the auto-tutorial group reported a lower mean (thought it was easier) than the lecture group.

Post-test only

Perhaps one wants to examine student attitudes or understanding at the conclusion of a course. Administration of a quantitative survey at the conclusion of a course can be useful. Many course evaluation programs are designed to do just this—ask students to rate the professor, content, engagement, feedback, assessments, readings, etc. All professors are familiar with this kind of assessment. How might we use it as data in our research? The answer is, it depends on your research question. Perhaps you are wondering "do young men and women feel the same way about my teaching and my course?" We could use final course evaluations to examine gender differences if gender is one of the demographic questions. Or "do more experienced students tend to rate the course higher than less experienced students?" Or "do students who anticipate receiving a higher grade in the course rate the course more favorably?" These kinds of questions can be examined using end-of-term course evaluations (perhaps by adding some additional demographic data or questions). Often though, the course evaluation is just one source of evidence among other data sources that we can use to triangulate our data (support from different angles/perspectives/approaches).

Other single-group surveys can be useful as well. Gathering feedback from students about a new pedagogical strategy or their affective responses to particular classes or activities may require the use of a good quantitative survey instrument.

SURVEY DEVELOPMENT

Creating a good survey can be challenging. However, starting with good research questions can help. For instance, we may wonder "are there gender differences in the perceptions of the think-pair-share activity?" Or "did students feel that the use of blogging in my course was useful?" Or "did students who opted to go to supplemental help sessions do better in the course?" These questions will help guide the kind of survey you may want to create, the nature of the evidence you will need, and they type of demographic data you may want.

Demographic Data

Demographic data include information about your participants such as race, gender, social class, age, major, minor, year in school, hometown, career aspirations, Grade Point Average (GPA), and so on. These are factors about the participants that may be important or interesting but not directly "tested" in the survey. You don't want to ask for unnecessary demographic information to make your survey unnecessarily long, but you do want to consider what information about your respondents may be relevant for the analysis of your research question.

You never have a second chance to go back and get demographic data in an anonymous survey. Why does this matter? What if you start your data analysis and notice a strange trend in your data—maybe it is related to a demographic factor such as gender or year in school or experience in the major.

Likert and other Rating Scales

Likert scales typically ask respondents to comment on a statement and rate their degree of agreement or disagreement. For example:

Engaging in the debate on affirmative action helped me better understand both sides of the conflict.

1=strongly disagree 2=disagree 3=neutral 4=agree 5=strongly agree

It is also possible to create different kinds of rating scales, for example having respondents rate on a ten-point scale the degree to which they felt confident about a certain surgical procedure: "Rate on a scale from 1–10. 1=completely unconfident 5=neutral 10=confident." This provides the respondent with a greater range of possible answers. Make sure that your statements are worded as statements and are clear to a variety of different people (field test them if possible beforehand).

Asking questions is possible, but the scale will be different. You could provide respondents the following possible responses to a question:

Do you feel that this project helped you critically examine the limitations of neuroscience research?

1 = Not at all
2 = Somewhat
3 = Yes, quite a bit
4 = Yes, a great deal

Or have them rate on a scale of 0–10 where 0 is "not at all" and 10 is "a great deal."

These scales are categorical and may be limited as far as the nature of the data and statistical analysis that can be conducted. You can be creative in your possible responses, but try to make categories mutually exclusive if you can. Examples include "often", "sometimes", "never", or you can be more specific, such as "how much time do you spend thinking about course content?" (more than 2 times per day, daily, 2–6 times per week, etc.). Make sure the categories do not overlap and are mutually exclusive, so 1–2 times per day, 3–4 times per day, 5–6 times per day, and so on. If you choose a category such as "multiple times per day" this may make sense for the question you ask, but realize that what may be "multiple times per day" for one person can vary to others.

COMMON STATISTICAL ANALYSES IN CLASSROOM RESEARCH

For those who may be somewhat math phobic or reluctant to engage in mathematical statistical analysis, rest assured that there are some very basic mathematical strategies that will yield some interesting and useful evidence without engaging in sophisticated statistical analyses. However, some sophisticated analyses are possible as well. At the most basic level is describing the mathematical trends in the data. The most sophisticated we will get in this book is the inferential statistics of the chi-square, t-test and correlation.

Statistical analyses depend on the nature of the data we collect. Not all numerical data is the same.

Levels of Measurement

Nominal—nominal data tend to be more qualitative although they can be analyzed quantitatively. Typically these are categorical data collected as classifications of demographic data, such as gender, race, social class, religion, etc. There is no rating or ranking of one category being "better" than or "higher" than another. We can still look at the number of responses within these categories and conduct chi-squared analyses to determine statistical significance.

Ordinal—ordinal data is the first level of measurement that allows us to rank order and sort from high to low, but the degree of difference between the different measurement is not always clear. It may be that "yes/no" questions can count here if a "yes" is preferable to a "no" response. So "helpful" is preferable to "not helpful" and the Likert scale described above typically has these kinds of values where the differentiation between the numbers is not necessarily equal or clearly defined.

Interval—interval level data does provide a clear degree of difference between numerical ratings. There are clear distinctions, but there are not clear ratios. For example, there may be clear differences between 4 and 2 degrees Celsius, but 4 degrees Celsius is not thought to be twice as hot as 2 degrees Celsius. These kinds of variables are also sometimes called scaled variables. Some good quantitative rubrics may qualify as interval level data but typically they are more ordinal in nature.

Ratio—There are some variables in classroom research that are ratio scale variables. These variables have an exact zero point and we can make statements such as "this is twice as long as that", or "this weighs twice as much as this", or that class is "twice as long as that." Mass, length, time/duration are thought to be ratio scale variables. We can think about class time, length of a course, etc. Sometimes exam scores are considered ratio values as well because an 80 percent score is considered twice as good as a 40 percent score. And there is an absolute zero.

These levels of measurement/types of variables allow us to perform certain kinds of statistical data analyses, so it is important to consider the nature of the data we have.

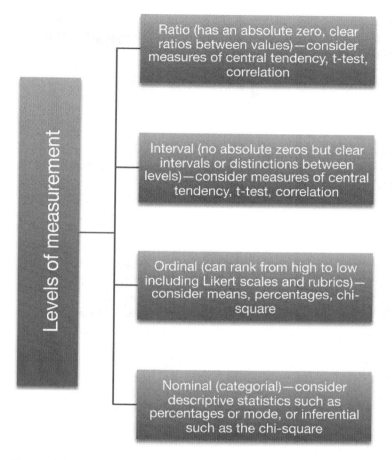

Figure 4.9

DESCRIPTIVE STATISTICS IN CLASSROOM RESEARCH

Descriptive statistics are meant to describe the data. Among the most commonly used in classroom research are measures of central tendency and percentages.

Measures of Central Tendency

Mode—typically when reporting nominal or ordinal (categorical kinds of data) the mode may be the best measure of central tendency to report. The mode is the most frequently occurring response or score. So if you ask a yes/no question, you could report whichever response was the more often reported as the mode or on a quiz whichever score occurred most frequently. These can be reported as percentages as well (see below).

Median—median is the number that appears at the midpoint of the dataset. So when a dataset is split in half it is the value that separates the higher from the lower half. In order to have a median, numerical data must be able to be separated into higher and lower values and ranked. We can report a median in Likert scale data. For example, if we have a course evaluation rating such as "my professor is available for help" 1=strongly disagree 2=disagree 3=agree 4=strongly agree, you can report the median, which is the number that splits the total sample in half. If you have the ratings 2,3,3,3,4,4,4, then the median is 3. With this example we can also report the mean.

Mean—the mean is the average. By adding up all the values and dividing by the number of values, we get the mean. So in the small Likert scale dataset above the average of these scores would be 3.29. Based on our four-point scale this means that the average is closer to agree than strongly agree. Let's say we had these same seven students use the same Likert scale to respond to the statement "The final research project helped build my skills as a researcher." If we see scores such as 3, 3, 4, 4, 4, 4, 4 the mean is 3.7—closer to strongly agree. We see more favorable ratings of the project than the professor's availability.

Variance and standard deviation—Once central tendency has been determined, the next step is often to determine how much variability there is in the data—how spread out it is. This involves computing the standard deviation (the average amount of variability in the sample).

Percentages—Sometimes, presenting percentages can be sufficient. Often with demographic data this can be an effective way of communicating these different categories. Consider these examples from Jared Hale's project:

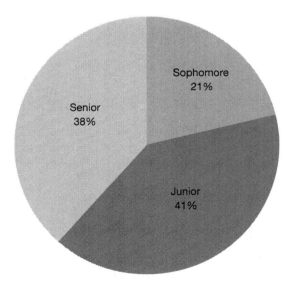

Figure 4.10

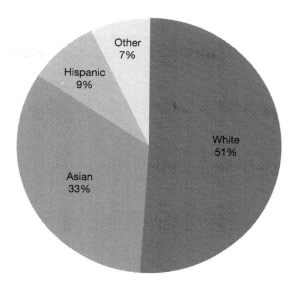

Figure 4.11

Sometimes just reporting the distribution of numbers can be useful, as Jared presented in the number of help sessions students reported attending.

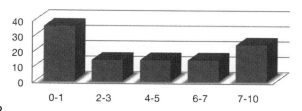

Figure 4.12

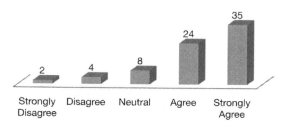

Figure 4.13

Below we see the percentage scores on the two major exams/prelims grouped by the number of problem-solving sessions students attended. We see interesting trends in the data that led him to title his project: "Optional Problem-Solving Sessions in Genetics: All or Nothing?" We can see that students who attended nearly all the sessions (9–10) did only slightly better than those who only attended 1–2. And oddly those who attended 6–8 sessions did the most poorly of any group—including those who went to no sessions at all. Strange trends indeed. The numbers alone are not sufficient. Fortunately as we will discuss in mixed method design, Jared's qualitative data helped explain some of the trends.

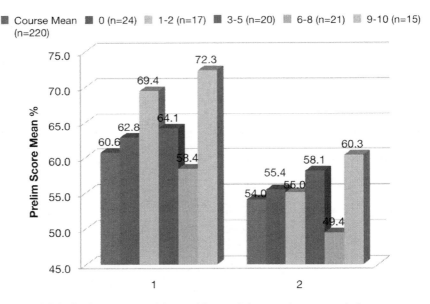

Figure 4.14 Prelims grouped by problem-solving sessions attended.

INFERENTIAL STATISTICS

Sometimes we want to find out whether what we have found is statistically significant. For example, the next logical question in Jared Hale's study is "is the difference between the scores of the students who attended all the problem-solving sessions significantly different than those who did not attend any?" The reality is that because this was a preliminary project, he was not interested in statistical significance as much as reporting the numbers and trends for consideration in curriculum planning. However, in Emily Pollina's example below, she provides statistical comparisons of pre- and post-test data comparing groups that provides some inferential statistics, examining for statistical significance.

The T-Test to Compare Means

Once we have the mean and the standard deviation we can compute whether the difference between two means is statistically significant. The t-test is an inferential statistic designed to compare two means to determine if the difference is significant. If, for example, you want to compare students' means on an assessment before an academic experience and then after, you can compare the means of the pre- and post-test and determine, using the t-test statistic, if the probability value (p-value) is less than .01 or .05 (depending on your determined probability that you can accurately reject the null hypothesis). Typically if the $p<.01$ you have a very strong likelihood that you can reject the null hypothesis (that your evidence supports your hypothesis) and between .01 and .05 you still have strong claims that you have statistically significant results. Notice in the example below how Emily Pollina uses the t-test statistic to examine whether there are statistically significant differences between her groups.

Examples of Research from the Classroom

Students' Perceptions of Efficacy

Emily Pollina

While I perceived important progress on student writing, I wanted to understand how students perceived their comfort with writing, primary literature, and the scientific community. One of the goals of this project was to help students become more confident in their abilities to locate and use primary literature, and to help them feel more a part of the scientific community. To measure their feelings on these topics, students were given a survey before most of the primary literature workshops and at the end of the course.

In the "Writing in the Majors" course (WIM), students showed trends towards increasing comfort with primary literature. WIM students reported a marginally significant increase in their comfort in identifying primary literature articles ($t = -2.20564, n = 11, p = .0519$, Figure 4.15), and awareness of how primary literature is used as evidence in a scientific article ($t = -2.20564, n = 11, p = .0519$, Figure 4.15). However, they did not show significant improvement in comfort with using primary literature to verify information for a non-scientific audience ($t= -.93761, n = 10, p = .3705$, Figure 4.15). This may be because this class did not focus as much on writing for non-scientific audiences as the FWS (first year writing seminar) class did. Interestingly, despite writing proposals on novel topics, they did not report a significantly greater awareness of current research topics in the area of ecology ($t = -1, n = 10, p = .3409$, Figure 4.15), though there was a trend towards greater awareness.

65

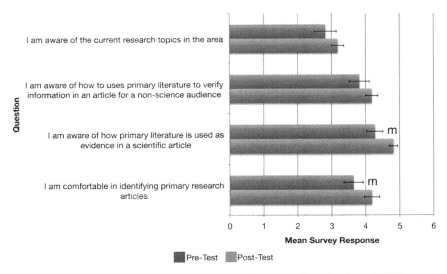

Figure 4.15 Student comfort with primary literature. Results from WIM students (n = 11). Error bars represent ±1 standard error. * represents pairs of means that are significantly different at p = .05, while m = pairs of means that are different at p < .07.

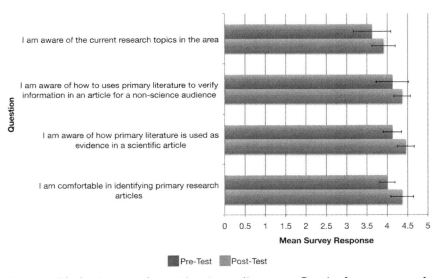

Figure 4.16 Student comfort with primary literature. Results from surveys of FWS students (n = 7). Error bars represent ±1 standard error. * represents pairs of means that are significantly different at p = .05, while m = pairs of means that are different at p < .07.

The FWS students struggled rather more with primary literature, and this is reflected in their survey responses. Students showed a non-significant increase in their comfort in identifying primary literature articles ($t = -1.92154, n = 7, p = .1030$, Figure 4.16), and awareness of how primary literature is used as evidence in a scientific article ($t = -2.12132, n = 7, p = .0781$, Figure 4.16). However, given the low sample size in this study, the fact that we were able to detect this trend towards increasing comfort in using primary literature for a scientific audience is perhaps encouraging. However, they, like their WIM counterparts, did not show an increase in comfort with using primary literature to verify information for a non-scientific audience ($t = -.67937, n = 10, p = .5222$, Figure 4.16) or greater knowledge of current topics ($t = -.67937, n = 7, p = .5222$, Figure 4.16).

They, do, however, report more confidence in writing for a scientific audience. They show a significant increase in the number agreeing that they felt comfortable writing a literature review ($t = -3.62738, n = 10, p = .0046$, Figure 4.17), a marginally significant trend towards being more comfortable writing an opinion piece for a newspaper ($t = -2.18543, n = 10, p = .0537$, Figure 4.17), and a non-significant trend towards being more comfortable choosing an appropriate voice for their audience (Figure 4.17).

Comfort in writing

FWS students made some important gains in their comfort with writing. FWS students reported significantly more comfort when writing with peers at the end of the semester ($t = -2.5, n = 7, p = .0465$, Figure 4.17). They also reported non-significant trends towards greater comfort in writing an opinion piece for a local newspaper ($t = -.6793, n = 7, p = .5222$, Figure 4.17) and a scientific literature review ($t = -1.74608, n = 6, p = .1412$, Figure 4.17). Interestingly, despite these trends in comfort with these two very different types of audiences, when surveyed directly about their comfort with audience, they reported no significant difference in comfort writing for a particular audience ($t = 0, n = 6, p = 1.0$, Figure 4.17).

However, the class did seem to increase their self-confidence in their writing, and possibly their meta-analytic skills. Students were significantly more likely to agree that their writing was excellent at the end of the course ($t = -4.58258, n = 6, p = .0038$, Figure 4.17), and they reported non-significant increases in awareness of how they learn best ($t = -1.54919, n = 6, p = .1723$, Figure 4.17) and their revision choices ($t = -2.12132, n = 6, p = 0.0781$, Figure 4.17).

In contrast, WIM students did not show such dramatic gains in confidence about their writing, despite my perception of their writing as good, and often excellent. They were not significantly more comfortable writing with peers at the end of the semester ($t = -1.17444, n = 10, p = .2674$, Figure 4.18), though this is likely because FWS students spent much more time writing with peers than did WIM students. In addition, they did not report more confidence in the excellence of their writing overall ($t = 0, n = 10, p = 1.0$, Figure 4.18), or greater meta-awareness of their learning styles

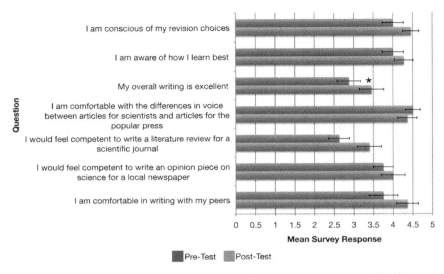

Figure 4.17 Student comfort with writing. Results from surveys of FWS students (n = 7). Error bars represent ±1 standard error. * represents pairs of means that are significantly different at p = .05, while m = pairs of means that are different at p < .07.

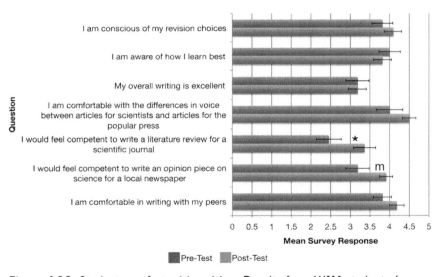

Figure 4.18 Student comfort with writing. Results from WIM students (n = 11). Error bars represent ±1 standard error. * represents pairs of means that are significantly different at p = .05, while m = pairs of means that are different at p < .07.

(t = 1.0, n = 10, p = .3409, Figure 4.18) or their revision choices (t = −.75955, n = 10, p = .4650, Figure 4.18).

Comfort with the nature of science

These workshops helped students to read and write effectively with primary literature. Sadly, the evidence for their efficacy in improving awareness of the nature of science is by no means as conclusive. Neither the FWS students nor the WIM students reported a significant increase in awareness of what scientists do at the end of the course (FWS: Figure 4.19, t = −1.54919, n = 7, p = .1723; WIM: Figure 4.20, t = 0, n = 10, p = 1.0.) Similarly, neither reported additional awareness of the limitations of scientific evidence (FWS: Figure 4.19, t = 0, n = 6, p= 1.0; WIM: Figure 4.20, t = .288675, n = 10, p = .7787), or of feeling like part of the scientific community (FWS: Figure 4.19, t = −.42008, n = 7, p = .1723; WIM: Figure 4.20, t = 0, n = 10, p = .6891).

However, both groups did report a non-significant trend towards a greater awareness of scientific techniques (FWS: Figure 4.19, t = −1, n = 7, p = .3559; WIM: Figure 4.20, t = −1.45556, n = 10, p = .1762). And the FWS students reported a significant increase in comfort with the dialogue of the scientific community (Figure 4.19, t = −2.5205, n = 6, p = .0453), though the WIM students did not report such an increase (Figure 4.20, t = −.24693, n = 10, p = .8100).

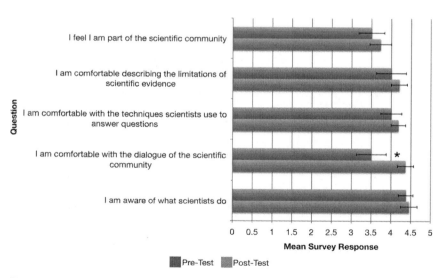

Figure 4.19 Student comfort with nature of science. Results from surveys of FWS students (n = 7). Error bars represent ±1 standard error. * represents pairs of means that are significantly different at p = .05, while m = pairs of means that are different at p < .07.

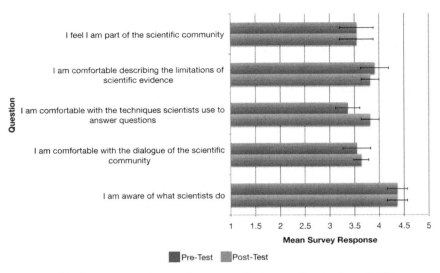

Figure 4.20 Student comfort with nature of science. Results from WIM students (n = 11). Error bars represent ±1 standard error. * represents pairs of means that are significantly different at p = .05, while m = pairs of means that are different at p < .07. FWS students showed the greatest gains in confidence in scientific dialogue, but neither group reported more confidence in evaluating scientific evidence.

Emily's classroom research study provides excellent examples of the ways we can use inferential statistics to examine statistical significance. Here she relies on the t-test (perhaps the most popular of the inferential statistics when comparing groups such as these on exams, or rubric performance, or in means on student rating scales). Most software programs will compute t-tests, even Excel. However, make sure you have the right kind of data for the analysis and that the t-test answers your question appropriately. Typically, when comparing two means from two sets of data (typically paired data at the ordinal level at least), the t-test is useful. We look at the "p" value, which is the probability that we can reject the null hypothesis. As a rule of thumb, p<.05 is thought to provide a high enough level of statistical significance to reject the null hypothesis.

For example, the null hypothesis may state: There are no significant differences between the pre-test scores and post-test scores on the attitude survey. Our research question may be to determine if there are significant differences, and we may hope to see some improved attitudes as a result of our instruction. However, typically the "null hypothesis" is the hypothesis if there was no impact or difference.

The standard error is shown in Emily's above project with her use of error bars in the diagrams. Standard error gives a sense of statistical uncertainty or our confidence interval for the tests—in this case, given the use of the t-test statistic the error bars give a sense of how certain we can be in our findings given the sample size and the variance. The statistic takes into account the sample size and allows us a greater degree of certainty that the difference is not due to chance alone, but to something related to the intervention. It gives a bit of wiggle room to suggest that there is room for error in the findings.

Chi-square for categorical data

The chi-square test is a useful inferential statistic when you want to examine differences between groups for which you have nominal (categorical) or even ordinal data. The chi-square statistic allows you to determine whether the groups are significantly different. For example, perhaps you are comparing two groups and categorizing students based on who got a particular question on an exam correct or not. This would be categorical data—they either got the question correct or not. Your data could look something like this:

Table 4.1

	Question 1 correct	Question 1 incorrect
Class 1	20	20
Class 2	10	30
Total	30	50

The question you may have as you look at these data is "is this difference between my first class and my second statistically significant (greater than would happen by chance)?" You could do a chi-square analysis (which considers the actual observed frequencies in each category and makes projections about what the "expected" frequencies would be if the difference was just based on chance alone). If you run a chi-square statistic you can then determine whether or not the probability (p-value) shows statistical significance, and thus whether these differences are enough to be explained by chance alone or attributable to your intervention (or something else).

Correlation and regression to examine relationships and make predictions

Sometimes we may want to know if there is a statistically significant relationship between two variables. Perhaps we want to know if exam grades are correlated with class attendance or if performance on a particular paper is related to one's class year. Correlation, and specifically the "Pearson's r," allows us to determine the relationship between two variables. You will get a number between −1 and 1. The closer to −1 the value is, the more negative the relationship—meaning, as one value goes up, the other goes down. The closer to positive 1 the value is, the more positive the relationship (as one goes up the other goes up). The p-value will allow you to make claims of significance, but the value tells you direction of relationship and strength of correlation. We cannot make claims of causality—one variable does not cause the other to change.

In regression analysis, we are able to make some claims of predictability. So the correlation shows us the slope of the linear relationship, but the regression analysis makes statistical predictions based on that. As with most statistical tests like regression there are different types (linear regression, simple regression, logistic regression, and so on). A simple linear regression allows you to examine associations between a particular variable (nominal, ordinal) and a variable that is more continuous. So an example might be how well class attendance predicts exam scores or performance on a paper using a rubric. A multiple regression model allows you to examine more than one variable to determine how well it predicts the dependent variable. Generally, however, this statistic is focused on making predictions or forecasting based on the relationships between or among variables. When conducting a regression analysis, one will still get a p-value, which will indicate the statistical significance of the result and the probability that you can reject your null hypothesis.

Consider the following example in which we see that there is a perfect positive linear relationship between SAT verbal scores and SAT math scores (the correlation coefficient is +1.0), indicating that these two scores have a perfect and positive correlation—meaning as one goes up, so does the other in perfect unison. The regression line shown in Figure 4.21 is useful in seeing how we may predict one score if we have another.

If we know a score is 400 on one, then using the regression line we could predict that the score on the other would also be 400.

OVER-SIMPLIFICATION OF THE STATISTICS

This discussion of the statistical possibilities within classroom research is definitely an over-simplification. The purpose here is not to provide a detailed description of the statistics, but to provide a discussion of the kinds of statistics you might want to consider when analyzing the numerical data you might gather within a teaching-related research project.

The other goal here is to provide enough information for those without statistical backgrounds that they can make sense of others' studies that they may encounter when locating their own projects within the research literature. Online

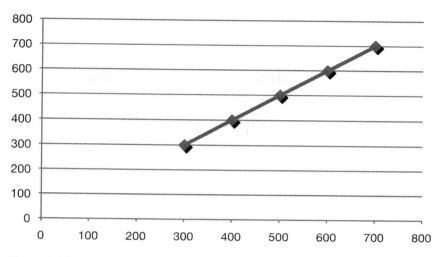

Figure 4.21

statistical tutorials exist, as does excellent statistical software with help features. For example, there are tutorials connected to software such as those associated with popular statistical software programs such as SPSS (www.spsstools.net/spss.htm) or SAS (http://support.sas.com/training/tutorial). There are also websites with general overviews, for example www.psych.utoronto.ca/courses/c1/spss/toc.htm.

Chapter 5

Using Assessment Data as Research Evidence to Improve Teaching and Learning

In this chapter:

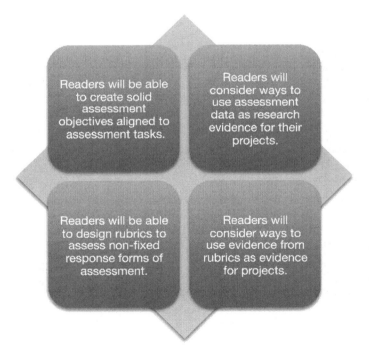

Readers will be able to create solid assessment objectives aligned to assessment tasks.

Readers will consider ways to use assessment data as research evidence for their projects.

Readers will be able to design rubrics to assess non-fixed response forms of assessment.

Readers will consider ways to use evidence from rubrics as evidence for projects.

The language used in the boxes above is based on the language of constructing learning outcomes/objectives. In these boxes you, as the reader, are being told early in the chapter what the learning outcomes for the chapter are. Ideally we do this in our courses on our syllabi. We state the learning outcomes and explain these to our students. We then construct assessments to determine if our students (or the degree to which our students) have learned what we stated in our learning outcomes/objectives.

Using assessment data as classroom research evidence is incredibly beneficial. Why? Because good assessment data should provide us with good evidence about what is happening in our courses. We collect assessment data on students regularly. These data should be linked to what we want students to gain from their involvement in the course (our stated learning outcomes/objectives). We can collect and analyze these data purposefully to better understand what is happening in our course(s). Professors have these data as part of the classroom experience, so using them as part of data analysis in classroom research projects can be quite useful and add an additional level of engagement with our data.

We are all engaged in the act of assessing every day. We assess whether our clothes fit, whether we have enough food in the house, how much time a particular task will take, and so on. In the classroom, we collect information and make a judgment and typically act based on that judgment. The same is true with classroom assessment. We collect information, typically in the form of student work; then we provide a judgment on that work and then act accordingly. We provide feedback to students throughout the course of a semester or term (formative assessment), and we are expected to provide some kind of grade or feedback at the end of the course/semester (summative assessment). Both formative and summative assessment can be very useful in classroom research.

Selecting from the myriad of possible assessment strategies can be overwhelming—should we give a traditional test? Should we assign a paper? Should we have students give a presentation? How can we best get students to show us what they have learned/mastered as a result of our learning event(s)?

Before determining which assessment strategy or task to select, one must determine what we should assess. We must clearly state what our outcomes are for a particular learning event (in the case of formative assessment) first. The next consideration is what we ultimately hope students to master as a result of taking the course. That is, what do we hope students will be able to do or know as a result of the learning experience? Do we expect a level of mastery? If so, what do we want them to retain as a result of this experience beyond the day, week, month, year?

FORMATIVE VERSUS SUMMATIVE ASSESSMENT

1. Formative assessment asks: How will we assess students along the way to see how they are progressing on our stated learning objectives/outcomes?
2. Summative assessment asks: How will we determine at the end the degree to which our students have met the stated learning objectives/outcomes for the whole course?

75

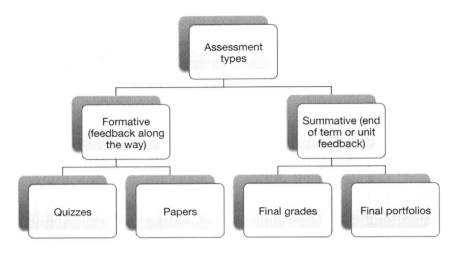

Figure 5.1

How Can We Assess Students Formatively and Summatively?

Traditional versus authentic assessment

Traditional assessments have typically involved outcome-testing methods such as multiple choice, matching, and "fill in the blank". We use traditional methods in the classroom for both formative and summative assessments. In addition, these methods are useful for comparing large groups of students—such as the case with state or local exams, including high stakes tests.

Authentic assessment (also known as alternative assessment) uses non-testing forms of assessment including observation and what are known as the "4 Ps": Process, Performance, Portfolio, and Production.

Process—students engage in a process and are assessed based on this. For example, to get a drivers' license, young drivers must be assessed using a driving exam where they actually drive a car. Evaluators have a checklist of behaviors of successful drivers that they use to determine whether a student passes or fails.

Performance—students engage in a performance and are assessed on the quality of the aspects of it. For example, many musicians must engage in performances and are assessed on how they do. In some classrooms students must do oral reports or engage in debates where they are judged based on their performance.

Product—students often create tangible products that teachers judge or assess. For example, students create products for the science fair or they create work products of all sorts, including original written pieces or clay structures.

Portfolio—there are a variety of types of portfolios to choose from depending on what the assessment outcomes are. If your outcome is to examine growth over time, you may want to have students create a process portfolio—with samples of work that show progress over time. If you want more of a summative portfolio, then you'll want to have students gather artifacts that represent their best work. There are also electronic portfolios that may be used to examine progress over time or best work samples.

Regardless of the type of authentic or alternative assessment, to be consistent in assessing student performance on these measures, one must create clear guidelines and have these guidelines match outcomes, and ultimately match the criteria outlined in an assessment rubric.

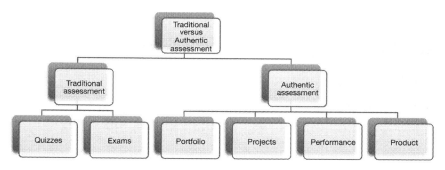

Figure 5.2

Angelo and Cross, in their book *Classroom Assessment Techniques: A Handbook for College Teachers*, provide detailed examples of possible classroom assessment strategies. Below is a non-exhaustive list of some of the examples they provide:

Content understanding / knowledge / skills
- Background knowledge probe
- Focused listing
- Muddiest point
- Misconception check
- Memory matrix

Analysis and critical thinking
- Categorization grid
- Defining features matrix

77

- Pro and con grid
- Analytic memo

Creative thinking and problem solving
- One sentence summary
- Analogies
- Problem recognition tasks
- Documented problem solutions

Learner attitudes and self assessment
- Class opinion polls
- Ethical dilemmas
- Self-confidence surveys
- Autobiographical sketches
- Self assessment

Many more assessment strategies exist, but before choosing the correct assessment tool from the toolbox, it is important to figure out what you want to assess and the kind of information you need.

Start with Outcomes

Before designing assessment, we must first figure out what our learning outcomes are—that is, what do we want students to be able to know or do as a result/outcome of the instructional experience we are designing. These should:

- be student-centered
- have a measurable, action, learning-related verb
- be related to the instructional experience.

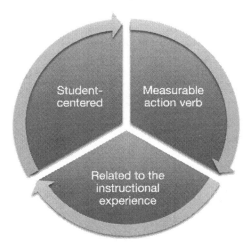

Figure 5.3

For example, perhaps for one of your learning outcomes you want students to be able to provide some substantiated explanations for global warming at the end of your instructional time. If this is the case then your learning outcome could be as simple as: "Students will be able to provide substantiated explanations for global warming."

To create an assessment objective/outcome from this learning outcome, you need to include:

1. The task under which you will observe the performance.
2. The criteria for acceptable performance (or, ideally, mastery).

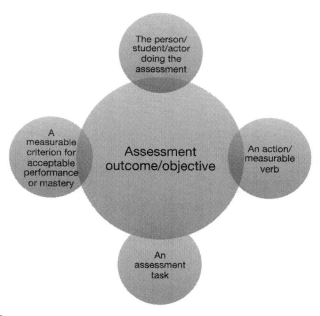

Figure 5.4

So an assessment objective/outcome contains:

1. The subject/person/student/actor who will be doing the assessment/performance. In most cases for teachers writing outcomes, this will be students.
2. An action or measurable verb—ideally one that works at higher levels on Bloom's taxonomy (see Figure 5.6 below for ideas—also consider what kind of THINKING the student being asked to do, e.g., causal reasoning, categorizing, describing, etc.).

3. An assessment task (performance, exam, paper, etc.) during or after which you will observe or can measure whether the outcome has been met (that is, the strategy the student is using to represent his/her cognition/understanding).
4. A measurable criterion for acceptable performance or mastery.

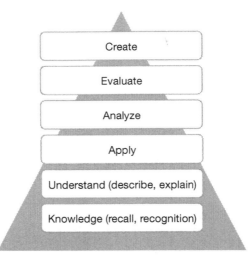

Figure 5.5 Bloom's revised taxonomy (based on an adaptation of the American Psychology Association from Anderson and Krathwohl 2001).

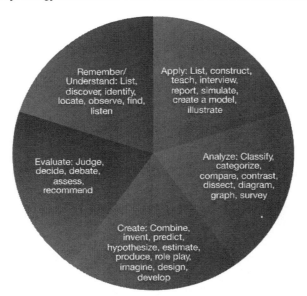

Figure 5.6 Bloom's wheel of words for creating outcomes/objectives.

Within the "wheel" we see the thinking/outcome type in the middle and then some verbs that may help in the design of the outcome/objective, and then some possible assessment tasks or "products" you may assign to achieve these.

In our first example we stated that we wanted students to be able to provide some substantiated explanations for global warming at the end of the instructional time. How will we know if students can do this? We could ask them to write a short paper. We could have them take a quiz? We could have them submit a lengthier paper or report for homework that incorporates more evidence they must find on their own. Many options are possible. So, let's say we choose to simply have students write a short paper at the end of class and we expect that they can provide at least three substantiated explanations for global warming. Now, our outcome becomes clear: "Students will be able to provide at least three substantiated explanations for global warming in a short essay."

The "at least 3 substantiated explanations" is our "criterion" for acceptable performance. The "short essay" is the assessment task, during which they will show the degree to which they have learned these explanations. So, our rubric may be brief but should be aligned with the outcome and the criterion.

	Needs improvement = 1 point	Acceptable = 2 points	Exceptional = 3 points
Provides substantiated explanations for global warming.	Provides one substantiated explanation.	Provides two substantiated explanations.	Provides three well-substantiated explanations.

Let's say we also want students to include evidence to back up their explanations. This would require another outcome: "2. Students will cite credible evidence to support each of their explanations of global warming." This assessment objective assumes that the ideal is to provide credible evidence to support all three examples. Then we need to add it to our rubric:

	Needs improvement = 1 point	Acceptable = 2 points	Exceptional = 3 points
Provides substantiated explanations for global warming.	Provides one substantiated explanation.	Provides two substantiated explanations.	Provides three well-substantiated explanations.
Provides credible evidence to support explanation.	Provides credible evidence for one explanation.	Provides credible evidence to support two explanations.	Provides credible evidence to support all three explanations.

TYPES OF RUBRICS

There are different basic categories of rubrics, including *analytic* and *holistic*. Generally, so far, this chapter has focused on analytic rubric development. If you are engaged in more summative assessment you may want to create a holistic rubric that addresses levels of mastery to help determine a student's final grade as a representation of a percentage of mastery of your stated outcomes.

Generally, a holistic rubric yields a single score/number/grade with all criteria for mastery included. So, for example, a holistic rubric might be created to help with the determination of a final grade for a course—or a final grade on a more summative-like assignment. The result is a single score/grade that represents perhaps many ideas in one final grade. The rubric makes clear what is being considered in that number or grade.

Example Holistic Rubric for Class Participation

A: Attended every class session; completed all in class assignments and tasks with at least a check-plus; group members rated as participating/helping/sharing in small group regularly.

B: Missed 1–2 class sessions; completed all but 1–2 in class assignments; group members rated as generally helpful and participative in small group activities.

C: Missed 3–4 class sessions; completed all but 3–4 assignments in-class assignments; group members had some positive rankings of participation in small group.

D: Missed 5–6, completed all but 5 assignments; lacked group positive rankings.

E: Missed more than 6 class sessions, completed fewer than 5 assignments, group members gave negative feedback about participation.

USING ASSESSMENT IN CLASSROOM RESEARCH PROJECTS

One of the ways we can use classroom assessment is to help us determine if our objectives/outcomes for student learning have been met. Our assessments provide evidence about student performance on outcome measures. Assessments also allow us to see how groups of students are performing on particular issues.

For example Emily Pollina was teaching a first-year writing seminar in the natural sciences and a more advanced "writing in the majors" course. She used rubrics for both courses and wanted to determine (among other things) the degree to which students were able to engage with scholarly sources. She engaged in a series of workshops with her students and then examined the themes that emerged from her comments on student papers, as well as student performance, using the rubrics she created to assess her students' writing. She found the following themes that emerged based on her analysis of student assessment and her feedback.

Examples of Research from the Classroom

Instructor evaluations of student writing

Emily Pollina

The difference between the two sections of my writing courses in terms of student comfort with primary literature was evident in student writing assignments. Nonetheless, students in both sections were able to make important gains in the sophistication with which they used primary literature. Examples of what constituted an increase in sophistication varied between students, partially because some students had much more trouble using primary literature effectively at the outset. Below are some examples of ways students used primary literature more effectively in secondary drafts than in early drafts, as demonstrated by their performance on the rubrics I created for the assignment grounded in the outcomes for the course.

Paraphrasing rather than quoting: In formal scientific writing, quoting is rare and stylistically eccentric. Students would be encouraged to paraphrase and cite, rather than quoting directly. This represents a challenge, however, as effective paraphrasing requires a solid understanding of the technical work one is paraphrasing. Students who were able to effectively paraphrase demonstrated their ability to summarize the important points of an article in their own words.

Amassing a greater amount of primary evidence: Some of the student gains in writing sophistication simply meant delving deeper into the body of knowledge on a particular topic—finding and citing a wider variety of literature on a particular subject. While this seems like a simple task, realizing that you need more information and doing additional research is actually a challenging skill for some undergraduates (Sommers 1980), and willingness to do this represents an increase in skill for some students.

Organizing more proficiently the evidence used: Many students struggled with the organization of their written pieces, and were citing similar information in several paragraphs. Through discussions, in-class writing responses, and comments, several students were able to re-organize information to group themes and improve the flow of their argument.

Synthesizing articles rather than simply listing their information: Several students, distributed across the two classes, struggled to put their articles together into a coherent argument. Their papers read like a series of summaries on the previous literature on their topic. Through repeated drafting, one of these students did an excellent job at pruning the summaries and integrating the information in them into his own argument.

83

The other student who struggled with this also made some progress, including more of his own analysis, although there were still many "summary paragraphs" in his final report.

Using a broad range of primary scholarship, including non-science (e.g., anthropology, economics, ethics): Many of the students were studying topics that had a social, ethical, or economic component. These students were able to locate primary sources from the appropriate discipline and cite these studies. While this does not indicate greater comfort with primary scientific literature, it does suggest a respect for primary intellectual scholarship—the source of original scholarship that is a crucial part of any field. While the previous types of gains in student writing and primary literature use were distributed across both classes, certain types of sophistication gains were only seen in the WIM class.

Using papers as models for technique as well as sources of background information: Several students realized that they could bolster their proposals by citing methods that other people had successfully used to answer related questions. This type of citation moves past using scientific articles merely for background information, to realizing that scientific articles can contain models for how to practice science.

Including a wider variety of justifications for studies: Most students' work was very application focused. When asked to explain why their proposed research was important, most students discussed things that their research would help make or build. For example, my student studying genes conferring salt tolerance discussed the possibility of genetically engineering salt-tolerant plants. Through discussion, students broadened the focus of their justification to include the joy of knowing the answer. Students began to realize that for the scientific community, answering a question that has never been asked is justification itself.

Pointing out articles that disagreed with each other and proposing research to resolve the dispute: One student noticed inconsistencies in the published literature on the effect of wild dog pack size on prey capture efficiency. She therefore proposed her study to (among other things) resolve this dispute in the literature. Identifying scientific debates from reading and synthesizing a body of literature is a crucial skill—one practiced by many scientists looking for their next project.

Disagreeing with published articles' methods: Several students criticized the methods of published studies, either in their writing or in class. Willingness to disagree in this way represents a major intellectual gain for students, as most students see themselves as inexpert and are reluctant to criticize published works. This type of robust critique is an important part of scientific dialogue (it happens at every journal club I've been in), and becoming familiar with it helps students to practice a key part of scientific thinking.

In Joel Anderson's humanities-oriented first-year seminar course "Medieval Books in the Digital Age" (also a first-year writing seminar class), he worked to analyze his comments and feedback on student writing. He looked for themes that emerged based on his feedback, including his comments in the margins of student work. He gathered together all of his handwritten marginalia and examined these for themes—what were the kinds of comments he made regularly.

In my own experience in teaching graduate students in my course entitled "Theories of Learning and Cognitive Development," I have analyzed my comments and found consistently the following themes: I tend to focus on pushing students to "use good evidence" and to "critique evidence" in their papers. This theme of evidence is a bias that I know I have. I do consistently tell students that becoming critical consumers of information is perhaps one of the most important skills they can learn as teachers in the information age, so this can help students gain these skills. This is one of my stated objectives in the course. My feedback is connected to this overarching educational goal that I have and comes through in my feedback. It is also reflected within the rubric:

Rubric for Assignment 3	1–3 points	4 points	5 points
Thesis and conclusions	Thesis and/or conclusions are limited.	Thesis and conclusions are somewhat grounded in research and are relevant or compelling.	Thesis and conclusions are grounded in the research literature and course content— relevant and compelling.
Research literature used	Studies included are dated or it is not clear that they are from peer-reviewed sources.	Some good contemporary studies included—3–4 from peer-reviewed sources.	Good contemporary studies included—used a minimum of 5 from peer-reviewed sources.
Analysis of research literature	Lacking good analysis and few connections.	Some good analysis of evidence with limited connections.	Carefully analyzed evidence and critique of evidence—connections made between and among studies.
Inclusion of other course readings/ materials/ concepts	Lack of connection to course content.	Makes some good connections to course content.	Makes several clearly considered connections to multiple course sources.
Application to personal or professional life	Provides limited application of topic to personal or professional life.	Provides some good applications.	Provides strong applications of topic to personal and/or professional life grounded in the research.

Some of the terminology used in my rubric emerged from analysis of my margin comments. In addition, I have made adaptations to assignments and assessments based on the consistent feedback I find myself giving students. I do recognize when analyzing the above rubric that terms such as "good" or "relevant" or "compelling" are highly subjective. I typically counsel faculty to take ambiguous or subjective terms out of a rubric because it can lead to inconsistent judgments (unless you can explain to students what you mean explicitly). I will tell students that words such as relevant and compelling are subjective and that I expect they will defend why they found particular issues/evidence/topics relevant and compelling and why they are considered so in the contemporary research literature. We must be mindful of the ambiguous, highly subjective terms we use in rubrics and I would advise, particularly if you are new to rubric development, avoiding them and staying as concrete and measurable as possible. Doing this can be very challenging.

Rubric to Assess Classroom Research Projects

There has been a push to create rubrics that have gradations of performance listed categorically (like the one above). However, sometimes a checklist-style rubric is more appropriate—particularly if there are not really levels of performance, but rather clearly articulated components of an assignment that must be present, and if missing result in poorer quality work.

This is a rubric that I developed to assess classroom research projects for doctoral students and faculty:

RUBRIC TO ASSESS RESEARCH PROJECTS

Adapted from Gay, Mills and Airasian

Note: This rubric will be used during the drafting process and for self and peer formative and summative assessment

Abstract

- Is the problem restated? _____/1
- Are the number and type of subjects and instruments described briefly? _____/1
- Is the design used identified? _____/1
- Are procedures described? _____/1
- Are the major results and conclusions restated? _____/1

Total _____/5 points

Introduction

- Is the problem stated? ____/1
- Is there a hypothesis statement (for quantitative research) and objectives listed (for qualitative research)? ____/1
- Is the problem able to be researched? Can data be collected or analyzed or can the topic be investigated as stated? ____/1
- Is background information presented and is the importance described? ____/1
- Are variables or issues clearly defined and described without use of jargon where possible? ____/1
- Does it set up the paper and what exactly is to follow? ____/1

Total ____/6 points

Comments:

Review of literature

- Is the review comprehensive (involving a variety of substantive original research)? ____/1
- Are references cited related to the research question? ____/1
- Are most sources primary (that is, they are original research articles, not summaries of research)? ____/6
- Is there a critical analysis of the literature included and relevance to the study explained? ____/1
- Is it well-organized and does it flow well? ____/1
- Is there a conclusion paragraph that summarizes the literature in general? ____/1
- Does the literature review logically set up the hypothesis or objectives that follow? ____/1
- Is APA style used to cite references appropriately within the text? ____/1
- Is APA style used appropriately in the reference section? ____/1
- Is the hypothesis or objectives clearly stated? Are important terms defined? ____/1

Total ____/15 points

Comments:

Method

- Are participants' characteristics described? Nature of the participants (gender, race, socio-economic class, special characteristics relevant for study)? _____/1
- Number of participants? If a small number describe in greater detail. _____/1
- How were participants selected or chosen? Are potential biases issues of power, etc. described if appropriate? _____/1
- For quantitative: Are instruments used/created/or selected described in terms of their validity, reliability, purpose, and content (sample questions, how created, etc.)? _____/1
- For qualitative: Are strategies use appropriate given the objectives stated? _____/1
- Is the research design appropriate to address the objectives OR adequately test the hypothesis of the study? _____/1
- Are the procedures described in enough detail that another researcher could replicate them? _____/2
- Are procedures and hypotheses OR objectives linked appropriately? 2 points _____/2
- Is the context of the study described in detail? (The school? The classroom? The program, etc.) _____/1

Total _____/11 points

Comments:

Results

For quantitative:
- Are appropriate statistics chosen given the nature of the study and the data? _____/1
- Are statistical significance levels given? _____/1
- Are tables or figures appropriate and easily understood? _____/1

For qualitative:
- Is there an explanation of how data were analyzed (constant comparative or some other method of analysis)? _____/1
- Are themes logically derived from the data? _____/1
- Is there more analysis than description? _____/1

For both:
- Are results clearly stated? ___/1
- Do data provided and results make sense? _____/1

Total _____/8 points

Comments:

Conclusions/discussion/recommendations

- Do conclusions logically flow from the data provided? ____/1
- Is the discussion based on original hypothesis or objectives presented in the beginning? ____/1
- Generalizability issues described? ____1
- Limitations discussed? ____/1
- Future research or action needed? _____/1

Total ____/5 points

Total ___/50 points

As you write up your own classroom research projects, this rubric can serve as a way to self-assess your project. I have classroom researchers use this rubric to self-assess before submitting their final project. The point values are for computing final grades, but certainly the rubric could be used without points, and just to provide feedback.

Rubrics to Assess Values and Creative Work

Often when working with faculty or future faculty on rubric development, I hear the desire to assess qualities that are difficult to articulate in rubric form, such as "creativity" or a "positive feeling about the subject matter" or in group work "working cooperatively." These are possible to measure using rubrics. The Association of American Colleges and Universities has created some examples of rubrics designed to assess values. They have created and posted several VALUE rubrics. VALUE stands for Valid Assessment of Learning in Undergraduate Education, but the rubrics focus on assessing areas that are not a demonstration of content understanding, but more about values, teamwork, creativity, and other aspects of student performance that are often difficult to assess. These VALUE rubrics are available to download from their website www.aacu.org/value/rubrics/index.cfm.

The rubrics cover the following domains: intellectual and practical skills (e.g., inquiry and analysis, critical thinking, creative thinking, written communication, oral communication, reading, quantitative literacy, information literacy, teamwork and problem-solving); personal and social responsibility (e.g., civic knowledge and engagement both locally and globally, intercultural knowledge and competence, ethical reasoning, foundations of skills for lifelong learning, global learning); integrative and applied learning.

Teamwork is a task that many professors require but few have strategies for assessing. Often we have stated outcomes that we want students to work well in groups, but we lack ways to measure that. A rubric like the one available from AAC&U may be useful—and modifying it to meet your individual task-specific needs may be even more helpful to align the rubric with your own expectations for student outcomes.

Another difficult educational outcome to assess is "creative thinking." I have often heard from faculty members reluctant to design rubrics that they are concerned they will limit student creativity and creative thinking. Admittedly, this is a genuine concern. As I have heard "whatever I put in the rubric is all that I'll get—students won't go above and beyond." To that I often say "then make sure your rubric truly covers everything you want students to address in their project/paper/assessment task." We can include aspects of creativity in our rubrics. Consider using examples from the AAC&U rubric that is focused specifically on creative thinking. Some of the categories considered in the "creative thinking" rubric are solving problems, embracing contradictions, innovative thinking, and so on. They offer specific behaviors that represent these such as "integrates alternate, divergent or contradictory perspectives or ideas fully," and "extends a novel or unique idea, question, format or product to create new knowledge or knowledge that crosses boundaries." The rubrics are available to download for free from the AAC&U website and can be used to develop your own that address affect and values. These rubrics, along with others on the website, provide some suggestions for ways that creativity and collaboration can be assessed.

It is possible to assess aspects of student development that have previously been so subjective that we have not been able to truly assess them effectively. The AAC&U rubrics give a starting point for consideration of purposefully examining more carefully how our students are meeting our stated outcomes in these particular areas.

Grades as Representing Percentage of Content Mastery: A Useful Source of Evidence

A complicated, often misunderstood, but critical part of student assessment is assigning grades. As faculty members, we assign grades for formative kinds of work, such as individual student projects, tests, papers, or other project work.

We also assign summative or final/overall grades for a unit, quarter, semester, or year. The general rule of thumb is that the grade should reflect a percentage of the content that the student has mastered. This, however, is much easier said than done. When one has good lesson and unit outcomes that are measurable with clearly stated expectations, this task becomes easier. However, creating a grading strategy that clearly articulates the relative percentage of mastery for different concepts can be very useful.

Much like the creation of the rubric in the examples on the previous pages of this chapter (which should represent a percentage of mastery for a particular project or lesson), to create a final summative grade that represents a percentage of mastery for a final grade, we need to expand the same idea further. That is, we need to determine the relative weight of each assessment and make sure that these weights truly represent the weight of the assignments in relation to the stated outcomes and content of the course.

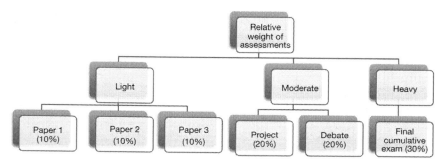

Figure 5.7

Now, rather than having four assessments, each given a grade of A, B, C, D, F or some percentage and the mean/average for all assessment represents the final grade, the grade will represent the relative weight of each task in relation to the stated course outcomes and content. A short paper that covers content from only a few weeks of the content for the semester, should reflect a percentage of the material covered (e.g., 10 percent). A formal debate that relies on the student drawing from about 20 percent of the content material should reflect that as a percentage of mastery. A good end-of-term exam or culminating project should require students to engage with all the major content/concepts of the course, and thus may weigh more heavily than smaller assignments combined. Consider the degree to which different assessments reflect a percentage of mastery of the course content, so the summative grade reflects what students have learned and achieved in a course.

Using Assessment Data to Inform Practice

When you have good formative and summative assessment data that accurately reflect instructional outcomes and carefully and explicitly examine student mastery of content, you can analyze this evidence both qualitatively and quantitatively to inform and improve instruction.

Students and teachers doing data analysis

We learn a great deal from our mistakes. However, we learn more from our mistakes if we are allowed time to reflect and process the mistakes we make. As students and teachers, we are naturally self-reflective about our performance, but we can improve our practice, and improve our content understanding and performance if we go through a purposeful strategy to analyze student performance on assessments, and perhaps even encourage students to go through the process too.

The following is a strategy that we might consider encouraging our students to complete to get them to use their own feedback on assessments as data:

1. Student engages in assessment task
2. Student reflects on performance of the assessment experience specifically considering:
   ■ What did I do well?
   ■ What did I not do well?
   ■ What needs more work?
3. Student considers: What can I do to improve and gain mastery on these concepts?
4. Student creates a specific action plan to improve/gain mastery.
5. Student may redo the assessment or similar assessment to see if s/he has improved.

See Figure 5.8 below, which shows this process for students (but the same process can be used for anyone, including teachers reflecting upon their lessons).

Figure 5.8

As college and university professors, we use a similar process when reflecting on assessment data and consider using assessment data in our classroom research projects:

1. Collect assessment data for all students.
2. Analyze the data for themes and consider the following questions: What did students do well? What did they do poorly? What kinds of mistakes did they make? What still needs to be done for them to achieve mastery?
3. Brainstorm possible strategies that could help—based on the data (perhaps what has worked well in the past, what specific issues students are having, etc.).
4. Create a specific plan to improve students' mastery.
5. Redo the assessment (or similar one) to determine improvement.

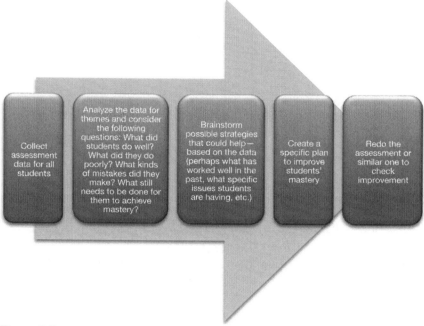

Figure 5.9

Students and teachers alike can go through this reflective process of using assessment data to inform and improve teaching and learning. This process can be used with exams, papers or any assessment task. Too often we see students get an exam or paper or project feedback and shove it in their backpack without ever looking at it again. In order to improve, helping students process the feedback they are given in a meaningful self-reflective way can be wonderfully instructive and lead to long-term learning. If we as professors use data from our assessments as feedback about our instruction, we can use the data to improve our teaching and student learning as we work toward student mastery.

Using good assessment for classroom research

Once one has created good educational outcomes and then designed good assessment grounded in those outcomes, using the evidence obtained from those assessments to inform the research project can be very useful. There are a variety of ways to examine this assessment evidence:

- Analyze for common themes that emerge from your written feedback and feedback using rubrics.
- Track scores numerically on rubrics to include the nature of the mistakes, topics mastered by most, column and row totals for analytic rubrics.
- Use "question analysis" from exams—that is what questions were most often missed? Is there a common topic area that students missed? How were questions missed? By which students?
- Pay attention to the written feedback you give students and what you say to students in class and out, in one-to-one meetings during office hours, and before, during and after class. What kinds of questions do students ask about assessments? What kinds of answers do you provide?
- Make keen observations of the kinds of questions students ask about their assessment feedback and your responses (in class, during office hours, etc.)

When tracking student performance over time using a rubric for a writing task or writing improvement (as in the case of Emily Pollina's example) you may want to examine both qualitatively and quantitatively—that is, looking for themes as well as actual numeric scores as they shift and change over time. Make sure that your rubric is solid enough to reflect the kinds of changes you expect to see, and you let students know that they should see improvement and they will not be penalized as they are making improvements. This notion of mastery learning can be useful in the classroom—to encourage students toward mastery of skills or concepts and allow multiple chances to build mastery over time. This requires a shift in our traditional ways of teaching that allows students one opportunity to show what they know. If your goal is to work toward student mastery of class content, then providing feedback that allows students to learn from mistakes, grow, learn and aim toward mastery requires us to give thoughtful, regular, consistent and immediate feedback and student opportunities for revision and resubmission.

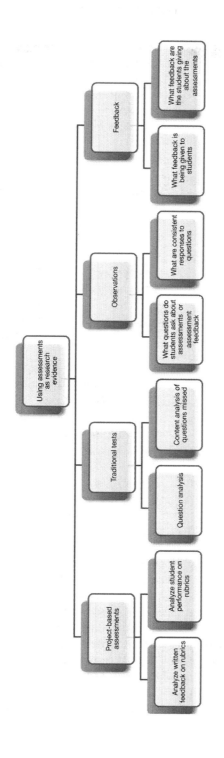

Figure 5.10

If we use the data from these assessments and analyze them using qualitative and quantitative strategies identified in previous chapters, we can also revise and hone our courses to meet the needs of our learners.

In an interesting example of using student assessment data in the form of student compositions, Adem Birson in the Music Department explains a course he was teaching and the evidence he used to determine whether teaching composition alongside theory in music would help inform both.

Examples of Research from the Classroom

Engaging with Mozart: Using composition to teach music theory

Adem Birson

What I did and why

Most college students learn music theory from textbooks and are assessed for their musical aptitude based on written exams and homework assignments. My theory course was designed to help music majors engage with theory through practical application in performance, composition and improvisation at the keyboard. Since music theory in college specifically refers to European Classical music, a genre with which most current music majors are not very familiar, I believe that this form of active learning is essential for cultivating and maintaining student interest in music theory. Through performance, students would develop a familiarity with the Classical repertory their textbook only describes; through composition in the Classical style, they would begin to appreciate the creative process of this music, as well as take creative ownership over the quality of their musical work; and through improvisation, they would learn to conceive of music theory in terms of musical language in a stimulating real-time setting, my ultimate goal for the course. Since the keyboard was traditionally the theoretical instrument of the Classical period, and all composers trained, composed and improvised on the keyboard, I felt it most appropriate to focus on developing the aforementioned skills through the medium of the keyboard. As opposed to the traditional textbook model, I hypothesized that using music composition as the focal point around which the course revolved would not only be a more logical approach to the study of music, but also would enable the students to generate their own questions or aid in unexpected solutions to problems that are not necessarily addressed in theoretical textbooks. The students for my sections totaled five, and ranged from one to nine years of prior keyboard training.

The repertory I selected consisted primarily of Classical-era keyboard minuets by the three most important composers from that period: Joseph Haydn, W. A. Mozart and Ludwig van Beethoven. I chose to use minuets, one of the most popular and widely-composed dance pieces in eighteenth-century European courts, because many eighteenth-century musicians and theorists (including Mozart himself) described the minuet as the most basic form for practicing composition, and recommended that beginners start by composing them. Having the students learn using these minuets was crucial in providing a constant source of reference for their own creative activity, as well as a crucial aid to the effectiveness of my teaching. Any time a student was having difficulty composing or improvising, we were able to refer to one of the minuets we had studied over the course of the semester to work out theoretical issues. The students asked meaningful questions, and I was able to offer them meaningful answers using an active learning model.

Using minuets also enabled me to provide the students with a simple mold into which they could pour their musical ideas, so to speak. A generic Classical minuet would normally consist of two sections, each eight measures in length, corresponding with what modern theorists have termed "binary form." Each of these two sections, moreover, is further divided into two sub-phrases of four measures each. I was thus able to use these small, subdivided sections to gradually build my students up to composing an entire minuet, step by step. Over the course of the semester I devised a series of ten, weekly composition assignments/assessments, which increased in complexity, from the smallest units of composition to complete musical forms such as the minuet. I gave students feedback on their pieces and analyzed their progress on these assignments. The advantage of this approach, however, was that it did not limit us to composing minuets alone. By the end of the semester, I had already got them to comfortably compose in other mediums, such as the theme and variations and the rondo, two types of composition that use the same building blocks of the minuet, yet extend well beyond the sixteen measures of a simple binary dance form. This practical framework, built on a foundation of repertory and the building blocks of musical form, also structured the improvisation element of the course, as students could think in terms of small phrasal units while being asked to invent their own music on the spot.

What I found

Over the course of the semester, I was able to gather data through empirical observation/assessment of their in-class improvisation and performances, analysis and assessment of their weekly composition assignments, and a mid-semester evaluation I conducted just prior to spring break. The biggest obstacle to their achieving total musical fluency through the medium of the keyboard was their prior experience at the keyboard. The most advanced performers of the Classical minuets and the best improvisers were the students who had the most prior experience at the piano. The mid-semester evaluations provided further supporting evidence that those with less keyboard training seemed to enjoy the performance and improvisation course components the least, as the two students with less than one year of piano lessons ranked those two methods as a neutral three on a Likert scale survey ranging from one to five. The composition assignments were the most successful course component, as the students could take a week to work on their compositions without the stress of in-class improvisation or lack of keyboard skills in performance. These assignments took on a life of their own, as the students identified with and took pride in their creative work. The class became fun for them because they looked forward to sharing their music with their fellow classmates and me. In a free-response question on the mid-semester evaluation, four out of five students mentioned the composition assignments as one of the most effective aspects of the course. Furthermore, I was able to better assess whether they had satisfactorily understood a musical concept based on their ability to replicate it in composition than had they only been asked to define it on a written exam.

How these findings have informed/will inform my practice

I have been convinced that an active learning approach to music making in the music theory classroom is the most effective and engaging way to teach Classical music theory that I have experienced so far, both as a student and as a teacher. While music theory textbooks can be useful as a reference for vocabulary and terminology, the use of music, both pre-composed masterworks and spontaneous improvisation and composition in the Classical style, offered a more fertile learning ground for these undergraduate music majors. By semester's end, not only were they able to define all the theoretical terminology contained in music textbooks on more traditional assessments, they could perform a handful of Classical minuets, draw from a portfolio of their own compositions, and even attempt improvisation. These results, in my opinion, are outcomes far preferable to paper analyses of musical scores and written responses on examinations. In the future, I would hope to see more of an emphasis on creative musical production from music majors in theory courses at the university level, and less of an emphasis on written definitions and traditional exams. Not only is it more effective as a pedagogical tool, it is something the students seem to appreciate and look forward to.

However, the range in prior keyboard experience was a factor that the course design was not able to overcome. The students who could already play piano performed far better in the repertory and improvisation course components, in spite of my efforts to get them all playing at a high level. That being said, all the students improved their theoretical understanding at the keyboard, and even those with little prior experience were able to use the course as a training ground for establishing their physical keyboard technique. In the future, however, I would have to reconsider how much emphasis I place on keyboard for the performance and improvisation components. Some of the students indicated other instruments, such as violin, flute, voice and guitar, as primary and I may find it more fruitful to allow them to utilize their more comfortable medium for more stressful activities like performance and improvisation. I would also weigh more of the total grade towards the composition exercises, since all students enjoyed and excelled at these assignments similarly.

We can see in Adem's example above that the assessments were useful sources of evidence: the compositions, the traditional assessments, and the student performances (including improvisation). This example is useful because it is important to see that not only are more traditional assessments useful, but so are more authentic performance measures and those where students are given opportunities to be creative. Even without rubrics, Adem was able to see what kinds of themes emerged from the student work. Sometimes when developing a rubric, allowing students the opportunity to complete a "trial" or pilot example of the assignment (without a rubric) can provide useful information about what students will do on their own without a specific grading rubric. This information can be useful when generating the rubric for the assignment for later groups. In Adem's case, students were asked to craft particular kinds of compositions, and he wanted to see what they would be able to do. He learned a lot in this pilot project about some of the challenges and what students could accomplish. This understanding may influence his development of a rubric in the future as he refines the assignment.

In conclusion, classroom assessments can provide rich data from which to conduct our classroom research projects—both the student performance on the assessments themselves and the feedback we provide on assessments. To be as effective a measure or evidence tool as possible, assessment should be linked to educational outcomes/objectives of the course. For example, rubrics should be aligned with task-specific outcomes and can be used to grade papers/essays/longer response answers on exams and provide feedback on presentations, projects, and performances. Good rubrics can show our feedback to students, and using these rubrics can provide useful data about the nature of feedback given, as well as an examination of student performance. More traditional assessment strategies, such as exams, should also be aligned with course outcomes and can be useful forms of data/evidence for classroom research. Comments on student work or observations of student interactions/discussions can provide useful evidence for classroom research as well, and the evidence from assessments can be analyzed both qualitatively and quantitatively. In the next chapter, we will discuss ways of doing both qualitative and quantitative research strategies within the same project, and why this can be beneficial.

Chapter 6

Mixed Methods and Triangulation of Evidence

In this chapter:

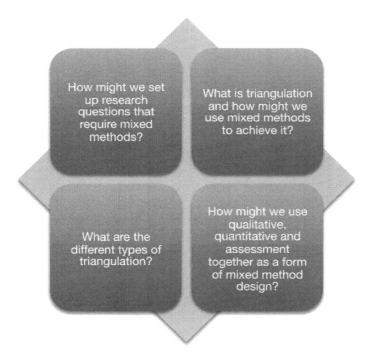

How might we set up research questions that require mixed methods?

What is triangulation and how might we use mixed methods to achieve it?

What are the different types of triangulation?

How might we use qualitative, quantitative and assessment together as a form of mixed method design?

WHAT ARE MIXED METHODS AND TRIANGULATION AND HOW CAN WE USE THEM IN CLASSROOM RESEARCH?

Mixed-methods Research

Mixed methods research (combining qualitative and quantitative research methods and analysis) is becoming increasingly popular and more clearly articulated within classroom research as a third alternative to qualitative alone or quantitative alone. Johnson, Onwuegbuzie and Turner (2007), in their article "Toward a Definition of Mixed Methods Research," wrote about the complexities of defining mixed methods research after analyzing many sources of evidence and several definitions of mixed methods. They offer a particular definition that takes into account their review, in addition to input from other academics who do mixed methods research:

> Mixed methods research is an intellectual and practical synthesis based on qualitative and quantitative research; it is the third methodological or research paradigm (along with qualitative and quantitative research). It recognizes the importance of traditional quantitative and qualitative research but also offers a powerful third paradigm choice that often will provide the most informative, complete, balanced, and useful research results.

They argue further that this new paradigm "partners with the philosophy of pragmatism in one of its forms (left, right, middle)" and "relies on qualitative and quantitative viewpoints, data collection, analysis, and inference techniques combined according to the logic of mixed methods research to address one's research question(s)." And they argue that those employing mixed methods research are "cognizant, appreciative, and inclusive of local and broader sociopolitical realities, resources and needs" (p. 129). Given these considerations within the definition, it becomes clear why mixed methods research is well-suited for classroom research that attempts to be inclusive of these "local and broader" realities and relies on a variety of viewpoints to better understand these different contexts.

Triangulation in Classroom Research

Ideally, when designing classroom research projects, using a variety of methods including qualitative, quantitative, and careful analysis of assessment data affords the ability to *triangulate* our data. According to Bogdan and Biklen (2006), the authors of books on qualitative research and its use in education, triangulation can be a very powerful strategy that allows us to validate data through the use of multiple sources of evidence that examine the same phenomenon and find similar

101

results. We use triangulation in classroom research projects to try to increase the credibility, validity, and perhaps generalizability. Different scholars have attempted to define the concept of triangulation. For example, Cohen, Manion and Morrison (2000) define triangulation as an "attempt to map out, or explain more fully, the richness and complexity of human behavior by studying it from more than one standpoint." Whereas O'Donoghue and Punch (2003) view triangulation as a "method of cross-checking data from multiple sources to search for regularities in the research data." And more recently, Altrichter et al. (2006) argue that triangulation "gives a more detailed and balanced picture of the situation" under investigation.

These definitions demonstrate the ways that triangulation can allow researchers to cross-check and get a more robust picture of what is happening in their research. As researchers we collect a variety of different types of information in an effort to gain the most accurate results possible that will ideally provide greater certainty for our claims. However, we are not always concerned with triangulating data or generalizing from our findings when we undertake classroom research. The multiple forms of evidence can provide us with a depth and breadth of understanding that we might not otherwise get with a single approach.

There have been four different types of triangulation defined:

- *Data triangulation*: examines time, space, people, and other data sources and uses these different data sources to determine if they support (or not) findings from each single data source.
- *Investigator triangulation*: considers perspectives of multiple researchers in an investigation (Do they share the same findings? Do they have different perspectives?)
- *Theory triangulation*: using more than one theoretical framework when interpreting the phenomenon and evidence.
- *Methodological triangulation*: using multiple methods to gather data, such as interviews, observations, questionnaires, student work, and documents (Denzin 2006).

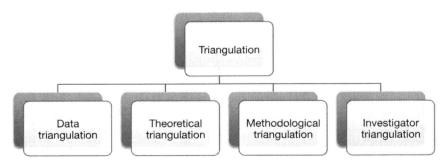

Figure 6.1

Mostly for the purposes of classroom research conducted with one's own classroom, the focus is typically more on methodological triangulation. However, if you call upon outside help (as discussed in Chapter 8) you may want to use investigator triangulation.

The Purpose of Triangulation

While some may argue that the purpose of triangulation is to validate data that support a single theory or perspective, others such as Guion, Diehl and McDonald (2011, para. 1) have argued this is not the case:

> Validity, in qualitative research, refers to whether the findings of a study are true and certain—"true" in the sense that research findings accurately reflect the situation, and "certain" in the sense that research findings are supported by the evidence. Triangulation is a method used by qualitative researchers to check and establish validity in their studies by analyzing a research question from multiple perspectives. Patton (2002) cautions that it is a common misconception that the goal of triangulation is to arrive at consistency across data sources or approaches; in fact, such inconsistencies may be likely given the relative strengths of different approaches. In Patton's view, these inconsistencies should not be seen as weakening the evidence, but should be viewed as an opportunity to uncover deeper meaning in the data.

This approach is an interesting way to consider inconsistencies in our data when we triangulate. Inconsistencies do not necessarily weaken what we have found, but allow us to dig even deeper into our findings and explore other possibilities. In her article Sandra Mathison (1988) also suggests that:

> Typically, through triangulating we expect various data sources and methods to lead to a singular proposition about the phenomenon being studied. That this is not the case is obvious to most researchers and evaluators. Given that this expectation is unrealistic, an alternative perspective of triangulation is presented. This alternative perspective takes into account that triangulation results in convergent, inconsistent, and contradictory evidence that must be rendered sensible by the researcher or evaluator.

It is quite likely that as we attempt to triangulate we continue to find conflicting evidence (or at least data that seem to contradict what we think we have found). Do not let this discourage you. These divergent types of findings can sometimes be the most useful in expanding our understanding of classrooms and teaching and learning within them.

103

Although researchers often turn to triangulation to validate findings or create a unifying theory from our data, this may not always be the case. Particularly in classroom research, we may very well find "convergent, inconsistent and contradictory evidence." Any professor who has ever read student comments on course evaluations can attest to this—that twenty-five students asked to provide feedback on a classroom event will often have twenty-five different opinions, even when asked in several different ways. As classroom researchers we don't need to discount the outliers or the data that don't converge neatly with what we have already found. We can attempt to explain it, try to make sense of it, or offer it to readers for their examination. Sometimes we have data that are interesting, useful and important, but that we cannot always explain. Sometimes these data generate more questions for future research.

The beauty of mixed methods in classroom research is that this methodological framework is designed to not only provide answers to research questions, but also to help us generate additional questions. As Johnson, Onwuegbuzie and Turner (2007) argued, "the mixed methods research paradigm offers an important approach for *generating* important research questions *and* providing warranted answers to those questions" (p. 129). Classroom research projects using mixed methods research will certainly generate research questions, as well as providing evidence that may help with understanding a particular phenomenon within the classroom, curricula, student engagement, and so on.

Example of a Project that Employed Mixed Methods, including Assessment

Lauren Schnabel, a board-certified veterinary surgeon and faculty member teaching surgical courses in veterinary medicine, engaged in mixed methods in her classroom research project to examine the effectiveness of a formal assessment instrument she created and piloted for assessing veterinary students' surgical skills (Schnabel *et al.* 2013). Because she was interested in determining the validity and reliability of an assessment instrument for a surgery course, she wanted to engage in methodological triangulation. She engaged in observations of students and faculty using the instrument. She interviewed faculty to discover their thoughts about the usefulness of the instrument. She examined the results of student performance (evaluation data). She conducted a student opinion survey, and debriefed with students and faculty, sharing the findings. Her debrief session with students ended up functioning as a de facto focus group in which she learned more about student perceptions. Her study was published in *Veterinary Surgery Journal* and is reprinted here with permission in its entirety (with the exception of the instrument itself), because it provides an excellent example of the different forms of data collection discussed in this and the previous chapters (the published article is available at http://onlinelibrary.wiley.com/doi/10.1111/j.1532–950X.2013.12006.x/abstract).

USE OF A FORMAL ASSESSMENT INSTRUMENT FOR EVALUATION OF VETERINARY STUDENT SURGICAL SKILLS

Lauren V. Schnabel[1], DVM, Diplomate ACVS, Paul S. Maza[2], DVM, PhD, Kimberly M. Williams[3], PhD, Nita L. Irby[1], DVM, Diplomate ACVO, Carolyn M. McDaniel[1], VMD, and Brian G. Collins[1], DVM

[1] Department of Clinical Sciences, College of Veterinary Medicine, Cornell University, Ithaca, NY, [2] Department of Biomedical Sciences, College of Veterinary Medicine, Cornell University, Ithaca, NY and [3] Cornell University Center for Teaching Excellence, Cornell University, Ithaca, NY

Corresponding Author
Lauren V. Schnabel, DVM, Diplomate ACVS, VMC C3 105, College of Veterinary Medicine, Cornell University, Ithaca, NY 14853
E mail: lvs3@cornell.edu

Submitted April 2012
Accepted December 2012

DOI:10.1111/j.1532-950X.2013.12006.x

Objectives: To (1) evaluate the design and use of a global rating scale assessment instrument in veterinary medical education and; (2) examine the effectiveness of 2 surgical techniques courses for improving the surgical skills of veterinary students.

Study design: Instrument development; observational; survey-based.

Sample population: Students (n = 16) registered for 2 elective surgical techniques courses were enrolled on a volunteer basis.

Methods: A 5-point global rating scale instrument was designed for the evaluation of 12 basic surgical skills by faculty evaluators and used to obtain student start and end scores during the courses. Upon conclusion of the courses, students completed a survey from which their opinions on their improvement as well as their desire for feedback were obtained.

Results: All authors agreed the instrument was easy to use. As groups, 3rd year students, 4th year students, and all students combined had significantly higher total skill scores at the end of the courses compared to the start of the courses. Individually, 10 students (63%) had significant improvement in surgical skills as a result of their participation in the courses: 4 (100%) 3rd year and 6 (50%) 4th year students. Student survey responses revealed a strong desire for feedback as well as support of formal assessment methods. Only weak agreement was found between student opinions on their improvement and the authors' assessment scores.

Conclusions: Assessment instruments are useful for (1) student evaluation and (2) for providing students with feedback on their surgical skills.

Grant Sponsor: Cornell University Biological and Biomedical Sciences Graduate Research and Teaching Fellowship Program

Surgical principles and skills are often difficult to teach and evaluate[1] and further complicated by use of live animals or surgical simulators, typically in a laboratory setting, which is expensive and necessitates a large number of faculty to be effective.[1–3] However, it is highly desirable that veterinary students be well trained in surgery because veterinarians are expected to perform at least basic surgical procedures upon graduation without further specialty training.[1,4–6]

Several methods to evaluate veterinary student clinical skill training including surgical skills have been discussed[2,3,7] and are necessary as accreditation requirements continue to become more stringent for clinical competency outcomes assessment.[8–10] Both checklist[3] and point scoring systems have been described,[2,5,7] generally in the context of structured examinations such as the Objective Structured Clinical Examination (OSCE)[3] rather than on observations of students in clinical settings such as the Clinical Observed Performance Evaluation (COPE).[11] Whereas several Likert-type or global point rating scale evaluation instruments have been described for assessment of medical student surgical skills using OSCE and COPE,[12–14] we are unaware that similar instruments have been used for assessment of veterinary student surgical skills.

Thus, our purpose was (1) to evaluate the design and use of a global rating scale instrument in veterinary medical education and (2) to use the instrument to examine the effectiveness of 2 week-long surgical techniques courses for improving surgical skills in veterinary students. The 2 courses used for student observation and evaluation (VTMED 6528 Equine Surgical and Anesthetic Techniques and VTMED 6529 Food Animal Surgical and Anesthetic Techniques) have been taught for many years, but have never included a formal assessment of the students' surgical skills. Our first hypothesis was that student surgical skill scores attained by the end of the second week-long course would be significantly higher (improved) than those demonstrated at the beginning of the first week-long course. Our second hypothesis was that student opinions about their improvement in surgical skills, as determined by survey results, would agree with our findings. Both these hypotheses were based on previously reported findings from the medical education literature where medical students completing surgical skills training courses improved both their surgical skill proficiency level as well as their ability to perform accurate self-assessments of their proficiency level.[15,16]

Methods

The University Institutional Review Board (IRB) for Human Participants reviewed this study and found it to qualify for Exemption from IRB Review according to paragraph 1 of the Department of Health and Human Services Code of Federal Regulations 45 CFR 46.101(b).

Assessment instrument

A global rating scale instrument was designed for assessment of veterinary student surgical skills based on 2 instruments previously validated for the assessment of medical student, resident, and fellow surgical skills.[12,13] Notably, we chose to use a 5-point scale with response anchors placed at points 1, 3, and 5 as it was determined that it would be too difficult to differentiate skill levels into >5 categories. The first author created the initial draft of the instrument and then met with the other authors to further refine the instrument into its final version (Appendix). Each individual skill as well as the response anchors for each skill score were discussed and agreed upon by all authors as well as by the course leaders before use of the instrument in the courses. All authors expressed concern regarding both the wording on the assessment form and our ability to score skills 9 (hemostasis) and 12 (knowledge of the specific procedure) accurately because of the observational nature of the study and the complexity of the courses being evaluated. Both skills were kept on the assessment form, however, and their evaluation attempted.

Surgical techniques courses

The use of animals in these courses was approved and performed according to guidelines of the Institutional Animal Care and Use Committee.

The 2 week-long courses during which the students were observed and assessed were Equine Surgical and Anesthetic Techniques (VTMED 6528) and Food Animal Surgical and Anesthetic Techniques (VTMED 6529). These elective courses offered during the winter intersession in January were only open to 3rd and 4th year veterinary students. Despite the fact that students must give up 2 weeks of vacation to participate, there has always been a strong student response to the call for registration, and the courses typically fill to the enrolment limit necessitated by available facilities, equipment, and staffing. Each course is led by a board certified large animal surgeon and by 2 licensed veterinary technicians and further instructed by other board certified large animal surgeons, large animal surgery and anesthesia residents, veterinarians, and licensed veterinary technicians. Students work in groups of 3 per animal and rotate through the positions of surgeon, assistant surgeon, and anesthetist. Students receive printed notes on each procedure before the start of each course and also have access to videos for most of the surgical procedures performed. Although the students continuously receive informal feedback from instructors, they officially receive pass/fail grades only with no formal assessment about their performance or skill level.

The equine course occurs during the 1st week and includes the following procedures on live ponies: castration (with scrotal ablation) and ventral median exploratory celiotomy with pelvic flexure enterotomy and small intestinal resection and anastomosis (general anesthesia); abdominal laparoscopic exploratory and assisted rectal palpation (standing under sedation and with local anesthesia). The ponies are euthanized after the procedures and their carcasses are used for the remainder of the course in which students perform procedures including enucleation, split bone removal, periosteal stripping, palmar digital neurectomy, and inferior check ligament desmotomy. Additionally, students practice cast application on the limbs and have a laboratory session sponsored by Synthes Vet (West Chester, PA), in which they practice fracture repair techniques on synthetic bone models.

The food animal course occurs in the 2nd week and includes the following procedures on live animals: right paramedian abomasopexy and right paralumbar fossa exploratory celiotomy with enterotomy, typhlotomy, and omentopexy (sheep, general anesthesia); bilateral exploratory celiotomy and omentopexy or pyloropexy (cows, standing with local anesthesia); ventral median exploratory celiotomy with umbilical and apex of the bladder resection and umbilical herniorrhaphy as well as castration and enucleation (calves, general anesthesia). All animals that had general anesthesia were euthanized after completion of the procedures. The cows that had standing surgery were sold at auction upon recovery. Additionally, students use carcasses to practice udder/teat procedures as well as foot trimming and foot surgeries.

Student enrollment

Students registered for both courses were eligible for this study and enrolled on a volunteer basis. Preliminary enrollment occurred by email communication. Official enrollment took place once the students signed individual informed consent forms on the 1st day of the equine course. Students were informed of the purpose of the study but were not allowed to view the assessment instrument until after study conclusion and completion of the student surveys. So, students were aware that they were being assessed on their surgical skills, but were unaware of the specific skills being examined.

All students had received the same basic skills training throughout their 1st and 2nd years of veterinary school in 4 laboratories (1.5 hours each; 1/semester) on cadavers or models. The laboratories were staffed by surgeons and surgical residents and included the basic skills 1–9 and 11 included in the assessment instrument. All students had the same live animal practice in the fall semester of their 3rd year performing and assisting in feline ovariohysterectomy. Further, all students had online access to an instrument atlas, suture and suture pattern atlas, as well as knot-tying procedural videos at all times during their veterinary training, which they were made aware of at the start of their 1st year of veterinary school.

Use of assessment instrument

Four of the authors were assigned to score the students using the assessment instrument and are hereon referred to as evaluators in that context. All have taught surgical techniques courses in the past, either on large or small animals. To avoid biases, none of the evaluators were course instructors for the 2 courses in this study. Each evaluator was assigned a group of students to evaluate by the first author based on student proximity to each other. The evaluator scored that same group of students for both their start and end scores and scored each skill in the instrument. Each student was scored only once for start scores and once for end scores by that assigned evaluator.

Students were observed and assessed during equine abdominal surgery (exploratory celiotomy, pelvic flexure enterotomy, and small intestinal resection and anastomosis) as well as palmar digital neurectomy surgeries to obtain beginning (start) surgical skill scores. These procedures were performed on multiple days throughout the beginning of the 1st week because of interspersed laboratories not relevant to this study such as the casting laboratory. Students were observed and assessed during sheep abdominal surgery (right paralumbar fossa exploratory celiotomy, enterotomy, typhlotomy, and omentopexy) as well as calf surgical procedures (exploratory celiotomy, umbilical, and apex of the bladder resection, umbilical herniorraphy, and castration) to obtain final (end) surgical skill scores. These procedures were also performed on multiple days throughout the end of the 2nd because of interspersed laboratories not relevant to the study. To avoid biasing the study, evaluators did not assist the students unless there was an emergency and did not correct any improper techniques observed until the final procedures after end scores had already been obtained. It is important to note, however, that although the evaluators were not assisting or correcting the students throughout the courses, the course instructors were actively assisting the students and providing instruction and feedback on a daily basis.

Student survey

Upon completion of the courses, students were asked to complete a brief paper survey consisting of 4 "yes" or "no" questions. The first question "Do you believe that your surgical skills have improved significantly over the past 2 weeks because of your participation in VTMED 6528 (Equine Surgical and Anesthetic

Techniques) and VTMED 6529 (Food Animal Surgical and Anesthetic Techniques)?" was designed to generate data for testing our 2nd hypothesis that student opinions on improvement of their surgical skills would agree with our scored findings. The 2nd question "Did you feel that your participation in this study affected your learning in any way during the courses?" was intended to determine whether or not the students felt that the presence of the evaluators and the potential pressure of observation affected their learning in any way.[17] This question also included a response box that stated: "If yes, please state whether the effect was positive or negative." The 3rd and 4th questions ("Would you like me to review your completed Veterinary Surgical Skills Assessment Forms with you?" and "Do you think that future implementation of formal assessment methods for courses such as these would be of benefit to students?") were designed to assess student desire for feedback and student acceptance of formal assessment methods. The 4th question also included a response box that stated: "Please briefly explain the reason for your response." Because of the authors' use of the data generated from the 1st question to evaluate our 2nd hypothesis, student surveys were not anonymous.

Student debriefing

At study end and completion of student surveys, a voluntary meeting was held with the students in which the first author gave a presentation on the study background, methods, and results. The results were then discussed as a group and student opinions on both the assessment instrument and the surgical technique courses were obtained. After the group discussion, the first author met with each student on a voluntary basis to discuss their own scores and provide feedback on the skills that showed improvement and the skills needing additional work.

Statistical analyses

Our 1st hypothesis was that student surgical skill scores would improve during the 2 week-long courses. In statistical terms, our null hypothesis (H_0) stated that there was no difference between start and end surgical skill scores, whereas our alternative hypothesis (H_A) was that there was a significant difference (improvement) between start and end surgical skill scores. Paired t-tests were used to compare the differences in start and end scores for 3rd year students, 4th year students, and all students combined. Wilcoxon rank sum tests were used to compare 3rd and 4th year student start and end surgical skill scores as well as the differences in their start and end scores.

Our 2nd hypothesis was that student opinions on their improvement in surgical skills would agree with our scored findings. In statistical terms, our null hypothesis (H_0) stated that the probability of a student finding an improvement in their skills (yes or no) would equal the probability of our scores finding an improvement (yes or no), whereas our alternative hypothesis (H_A) was that the probability of a student finding an improvement in their skills would not equal the probability of our scores finding an improvement. A McNemar's symmetry (χ^2) test was used to assess the significance of agreement between student opinions and our scores above that of chance alone. A kappa (κ) coefficient was also calculated to quantify the magnitude of agreement.

All analyses were performed with software (Statistix 9, Analytical Software, Tallahassee, FL) and a value of $P \leq .05$ was considered significant to reject the null hypothesis. Data are reported as (mean $\pm$ standard error (SEM); range). Results of paired t-tests are reported as t(degrees of freedom) = t-value, P = P-value. Results of Wilcoxon rank sum tests are reported as $W_s(n_1;n_2)$ = lowest mean rank, P = P-value. The result of the McNemar's symmetry test is reported as χ^2(degrees of freedom, N) = χ^2-value, P = P-value.

Results

Student enrollment

Registration for both courses was 21 students per course. Of the 21 students, 17 (81%) registered for both the equine and food animal course and were eligible for this study. Of the 17 eligible students, 16 (94%) volunteered and were enrolled in the study, 4 (25%) of which were 3rd years and 12 (75%) of which were 4th years. The 3rd year students had not completed any clinical rotations before these courses, whereas 4th year students had completed ~1 year of clinical rotations, which may or may not have included surgical rotations.

Use of assessment instrument

As 16 students enrolled in the study, each of the designated evaluators scored 4 students. The 1st author assigned each evaluator their students based on student groups and surgery table locations so that the 4 students were as close to each other as possible, allowing for easier observation. The 1st author also provided each evaluator with an identification picture of each student as well as the printed assessment form on a clipboard. Instead of having 1 form for each student during the observation, all evaluators found it easier and more efficient to use 1 form only and to write each of their assigned student's initials under or next to the point number given for each skill.

Overall, all evaluators found the assessment instrument itself easy to use. As anticipated, however, the evaluators had difficulty scoring skill 9 (hemostasis) because of the type of surgeries being observed and the fact that they were terminal in nature. Because the authors felt that the students justly chose to spend their limited time performing the surgical techniques such as enterotomies and resections rather than spending the time controlling hemostasis in some cases during terminal procedures, skill 9 was eliminated from the study and excluded from any analysis. For this reason, skill 9 does not appear in the results figures and the maximum possible total surgical skill score for each student dropped from 60 points as indicated on the original assessment form (Appendix) to 55 points.

Skill 12 (knowledge of specific procedure) was also challenging for the authors to score given that some procedures were more complicated than others and some of the notes and videos provided to the students for preparation were more detailed than others. Nevertheless, the authors kept to their agreed upon anchors and were able to assign a start and end score to each student. For this reason, skill 12 was kept in the study and included in the analysis.

Other challenges faced while scoring the students were the rotation of students through the positions of surgeon, assistant surgeon, and anesthetist, and that some procedures were not originally planned to be sterile in nature for the purposes of the courses such as the limb surgeries performed on carcasses. Both of these challenges necessitated the 1st author and the 2 licensed veterinarian technicians who led the courses to ask students enrolled in the study to maintain sterile technique in instances where other students were not asked to. Additionally, in rare circumstances, students that had been filling the role of anesthetist had to be asked to specifically perform a procedure so that they could be scored.

Student surgical skill scores

Total surgical skill scores. Each student had an end total surgical skill score that was higher than their start total surgical skill score. When the differences in total start and end surgical skill scores were compared for 3rd year students (n = 4), 4th year students (n = 12), and all students combined (N = 16), each group had a statistically significant improvement as shown in Figure 1 (3rd year students: $t(3) = 5.47$, $P \leq .01$; 4th year students: $t(11) = 6.47$, $P \leq .01$; all students combined: $t(15) = 7.45$, $P \leq .01$).

As anticipated based on experience, the mean ± SEM start surgical skill score of 3rd year students (37.75 ± 2.78 points; range, 32–42 points) was less than that of 4th year students (40.00 ± 0.90 points; range, 36–45 points), but this difference was not statistically significant, $W_s(4;12) = 18.00$, $P = .51$. Although the mean end surgical skill score of the 3rd year students (46.25 ± 1.43 points;

range, 44–50 points) was higher than that of the 4th year students (44.83 ± 0.96 points; range, 38–50 points), this difference also was not statistically significant, $W_s(4;12) = 17.50$, $P = .46$. The mean difference in start and end surgical skill scores, however, was significantly higher in 3rd year students (8.50 ± 1.55 points; range, 5–12 points) compared to 4th year students (4.83 ± 0.75 points; range, 1–9 points) as shown in Figure 2, $W_s(4;12) = 7.50$, $P = .04$. Interestingly, the 4th year students that had the lowest differences in start and end scores (i.e. least improvement) were those with the lowest start scores.

Individual surgical skill scores. When differences in student start and end surgical skill scores were compared for individual skills, students (3rd and 4th year students combined) had significant improvement in all skills except skill 1 (surgical preparation: student) and skill 12 (knowledge of specific procedure) as shown in Figure 3. For skill 1 (surgical preparation: student), the mean end surgical skill score (4.38 ± 0.15 points; range, 3–5 points) was higher than the mean start surgical skill score (4.06 ± 0.19 points; range, 3–5 points), but this difference was not significant, $t(15) = 2.08$, $P = .06$. Skill 12 (knowledge of specific procedure) was the only skill in which the mean end surgical skill score (3.50 ± 0.16 points; range, 3–5 points) was lower than the mean start surgical

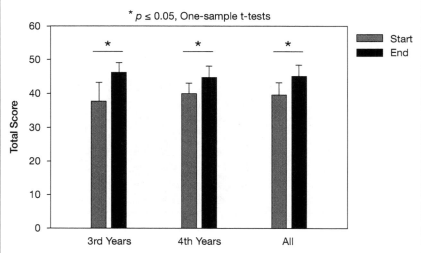

Figure 1 Mean ± SEM of 3rd year (n = 4), 4th year (n = 12), and all 3rd and 4th year students (N = 16) total start and end surgical skills scores. An asterisk indicates a significance difference between start and end scores for each group as determined using paired t-tests with significance set at $P \le .05$.

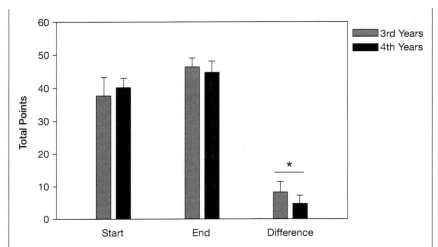

Figure 2 Mean ± SEM 3rd (n = 4) and 4th year (n = 12) student total surgical skill scores and differences in end and start surgical skills scores. An asterisk indicates a significance difference between the 2 groups as determined using a Wilcoxon rank sum test with significance set at $P \leq .05$.

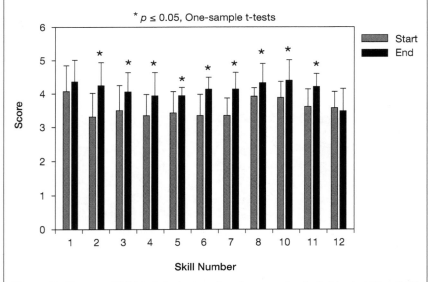

Figure 3 Mean ± SEM total start and end scores for individual skills of all 3rd and 4th year students. An asterisk indicates a significance difference between start and end scores for each skill number as determined using paired t-tests with significance set at $P \leq .05$. Note: Skill number 9 is not present as this skill was eliminated from the study.

skill score (3.56 ± 0.13 points; range, 3–4 points), although this result was not significant, $t(15) = -0.32$, $P \leq .75$. When individual surgical skill scores were examined for 3rd year students and 4th year students as separate groups, statistical significance for skills remained unchanged. Notably, however, the mean skill 12 end score for 3rd year students (3.75 ± 0.25 points; range, 3–4 points) was higher than their mean start score (3.50 ± 0.29 points; range, 3–4 points), whereas the mean skill 12 end score for 4th year students (3.42 ± 0.19 points; range, 3–5 points) was lower than their mean start score (3.58 ± 0.15 points; range, 3–4 points).

Individual student improvement. For individual students, a 5 point or more improvement in total surgical skill score was considered a significant improvement as determined by the authors. As such, 10 students (63%) had significant improvement in their surgical skills. Importantly, all 4 of 3rd year students had significant improvement, whereas only 6 (50%) of the 4th years had significant improvement.

Student surveys

All 16 enrolled students completed the paper surveys immediately after completion of the food animal course. In response to the 1st question, "Do you believe that your surgical skills have improved significantly over the past 2 weeks because of your participation in VTMED 6528 (Equine Surgical and Anesthetic Techniques) and VTMED 6529 (Food Animal Surgical and Anesthetic Techniques)?" 13 students (81%) answered "yes." Of these 13 students, 9 (69%) were also considered to have significant improvement in their surgical skills based on our criteria (with significant improvement defined as a 5 point or more improvement in total surgical skill score) whereas the other 4 (31%) did not. All 3 students who answered "no" to the 1st question were 4th year students. Of these, 2 (77%) were also considered not to have significant improvement in their surgical skills based on our criteria whereas 1 (33%) had significant improvement. Using a McNemar's symmetry test, the null hypothesis that the probability of a student finding an improvement in their skills would equal the probability of our scores finding an improvement was accepted ($X^2[1,16] = 1.80$, $P \leq .18$), however the calculated k coefficient of 0.24 revealed only weak to moderate agreement.

In response to the 2nd question, "Did you feel that your participation in this study affected your learning in any way during the courses?" 7 students (44%) answered "no." Of the other 9 students (56%) that answered "yes," all felt that their participation in the study affected their learning in a positive way. The most common explanation given by the students for this response was that the study made them more conscientious of their technique. Several of the 9 students also commented that they chose the responses "yes" and "positive" in anticipation of the feedback that they would receive from the first author.

In response to the 3rd and 4th questions that assessed student desire for feedback and student acceptance of formal assessment methods, the responses were overwhelming in support of both. Fourteen (88%) of students answered "yes" to the 3rd question "Would you like me to review your completed Veterinary Surgical Skills Assessment Forms with you?" and 14 (88%) of students answered "yes" to the 4th question "Do you think that future implementation of formal assessment methods for courses such as these would be of benefit to students?" Interestingly, the 2 students who answered "no" to the 3rd question were not the same 2 students who answered "no" to the 4th question. The most common explanation for the answer "yes" to the 4th question was that the students felt that it was important to get feedback so that they would know what they needed to work on in order to improve. The 2 students that answered "no" to this same question stated that they felt that actual assessments were not necessary for learning or improvement.

Student debriefing

Five students (36%) who responded "yes" to the 3rd survey question attended the voluntary evening meeting. Four other students who could not attend the meeting because of clinical rotation obligations contacted the first author to obtain feedback via email. During the meeting, the first author gave a brief presentation on the study background, methods, and results, and then discussed the study with the students as a group. Through this discussion, valuable insight was gained that was not obtained through the student surveys. For example, whereas none of the students who responded "yes" to the 2nd survey question "Did you feel that your participation in this study affected your learning in any way during the courses?" qualified their response in a "negative" way, several of the students at the meeting admitted that the presence of the authors performing the scoring and standing at their surgery table made them very nervous and that at times they felt that this nervousness took away from their experience in the courses. All of the students present at the meeting also expressed their frustration at not being able to ask the evaluators for help when they were standing right there at their table. Whereas this was a concern of the authors from the beginning, this was the first time that such a feeling was voiced by the students. Despite such feelings, all students expressed gratitude for the author's initiative to create an objective assessment method for evaluating their surgical skills and for providing them with feedback on their performance and how they could improve in the future.

The debriefing meeting with the students also yielded valuable feedback about the importance of access to videos of procedures for student preparation. For example, whereas students had access to videos of the procedures that they were assessed on for their start surgical skills scores, they did not have access to videos for the some of the procedures on which they were assessed for their end surgical skills scores including the umbilical and apex of the bladder resection, and umbilical herniorrhaphy. Students felt that this was the likely reason why their end scores for skill 12 (knowledge of specific procedure) were lower than their start scores.

Discussion

Our purpose was to both evaluate the design and use of a global rating scale instrument in veterinary medical education and to use this instrument for the first time to examine the effectiveness of 2 surgical techniques courses for improving the surgical skills of veterinary students. Although all evaluators found the instrument easy to use, some of the surgical skills were more difficult to assess than others. Also, the nature of the 2 surgical techniques courses created several challenges in performing the assessments. That students were evaluated during different surgical procedures to obtain start and end scores may have had an impact on our results. Nevertheless, this study provides readers with the basis of an assessment instrument that can be modified for use in specific veterinary colleges and/or specific courses. Additionally, our data reveals valuable insights into student desire for objective assessment methods and formal feedback mechanisms.

We believe that there is a clear need for assessment instruments like this in veterinary medical education. In designing such an instrument, we hoped to provide colleagues with one that would be easy to apply with or without minor modifications. For this reason, we chose to use a global rating scale instrument, which has been shown to be more reliable and consistent than checklist systems,[14] and to only include important basic surgical skills that would be easy for veterinarians of all levels of training to evaluate.[6] The summation of the individual skill scores, as previously described,[12,13] also allows for an overall evaluation of surgical skill proficiency. However, as we experienced, what seems like a basic surgical skill can be difficult to evaluate, particularly in the setting of a COPE, which lacks the structure and consistency of an OSCE. Because of challenges faced during assessment in these particular surgical techniques courses, we were forced to eliminate the critical surgical skill of hemostasis from the evaluation. Had the students been assessed one at a time performing a more simple recovery procedure such as a feline or canine ovariohysterectomy, we believe this particular skill could have been evaluated without difficulty. It would perhaps be better to use an instrument like this, especially initially, during a course in which each student performs an entire basic surgery by themselves in the context of a COPE or during a standardized surgical exercise in the context of an OSCE. Another option for using this instrument would be to have the students each perform one standardized basic surgical procedure before the start of the course and then again at the end of the course on which all evaluations would be made.

It is important when using an assessment instrument that all evaluators agree on every skill and every response anchor to avoid any confusion or inconsistencies in scoring. Although similar instruments used in human medical education have yielded excellent inter-rater reliability results,[12] we should have tested the inter-rater reliability of this instrument for use in veterinary medical education. This could have been performed on a trial group of students each performing the same surgical procedure and being evaluated by multiple evaluators whose scores were then compared. This also could have been tested by having the evaluators rate overlapping groups of students throughout the course of the study and then comparing the scores of the overlapping students assigned by the different evaluators. One potential way to make the process of multiple evaluators assessing the same student easier, and perhaps also make the assessment process more appealing would be to videotape students during surgery and then perform the assessments using videotapes.[7,18,19] Not only would this allow for more flexibility in scheduling, it also allows the evaluators to go back and watch a student multiple times before assigning a point value for a specific skill. Because each of the evaluators in this study had to assess 4 students simultaneously, there were certainly times when skill scores were assigned based on a single observation. Had students been videotaped, each performance of a specific skill could have been observed multiple times allowing for a more accurate assessment. In addition, had assessments been made from videotapes, student frustration at not being able to ask evaluators for assistance during surgery would have been avoided. It is important to note, however, that the use of videotapes alone to perform evaluations can be problematic as it is difficult to get the full perspective by camera on the performance of skills such as preparation of student and patient, especially scrubbing and draping.

Despite the previously described issues caused by the nature of the courses examined and the surgeries that the evaluators observed, the authors were able to draw several important conclusions from the data regarding student improvement in surgical skills and student acceptance of formal assessment methods. Whereas results based on only four 3rd year students must be interpreted with some degree of caution, a statistically significant difference between 3rd and 4th year students was found when comparing improvement in total surgical skill scores with 3rd year students having a 1.75 times greater improvement than 4th year students in terms of points. In addition, all 3rd year students had individual improvement in their total surgical skill scores compared to only 50% of 4th year students. Whereas it might have been expected that the 4th years students who had the least improvement were the ones that started with the highest start total surgical skill scores (i.e. those who did not have much room for improvement), this was not the case. The 4th year students that had the least improvement in their total surgical skill scores were actually the ones with the lowest start total surgical skill scores. There are a couple of possible explanations for this finding. The first is that these 4th year students may have had the unfortunate opportunity to learn incorrect surgical skills or "bad habits" before these courses either on clinical rotations or in other settings in which they may have received less guidance than they did in these courses. These "bad habits" would then be harder to correct whereas 3rd year students who are essentially starting de novo soon after their live animal practice are easier to train.[1,20] The 2nd possible explanation is that because of the increased number of 4th year students compared to 3rd year students, we were able to detect several 4th year students who perhaps lack natural surgical ability or manual dexterity.[7] Had we examined a comparable number of 3rd year students, a similar phenomenon in which several 3rd year students displayed little improvement in surgical skills despite the intensive learning environment of the surgical techniques courses may have been found. The significant difference between 3rd and 4th year students we observed raises some interesting questions about which students benefit most from surgical techniques courses such as these and suggests that such courses may be more effective earlier in the curriculum. This finding needs further examination in a larger group of students before any definitive conclusions can be made.

A strong and consistent theme throughout this study was student desire for feedback. Tied into this concept is student acceptance of formal objective assessment methods because they will result in meaningful feedback. This desire was evident in all aspects of the study from student enrollment through student survey results and information obtained during the student debriefing meeting. Students felt strongly that they needed more formal and regular feedback to know where they needed to improve. They also stressed that this feedback would be most useful if it could be given halfway through a course or clinical rotation while there is still time for improvement and preferably opportunities for re-evaluation. The benefit of feedback on long-term improvement in the surgical skills of human medical students has been previously reported[21,22] and there is no reason to believe that this would be any different for veterinary students. The use of an objective assessment instrument as we described, provides an excellent opportunity to give formal feedback either in a written format or verbally through meetings with students. That only a weak to moderate agreement was found between student opinions on their improvement in surgical skills and our assessment scores underscores this need for feedback.

Veterinary surgical skill assessment instruments like the one we designed are useful for student evaluation and for providing feedback they can use to improve as veterinary surgeons. Furthermore, formal assessments are necessary for objective student assessment as accreditation requirements continue to become more stringent for student learning outcomes. Additional work needs to be performed to determine the most efficient way to incorporate these assessments into the curriculum either through COPEs or OSCEs, and possibly with the use of videotaping. Additional work needs to be performed to determine how surgical techniques courses can be used most effectively to improve the surgical skills of veterinary students. Whereas our results suggest that these courses are more effective earlier on in the curriculum than after the students have already started their clinical rotations, the sample size is small and the courses examined are very specific advanced courses that may not be generalizable to all surgical techniques courses. In conclusion, we have developed a surgical skill assessment instrument that can be readily adapted and incorporated into outcomes assessment of a veterinary curriculum.

Acknowledgment

This study was supported by a Cornell University Biological and Biomedical Sciences Graduate Research and Teaching Fellowship Program (L.V.S). We thank Dr. Richard Hackett, Dr. Susan Fubini, Ms. Pati Kirch and Ms. Natalie Spaulding for their support during the surgical techniques courses.

References

1. Smeak DD: Teaching surgery to the veterinary novice: the Ohio State University experience. *J Vet Med Educ* 2007;34:620–627.
2. Smeak DD, Beck ML, Shaffer CA, *et al.*: Evaluation of video tape and a simulator for instruction of basic surgical skills. *Vet Surg* 1991;20:30–36.
3. Davis MH, Ponnamperuma GG, McAleer S, *et al.*: The objective structured clinical examination (OSCE) as a determinant of veterinary clinical skills. *J Vet Med Educ* 2006;33:578–587.
4. Bowlt KL, Murray JK, Herbert GL, *et al.*: Evaluation of the expectations, learning and competencies of surgical skills by undergraduate veterinary students performing canine ovariohysterectomies. *J Small Anim Pract* 2011;52: 587–594.

5. Welsh PJ, Jones LM, May SA, *et al.*: Approaches to defining day one competency: a framework for learning veterinary skills. *Rev Sci Tech* 2009;28:771–777.
6. Smeak DD, Hill LN, Lord LK, *et al.*: Expected frequency of use and proficiency of core surgical skills in entry-level veterinary practice: 2009 ACVS core surgical skills diplomate survey results. *Vet Surg* 2012;41:853–861.
7. Greenfield CL, Johnson AL, Schaeffer DJ, *et al.*: Comparison of surgical skills of veterinary students trained using models or live animals. *J Am Vet Med Assoc* 1995;206:1840–1845.
8. Rhind SM, Baillie S, Brown F, *et al.*: Assessing competence in veterinary medical education: where's the evidence? *J Vet Med Educ* 2008;35:407–411.
9. Turnwald G, Stone E, Bristol D, *et al.*: Assessing clinical competency: reports from discussion groups. *J Vet Med Educ* 2008;35:343–353.
10. Hardie EM: Current methods in use for assessing clinical competencies: what works? *J Vet Med Educ* 2008;35:359–368.
11. Markey GC, Browne K, Hunter K, *et al.*: Clinical observed performance evaluation: a prospective study in final year students of surgery. *Adv Health Sci Educ Theory Pract* 2011;16:47–57.
12. Bramson R, Sadoski M, Sanders CW, *et al.*: A reliable and valid instrument to assess competency in basic surgical skills in second-year medical students. *South Med J* 2007;100:985–990.
13. Chen CC, Korn A, Klingele C, *et al.*: Objective assessment of vaginal surgical skills. *Am J Obstet Gynecol* 2010;203:79.e1–79.
14. Martin JA, Regehr G, Reznick R, *et al.*: Objective structured assessment of technical skill (OSATS) for surgical residents. *Br J Surg* 1997;84:273–278.
15. Stewart RA, Hauge LS, Stewart RD, *et al.*: A CRASH course in procedural skills improves medical students' self-assessment of proficiency, confidence, and anxiety. *Am J Surg* 2007;193:771–773.
16. MacDonald J, Williams RG, Rogers DA: Self-assessment in stimulation-based surgical skills training. *Am J Surg* 2003;185:319–322.
17. DeCaro MS, Thomas RD, Albert NB, *et al.*: Choking under pressure: multiple routes to skill failure. *J Exp Psychol Gen* 2011;140:390–406.
18. Beard JD, Jolly BC, Newble DI, *et al.*: Assessing the technical skills of surgical trainees. *Br J Surg* 2005;92:778–782.
19. Macluskey M, Durham J, Balmer C, *et al.*: Dental student suturing skills: a multicentre trial of a checklist-based assessment. *Eur J Dent Educ* 2011;15:244–249.
20. Macluskey M, Hanson C: The retention of suturing skills in dental undergraduates. *Eur J Dent Educ* 2011;15:42–46.

21. Porte MC, Xeroulis G, Reznick RK, *et al.*: Verbal feedback from an expert is more effective than self-accessed feedback about motion efficiency in learning new surgical skills. *Am J Surg* 2007;193:105–110.
22. Ende J: Feedback in Clinical Medical Education. *JAMA* 1983;250:777–781.

(For a copy of the assessment instrument see the original publication—link is above).

Veterinary Surgery 9999 (2012) 1–9 © Copyright 2012 by The American College of Veterinary Surgeons

WHAT CAN WE LEARN FROM LAUREN SCHNABEL'S STUDY?

This study using mixed methods provides good examples of the nature of the evidence we may find, examine, and use. After searching the literature, Lauren found two medical instruments for assessing students' surgical skills for human medicine but none for veterinary medicine. These helped her generate the kinds of questions/statements necessary for her own surgical instrument that she wanted to test out in the surgical classroom. She collected a variety of qualitative and quantitative evidence from instructors and students, as well as her own observations. For her qualitative methods she engaged in systematic observation of the use of the instrument, focus groups and discussions with faculty using the instrument, focus group discussions with students after the use of the instrument. She used quantitative analysis of the outcomes of the student assessment using the instrument and engaged in statistical analyses to see skills before and after instruction, compared different levels of students, and she statistically examined the rating of individual surgical skills to see what areas needed more work. The instrument itself is designed as an assessment tool to aid with the assessment and feedback of students engaging in their surgical practicum to give them feedback on their performance. Thus, student assessment is also a critical part of this mixed methods study. She uses this information to make decisions about the instrument itself and its use, as well as thoughts about the curriculum in general.

The goal of using these methodologies together is that they give the researcher a really good picture of the phenomenon under investigation—in Lauren's case, a better understanding of her tool for assessing surgical skills. We can see in Lauren Schnabel's example the implementation of all of the strategies explored throughout this book so far: the need to examine the literature, the use of qualitative and quantitative methodology and student assessment and the use of triangulation and using all of this to inform and improve practice.

Chapter 7

Case Studies and Pilot Studies

In this chapter:

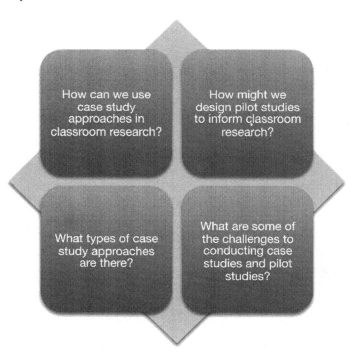

How can we use case study approaches in classroom research?

How might we design pilot studies to inform classroom research?

What types of case study approaches are there?

What are some of the challenges to conducting case studies and pilot studies?

WHAT ARE CASE STUDIES AND HOW CAN WE USE THEM IN HIGHER EDUCATION CLASSROOM RESEARCH?

Case studies seek to better understand or explain particular "real-world" contexts. The case study approach is quite well suited for research on individual classroom contexts or particular course contexts (e.g., departments, curricular issues, etc.). The appeal of case study is that it relies on multiple methods and approaches and analyzes various forms of data within a given context to better understand it. Often in classroom research, we want to better understand the context of our own classroom and what is really happening there.

Case Study Research: The Importance of Understanding Context

Case study research can be useful when planning and conducting college and university classroom research. However, the nature of case study research is often misunderstood. Yin wrote, "case study research continues to be an essential form of social science inquiry. The method should be one of several that a social scientist or team of social scientists would consider using." He adds that "despite its widespread use, case study research has received perhaps the least attention and guidance among nearly all social science research methods" (Yin 2011, p. 1989). He provides what he calls an "abbreviated definition" that all case study research

> starts from the same compelling feature: the desire to derive an up-close or otherwise in-depth understanding of a single or small number of "cases," set in their real-world contexts (e.g., Bromley, 1986, p. 1). The closeness aims to produce an invaluable and deep understanding—that is, an insightful appreciation of the "cases"—hopefully resulting in new learning about real-world behavior, and its meaning.
>
> (p. 1990)

He argues that central to case study research is an examination of the "context" of the case—that we seek to better understand the context and use multiple sources of evidence to gain a deeper understanding. For those interested in doing classroom research to gain a deeper understanding of what is happening within the context of the classroom, this approach fits perfectly.

Yin suggests further that there are certain situations and research questions that provide good opportunities for the case study methodology. One is the same for qualitative research more generally—when we ask research questions that examine a "descriptive" question such as an improved understanding of "what is happening or has happened?" (p. 1991). However, he also argued that case study research can answer a more "explanatory question," such as "how or why did something happen." Earlier in the book, when we discussed generating research questions, generally the former kind of question is used when framing questions best suited for qualitative methodology and the latter question is better suited for quantitative. What we see in this definition of case study is that we can rely on a variety of methods that allow us to better understand the "real-world context" within "natural settings" (p. 1992) including who, what, where, when, how, and why.

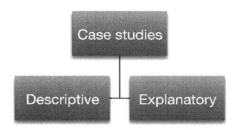

Figure 7.1

Yin (2011, p. 1994) describes four different case study designs (Figure 7.2 below is adapted from his original "Basic Types of Designs for Case Studies" table). We see that we can examine a single case holistically; a single case with multiple units/types of analysis; multiple cases holistically; and multiple cases with multiple methods/types/units of analysis.

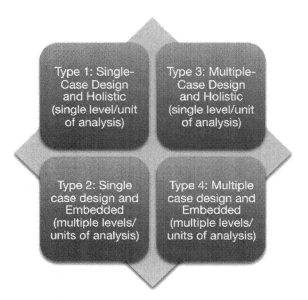

Figure 7.2

Yin also provides some useful examples of possible case studies that could be done in education, such as "how teachers form and make use of informal planning groups to improve instruction." He also lists the following as common evidence sources within case study research: documents, archived records, interviews, observations (including direct, participant or even non-participant) and actual artifacts. As seen in Figure 7.2, case studies can involve multiple cases or single cases and involve either a holistic or single unit of analysis or have multiple embedded sources of evidence for analysis.

There are many questions that might emerge as one considers following the case study approach, such as should I do a case study? This answer would be determined by the research question—if it is mostly descriptive and trying to better understand different aspects of a particular context through direct observational means, then case study may be the right choice.

What is the unit of the case for the analysis? For example what if you want to study your classroom—what is the "case?" That is, is the case your students? Your classroom setting? Your syllabus/course plan? Is it the entire semester? Month? Basically your research question determines the scope of the case and may help you identify how much time and effort would be involved in collecting data and what data you might want to collect.

In analyzing case study data, Yin (2004) had an interesting suggestion for those doing case study research:

> You might start with questions (e.g., the questions in your case study protocol) rather than with the data. Start with a small question first, then identify your evidence that addresses the question. Draw a tentative conclusion based on the weight of the evidence, also asking how you should display the evidence so that readers can check your assessment. Continue to a larger question and repeat the procedure. Keep going until you think you have addressed your main research question(s).
>
> (p. 21)

Examining context more deeply makes sense in classroom research—particularly when we want to better understand the complexities of our classroom context and the interplay among students, the curriculum, the professor, other instructors, the syllabus, the classroom setting, etc. Also, within teaching, we have many questions and many of us attempt to draw some conclusions, sometimes without much evidence, to try to figure out what may be happening. If we start with smaller questions first and then attempt to collect evidence that addresses this smaller question (and repeat the process if possible) we can create much better, evidence-based conclusions.

Recently, Ainley and Buckley (in Rodrigues 2010) wrote that there has been a shift in approaches to classroom research and how research questions are considered. They explain a dichotomy that is similar to the one Yin described above, but they separate the sides of the dichotomy into "variable-centered approaches and person-centered approaches." They suggest that "while this separation exists, it is also necessary to point out that these two approaches are complementary" (p. 7). *Variable-centered* approaches tend to use quantitative approaches with hypothesis testing and strategies discussed in the chapter on quantitative methods. *Person-centered* approaches tend to rely more on qualitative methodology. Case study allows these two approaches to complement each other (as does mixed methods design), while seeking to better understand a particular context or case. Case study allows us to examine the person and processes within a context. In classroom research, the case is often the classroom or course.

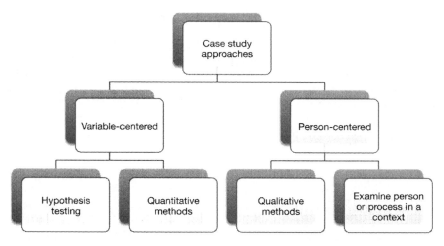

Figure 7.3

Also important to case study research is the focus on *direct empirical evidence*. So rather than a reliance on evidence by proxy such as surveys or interviews, where participants talk about or answer questions about a certain experience, attitudes, and so on, these behaviors are actually observed first hand. This is not to suggest that these proxy forms of evidence are not useful, but direct empirical data is preferred when striving to understand a particular context.

Considerations when engaging in case study research for classroom research are as follows:

1. What is the context? (e.g., the classroom, the laboratory, the department, the school, etc.)
2. What is/are your research question(s)? (consider whether descriptive or explanatory)

127

3. What kinds of evidence (qualitative and quantitative) can you collect that allow you to see what is happening in that context (consider direct measures rather than proxy measures)?
4. How do the data/evidence/findings fit within the questions asked/ considered?
5. What did you find that was compelling, consistent, inconsistent?
6. How do your findings help inform what you do in the future? What are the useful takeaways for you and your practice within this context?

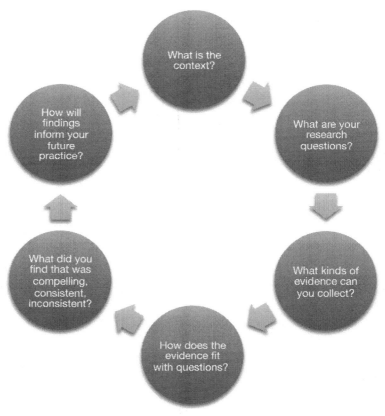

Figure 7.4

TAKING A STEP BACK: CHALLENGES TO OBSERVING OUR OWN ENVIRONMENTS

One of the challenges, as we conduct research within a context we are intimately familiar with or in which we play a major role, is the ability to step back and observe and notice aspects of the context that you otherwise might not. We are (as teachers/instructors/professors) influenced by our own biases, and sometimes veteran teachers can habituate to the classroom setting after years of experience, so much so that it may be difficult to notice behaviors or issues unless they are out of the ordinary. For novice teachers, doing case study research on one's own classroom may be overwhelming because so many aspects of the context are new and interesting and stand out. Regardless of whether the researcher is a novice or veteran teacher (or somewhere in between), doing case study research on one's own classroom *can* be challenging, but worth the effort. My advice to tackling the challenge of case study research within one's own classroom context is to keep a teaching journal.

The Importance of a Teaching Journal

Any new habit takes time and consistency to form. The habit of keeping a teaching journal is no different—it takes time, consistency and commitment to form. Try to start by jotting down important things you notice (before, during and after class) right after class is over or within a short period of time so the memories are fresh. Of course, this is similar to what you would do during an observation of your classroom, but thinking about these observations as you would a journal may help routinize it. Even if you don't intend to do case study research, a teaching journal can be quite useful in helping one think about and reflect more purposefully upon what happens in the classroom.

I know this seems like one additional task in the very busy schedule we have as faculty members, but in the end, as we become more reflective and use the observational evidence to inform our practice through a more formal research approach, the more efficient we will become.

CASE STUDY EXAMPLES: DIANA GARVIN (ROMANCE STUDIES/ITALIAN) AND INGA GRUß (ANTHROPOLOGY)

Diana Garvin was teaching an intermediate Italian course, and wanted to examine the context of that course and particular elements within that course using multiple sources of evidence. What was particularly intriguing about the context of her course, however, was that she was adding an online environment. As classroom environments become increasingly more complex (online and blended and traditional), the lines are becoming blurred as we attempt to define the context under investigation. Diana investigated not only her classroom context, but was particularly intrigued by the context of the online environment created within the student blogging assignment.

129

Examples of Research from the Classroom

Blogghiamo! Engaging students through autonomy, authenticity, and community

Diana Garvin

What I did and why

Recent debate in the Modern Language Association journal *Profession* considers how to effectively teach reading skills in the digital age. In this discussion, I noticed that many educators implicitly treated technology use as a goal rather than as a tool for learning how to read, write, or speak effectively. As a teacher, I select technology for my classroom on the basis of the lesson's learning outcomes, but as a researcher, I wondered how to characterize the benefits of technology and how to assess their effectiveness. My curiosity led me to this study, "Communicative Blog Writing for Student Engagement and Blended Literacy." In this research project, I investigated two questions related to this broader academic discussion. How does writing change when we move online? And how do we situate new technologies and their attendant forms of writing within the larger context of teaching students how to communicate through the written word? I framed these queries within the larger context of Communicative Language Teaching (CLT), which emphasizes authentic interaction in the target language as the primary means to promote student language development. In practice, teachers often focus on listening and speaking to the exclusion of writing, as they are often deemed to be less conversational than verbal and aural activities. Blogging serves as a natural addition to the CLT model because it involves authentic, written communication.

Holding the dual roles of teacher for ITAL 2090: Intermediate Italian Composition and Conversation and Graduate Research and Teaching Fellowship researcher provided the inspiration and weekly structure to methodically explore my questions. My Spring 2013 class of nine students, ages 18 to 22, three women and six men, participated in this case study. To start the Blog Project, I asked the students "If you could be an expert in any topic in Italian culture by the end of this class, what would it be?" Choices ranged from contemporary street art to sustainable agriculture to film. Students then followed that theme across four "realms" of the Italian Internet (blogs, Podcasts, Youtube, Facebook) to craft four different blog posts. They then commented on classmates' blogs and responded to posts on their own blogs, ultimately writing four 200-word posts and eight 100-word responses. I assessed their writing for personal input, originality, and consideration of audience.

To answer my two guiding research questions, I blocked out five specific project goals: characterize students' evolving conceptions of blogging as a form of communicative writing; determine what "engagement" means for students learning this form of writing; match blogging with outcomes in student engagement, cultural, linguistic, and technological fluency; explain how blogging fits within the traditional frame of communicative second-language skills such as listening and speaking; and point to the unique affordances that blogging provides within the larger context of writing skills. Because I wanted to know what "engaged" writing would look like and how effective it would be in increasing linguistic, cultural, and technological ability, I chose to combine quantitative and qualitative methods to track and assess these five areas. My methodology involved observations and analysis of student blogs and in-class discussions about the blogs, pre- and post-Blog Project online survey, wherein I compared means with a paired T-test and thematic coding, as well as a mid-semester focus group semi-scripted interview and student blog content, both analyzed with thematic coding.

What I found

As evidenced by my observations, examination of student work and student comments and the pre- and post-test online surveys, engagement in communicative writing began high and stayed that way over the course of the semester's work. Analyzing quote content pointed to three key themes that students associated with engagement. To characterize what we mean when speaking of "engagement" in writing, let's consider some of the focus group comments on their Blog Project experience: "[Blogging] gave me the chance to write about something I was invested in [and] just practice [what] I'd be looking up in Italy," "I liked reading everybody else's [blogs] . . . I learned a little bit from everybody's," "The assignments made me do it, but then I got into it and discovered it," "This was more about what I found than writing for the sake of writing," "I liked the blog cause you got to choose [the topic and material] you wanted," "I was actually learning, not writing just to prove I can." In describing engagement, students' comments clustered around these interrelated themes: autonomy, authenticity, and community. Autonomy emerged in terms of student choice of topic, material, tone; having "their own" blog. Many returned to descriptions of authentic voice and its effect. Students reported that writing online made them feel as though their voices mattered more and that they were more engaged. It also motivated them to immerse themselves in the technology as a means to achieve the goal of authentic communication. For students, autonomy linked with authenticity, which they defined as exposure to Italian materials written in slang and dialect and the idea that writing online felt "natural." The connection of autonomy and authenticity with engagement need not evoke the specter of the lonely crowd. In fact, students viewed community, that is, learning culture and vocabulary from classmates and contributing to Italian online forums, as an integral factor in online writing's draw.

Student blog content also highlighted what blended literacy looks like in practice. In brief, cultural, linguistic, and technological considerations intertwined. Comparisons between American and Italian culture, denotation of frequency, rarity, or absence of cultural forms evoked cultural literacy. For example, in one blog post and response two students discussed spaghetti westerns filmed in the USA and in Italy with reference to English and Italian titles. Interest in non-standard vocabulary, questioning the pervasiveness of Italianized English terms, emerging awareness of punctuation, and sentence length as markers of emotion suggested advances in linguistic literacy. We see this type of growth in the instance of a student who voiced her interest in the Italian etymology of the word "graffiti," meaning "little scratches" in a blog post on urban art. Finally, continued blog posting after the project's conclusion, independent research into other Italian Internet realms (Twitter, Wikis), interest in Italian blog maintenance and computer terms suggested the development of technological literary. While the primary goal of the project was not necessarily to teach tech literacy, the fact remains that traditional conceptions of literacy take on pluralistic forms involving culture and technology when we move writing online. Indeed, a key aspect of increasing technology literacy lies in teaching students how to write with increased attention, as the Internet projects their voices on a far wider stage.

How these findings have informed/will inform my practice

In approaching the issue of technology, we must consider both questions when studying teaching as research and then developing our best practices. Addressing the former question guards against fossilizing the definition of writing and rendering it old-fashioned, while confronting the latter assures that we do not lose sight of traditional modes of writing that still have something to teach. An additive approach to writing that allows one to select among choices, rather than a Darwinist model that advocates survival of the "best" way to write, increases the likelihood that our current definition of writing will not become obsolete when current technologies evolve, as they inevitably do with ever-increasing celerity.

Students reported that writing online made them feel as though their voices mattered more and that they were more engaged. It also motivated them to immerse themselves in the technology as a means to achieve the goal of authentic communication. Here we arrive at a key feature of online writing: users write on the Internet knowing that the world may read it. The inherent publicness of crafting text online thus heightens the importance of effective communication. To affectively convey a message to one's audience, the writer must target every element of writing, from content and structure to register and vocabulary, to this goal. Such attention to writing's recipient is not new — the epistolary novels, broadsheets, and circulars of years attest to the longevity of communicative writing and its formidable narrative thrall. But we do not write broadsheets. We write articles and essays, blog posts and status updates. Communicative writing provides a framework to hone the effectiveness of one's writing regardless of its placement in a print or online forum. We separate and dichotomize writing in this way at our peril. Integrating blogging to traditional curriculums provides a tool to teach integrated linguistic, cultural, and technological skills by appealing to students' needs for autonomy, authenticity, and community.

We see here that through Diana's experience examining her class and focusing specifically (although not exclusively) on the blogging project within that context, she learns and concludes quite a few ideas that shape her thinking about using blogging in the future as a way to increase language and cultural understanding. She found the project quite useful in meeting her espoused outcomes for her students and their engagement with writing and building fluency with another language. Among her qualitative and quantitative evidence, she has direct observations (of blogs and students in the classroom), along with proxy measures (surveys, interviews, focus groups), in an effort to triangulate her data and to gather as much as she can to fully understand the context from different angles.

In a somewhat similar fashion, in Inga Gruß's example of a first-year writing seminar (required of all first year students) offered within the department of Anthropology, we can see she is also approaching her research from a case study perspective—the context, once again, being her classroom and how issues of power and privilege were taken up within it and how students responded to these ideas—relying on her own classroom observations and student writing assignments, she uses strategies that are familiar within her discipline of Anthropology—participant observation and examination of student work to better understand the context of her classroom and student challenges confronting hegemony.

Examples of Research from the Classroom

Teaching as research project: "Writing my opinion or masking it as fact?" Learning/teaching (the implications of) positionality

Inga Gruß

What I did and why

During the spring semester 2013 I taught a first-year writing seminar at a large private research university. First-year writing seminars are designed to introduce first year students to academic writing in the disciplines. Most undergraduate students (exceptions apply) have to complete two seminars as partial fulfillment towards their undergraduate degrees. Students have a choice between taking the seminar in different departments that offer a wide range of topics. They submit their five favorite seminar choices and are usually assigned one of those choices.

The seminar I taught was offered through the Department of Anthropology and the course content provided students with an introduction to discourses about representation, power, and culture. Rather than focusing on few specific topics, I discussed a broad range of issues such as colonialism, class politics, gender and knowledge production, museum studies, religion, and politics in order to demonstrate the relevance of representation and power to a broad range of fields. A common thread throughout the semester that tied the various topics together was the emphasis on the position authors and audiences hold in constructing, analyzing, and understanding (academic) arguments. I taught the seminar for the second time and had revised the syllabus according to my experiences and student feedback in the fall semester.

133

Overarching goals that I had formulated for the course included developing the students' ability to grasp the importance of positionality, ideology, and power in researching, writing, and reading about cultures. Writing seminars are meant to introduce students to subject matter in a discipline, but more importantly aim to improve the students' writing skills. Argumentative writing is the foundation for any anthropological writing. I focused on enabling students to recognize the assumptions that inform their opinions and beliefs, since this is a skill that is not only crucial to anthropology, but would help them throughout their (non-)academic tenure. To learn to recognize one's own biases and value systems is a long-term process and I considered this seminar only one step in a much longer learning process.

The seminar was limited to sixteen students, of which eleven were females and five males. In general, students were required to read at least one academic article in preparation for class discussions. Articles were drawn from a variety of fields and mostly came from peer-reviewed journals. Students were encouraged to send in two discussion questions before each class session and received credit for doing so. Discussion questions focused on a broad range of issues: passages that students wanted to clarify, that they found interesting or confusing, or any other points they wanted to discuss about the articles during class time. I focused most class periods on understanding and evaluating the arguments the respective authors presented in their works. Students were required to participate actively since class discussions relied on their input and willingness to exchange and discuss their ideas.

I opened and ended the semester by critically engaging with the history of anthropology, in particular its role and compliance in colonialism and shaping popular beliefs about hierarchies among civilizations. My rationale in doing so was to illustrate that there is no contradiction in taking on a certain identity (in this case my identity as anthropologist), promoting it (by teaching anthropological subject matter) and to critically engage with this identity at the same time. The overall goal was to illustrate that membership of a particular group does not preclude critique of the same group. In contrast, membership in a group calls for critical engagement with the foundations of that groups' identity.

By framing the course in this way, I hoped that it would be easier for students to seriously consider points of critiques that were advanced in readings during the course. The majority of readings for the course were based on ethnographic research in the USA and many articles suggested ideas that were outside of most of the students' frames of reference (for example, see Haraway 1988; Howell and Shyrock 2003; Jensen 2010; McIntosh 1997). I had chosen these texts because it was more likely that the students would be familiar with the cultural assumptions that many of the texts aimed to deconstruct. While some readings drew on empirical examples from other parts of the world, the main goal of the course was not to familiarize students with ideas and concepts that people in other parts of the world hold. The goal was rather to defamiliarize the student's with their own perspectives and beliefs (Miner 1956).

134

During most classes, at first I discussed the article based on the questions the students had sent in. Discussions were closely related to the texts and students needed to have the texts on hand to be able to participate meaningfully. For the second halves of the class periods, I brought in additional materials that illustrated the concerns of the readings in an different context. The main purpose was to challenge students to think about the relevance of the respective articles to their everyday lives.

I started the course by illustrating the power of the author to shape the perspectives of the audience. An often-used text in introductory anthropology courses is Horace Miners' article "Body Ritual among the Nacirema," which defamiliarizes ordinary bodily techniques like brushing one's teeth by employing a distancing idiom. It becomes impossible for most students to recognize themselves as the object of Miner's ethnographic inquiry ("Nacirema" reads inverted as "American"). I asked students in class to write a similar shorter piece about an ordinary daily habit (showering, crossing the road, cooking, etc.) in a similar distancing idiom. They read the paragraphs to each other without announcing what process they were describing and other students in classes had to guess what they were hearing about.

An important concept of the course was the process of othering and the figure of the other that the students learned about by reading Abu-Lughod (1991) and Rosaldo (1989). In order to illustrate the power of othering in an everyday context, we watched an excerpt from the motion picture "300" that portrays a fictionalized, historical battle drama between Greeks and Persians. Afterwards students were asked to write a paper about the techniques of othering in the film.

Another example that illustrates the emphasis on transferring knowledge from one setting to the next comes from the class discussions on developmental politics and humanitarian aid. I had asked the students to bring any image from a humanitarian campaign that they came across during an Internet search. All the students put their photos on the blackboard and I asked them to describe common themes that they saw on these images. For this class, students had read an article that discussed the power of development to determine the representation of many industrializing countries (Escobar 1992). The images on the blackboard illustrated the point of the author and helped the students to understand that media representations powerfully shape their imaginations of other parts of the world.

What I found

Throughout the semester I collected written responses from students to assess their understanding of class activities. Furthermore, I held a survey at the end of the semester and class discussions also informed my understanding of the students' positions and thoughts.

At the beginning of the second week of the semester, I had asked all students to share their understanding of objectivity, subjectivity and the potential for objective representation in writing with me (What does objectivity mean? What does subjectivity mean? Can representation ever be objective?). Many students employ notions of objectivity and subjectivity to evaluate the validity of representations and have learned to consider objectivity as a positive value. One of the goals of the course was to sensitize students to the fragility of most claims of objective knowledge production (beyond some indisputable facts such as the existence of gravity or seasonal changes).

At the end of the semester I returned the same questions to the students and asked them again to respond in writing. I then returned them their responses from the beginning of the semester and asked them to write an additional paragraph that compared their answers from the beginning of the semester with their answers from the end of the semester. The purpose was to offer time for reflection and the opportunity for students to gauge their own changes in thoughts and opinions or absences thereof.

Most students suggested that objectivity can be defined as communicating information from an unbiased, disembodied position. Some samples from students responses: "Objectivity is being able to look at the situation and see it in an unbiased and unaffected light because you do not have any leanings." "Objectivity is a way of expressing thought that is fact and observation-based rather than opinionated." "Maintaining objectivity requires refraining from moral normative judgments." In contrast, subjectivity was defined as speaking from an embodied, personal position: "Subjectivity exudes a sense of bias and dependence on personal beliefs." "Subjectivity is when something is viewed from a unique perspective." There were few differences between the responses at the beginning and end of the semester. When asked to compare their responses from the beginning and end of the semester, most students stated that their understanding of the terms had not changed, but that their understanding of the importance and prevalence of the two terms had changed: "Subjectivity is looked down upon by scientists and many other fields focused on empirical facts. Many do not realize the extent to which we are all subjective (even when we are trying to be objective." "In a sense, I see the representor less as a passive observer with bias, but rather as someone with an agenda that wants to portray someone or something in a particular way." "It is important to identify what the author's intended 'stance' is. This way, the reader can better verify who is writing the piece, what it is about and why they are writing it. This gives the reader a deeper understanding and perspective on the writing." "I originally thought that objective representation was the only way to accurately represent an issue. However, I now recognize that because things are not necessarily cut and dry [sic], it sometimes is necessary to be subjective so that you can understand the people." Students' responses indicate that the seminar had sensitized them that any persons' positionality influences their individual representation of knowledge claims.

Furthermore, based on the survey, in- and out-class writing and class discussions, students seemed to appreciate the use of "real life" and contemporary examples, as these helped them make connections that they often had difficulties recognizing. Repetition of key aspects of positionality (race, gender, class, etc.) and using different materials from at least two different contexts may help students to recognize their own positionality. Making points explicit inside the classroom helps students to recognize relevant situations outside the classroom. It is crucial to recognize where students stand in terms of their understanding of their own privilege and/or positionality when the course started. It continued to be challenging for students to engage with criticism that might implicate themselves. While students readily accepted the larger implications for some topics (e.g., knowledge production in anthropology), the implications for other topics remained more difficult to grasp and understand (e.g., knowledge production in natural sciences).

How these findings have informed/will inform my practice

Students expressed their appreciation for the opportunities in class to share their opinions about articles, exercises and general course structure. I will continue to provide opportunities for students to share their thoughts since it not only facilitates the process of academic knowledge transfer to everyday contexts, but also serves to motivate the students. Providing room for everybody's opinion can be challenging as an instructor and emotional for students. I have learned to remind students to position their points of views vis-à-vis articles read for respective classes. This helps them to reflect on new ideas and at the same time prevents discussions from merely circling around similar unsubstantiated points.

Furthermore, it has been a useful practice to ask students to assess their own learning. I shared my learning objectives for the course with the students and, even if students might not reach all the stated learning objectives, there are additional issues that they might have learned about. Reading students' self-assessment has broadened my understanding of the goals of the course.

Last but not least, assigning fewer articles, discussing these in greater depth, and focusing on the implications can be important way of facilitating students' evolving understanding of academic arguments and the relevance of these to a broad range of topics.

Inga, like Diana, was a relatively novice instructor and, also like Diana, a reflective practitioner. She was able to step back and notice the challenges that students had in dealing with their own positionality, power and privilege as it related to white privilege. She also found that asking students, as they struggled through these difficult topics, to assess their own learning was very useful for her in terms of getting a better handle on individual student progress on stated learning outcomes. We can see in Inga's example that this kind of case study classroom research relying on a variety of research methodologies to dig deep and explore and describe the classroom setting can inform and improve teaching and learning in deep and meaningful ways.

In his case study, Lorenzo Fabbri was deeply interested in more closely examining and analyzing his completely unfamiliar teaching context, teaching in a maximum-security prison. In this context, everything was so new to him that he found the task of focusing on any particular aspect of the context overwhelming, but looked at many aspects at first before ultimately settling in on the lack of technology. In the end he focused on the lack of access to technology and information as a complex battle to overcome as a teacher in this context.

Examples of Research from the Classroom

Maximum security, zero technology: Teaching in a maximum-security facility

Lorenzo Fabbri

The program

The Prison Education Program was established to provide college courses to inmates at maximum- and medium-security prisons in New York state, and to engage faculty and students with the vital issue of the country's transformation into a "prison-industrial complex."

In the mid-1990s, when an act of Congress caused the collapse of taxpayer-funded College programs in most state prisons, a few faculty members undertook to offer a handful of classes on a volunteer basis at the local Correctional Facility (a maximum-security prison one hour from the university where I teach). In 1999, the university enabled these college classes to be given for credit, charging neither tuition nor fees.

Credits earned by inmates are transferred to the local community college, which is the degree-granting institution rather than the university.

My course and my students

I designed and taught an upper division philosophy course. My goal was to provide students with an opportunity to discuss crucial issues concerning human nature and social relations. In the tradition of Liberal Arts education and of the university's mission, I believe philosophy and arts are in fact essential to educating students to respect themselves and their fellow human beings.

I had 8 students, who were serving sentences that went from twenty-five years to life in prison. During the semester, through philosophy (e.g., Kant, Heidegger, Wittgenstein) and literature (e.g., Poe, Kafka, Hawthorne, Hemingway, Joyce, PK Dick) we discussed issues such as:

- Does free will exist?
- Does art exist for art's sake or does it have a moral value?
- Is it possible to understand people with different world-views?
- What is the defining trait of humanity?
- Is empathy acquired or innate? What about cruelty?

Students were required to:

- Write weekly response papers;
- Take three "take-home" exams;
- Write a philosophical fiction as their final project.

Security protocols

Once we arrived at the facility, the other volunteers and I would check for our gate pass. If for any reason someone is not on the list, he or she cannot get in. One week an inmate lit himself on fire and we were not allowed in. The guards treated the "incident" as normal administration.

In order to reach the school area, we are escorted through multiple checkpoints and gates. We walk through the yard. It is empty when we get in. The space is filled by the screams coming from the surrounding cell blocks.

After class, we retrace our steps. The yard is full at this point; inmates are enjoying their free time. They are playing basketball, standing in line for phones, and watching TV. As we walk by, they step back. After class, no contacts are allowed between the inmates and us.

Challenges

I expected challenges in two areas:

- students' behavior;
- lack of technology in the classroom.

My fears on these issues were not justified. Students were very respectful both towards me and towards each other. We engaged in lively, intense, yet considerate exchanges of ideas. The two hours of class would go by incredibly fast, even if I could not rely on any technological aid to support my teaching. This was a great surprise, for I have been taught that technology is crucial for the creation of an engaged classroom.

The "zero-technology" available for this course led me to rethink my assumptions, and ask the following questions:

- Is technology crucial for teaching?
- Does it enhance learning?
- Does it promote learners' engagement or does it encourage their apathy and passivity?

Reflection

Given the ever-increasing number of inmates detained in the United States, it is more crucial than ever to strategize on how to facilitate convicts' re-entry in society. Prison education programs have been shown to limit the dehumanizing effects of life in prison by providing inmates with occasions to practice dialogue and resolve conflicts without resorting to violence.

Prison education does not only improve the daily living conditions of both inmates and prison staff. It also prepares inmates for their re-entry into society. For this reason, investing in prison education programs equates to investing in society's future.

Lorenzo starts with his local focus of the context of his course within the prison, but cannot help but consider the broader context within which this course exists—how it fits with the mission of the university, the call within the prison system, and so on. Often case studies do call upon us to reflect on the larger social context and how these smaller contexts fit.

PILOT STUDIES: SMALL-SCALE PRELIMINARY PROJECTS

Pilot studies are often scaled-down or mini versions of a study you might be considering. These can be useful in classroom research projects. Sometimes if one has a research question and is not sure how to tackle it, or may not be able to approach it to the degree to which one wants to devote necessary resources to it, pilot studies can be a worthwhile alternative. Van Teijlingen and Hundley explained the two different ways of doing pilot studies: "It can refer to the so-called feasibility studies, which are 'small scale version(s), or trial run(s), done in preparation for the major study' (Polit *et al.* 2001, p. 467). However, a pilot study can also be the pre-testing or 'trying out' of a particular research instrument (Baker 1994, pp. 182–3)" (van Teijlingen and Hundley 2002, p. 33). For a classroom research project, a departmental research project, curriculum restructuring project or project that may become larger and increased in scope, pilot studies can help as a "trial run" or to "try out" to see what some of the potential challenges and pitfalls might be. They argue further that "one of the advantages of conducting a pilot study is that it might give advanced warning about where the main research project could fail, where the research protocols may not be followed, or whether proposed methods or instruments are inappropriate or too complicated" (van Teijlingen and Hundley 2002, p. 33). Pilot studies give classroom researchers a chance to test out or more closely examine ideas on a smaller scale and perhaps within a smaller context or within a smaller scope.

They list the following reasons for conducting pilot studies:

- Developing and testing adequacy of research instruments;
- Assessing the feasibility of a full scale study/survey;
- Designing a research protocol;
- Assessing whether the research protocol is realistic and workable;

- Establishing whether the sampling frame and technique are effective;
- Assessing the likely success of proposed recruitment approaches;
- Identifying logistical problems that might occur using proposed methods;
- Estimating variability in outcomes to help determine sample size;
- Collecting preliminary data;
- Determining what resources (finance, staff) are needed for a planned study;
- Assessing the proposed data analysis techniques to uncover potential problems;
- Developing a research question and research plan;
- Training a researcher in as many elements of the research process as possible;
- Convincing funding bodies that the research team is competent and knowledgeable;
- Convincing funding bodies that the main study is feasible and worth funding;
- Convincing other stakeholders that the main study is worth supporting.
  (van Teijlingen and Hundley 2002).

Kim (2011) in her article "The Pilot Study in Qualitative Inquiry" has lessons that are applicable to classroom research pilot studies at the college/university level. One of the advantages she suggests based on her own pilot studies in qualitative research is that

> the implementation of the pilot exercise proved to be essential in four ways. These comprise (1) finding issues and barriers related to recruiting potential participants, (2) engaging the use of oneself as a researcher in a culturally appropriate way and from a phenomenological perspective, (3) reflecting the importance of the epoche process and its difficulty in conducting phenomenological inquiry, and (4) modifying interview questions.
>
> (p. 190)

Her primary take away from her research experience is that the pilot study may allow researchers to create more "culturally competent" research strategies that are more mindful of the people involved in the study (p. 190). So as she suggests, "researchers may begin research by addressing an important but often overlooked question: how the research topic would be received by participants involved" (p. 203). As professors and instructors doing classroom research with our own students in our own classrooms, this question about the way our students may receive or experience our study/project is one to consider. Certainly in our ethical considerations and in applying for Institutional Review Board for Human Subjects

(IRB) approval we consider this question, but often, without a pilot, we may not know or have an idea about how participants may be affected by the project. Certainly any opportunity to examine our own cultural competence as researchers is welcome within the classroom.

Kim argued that "by its very nature, a pilot study may not be intended to produce results; this is probably one reason for the general underreporting of pilot works, as suggested by the editorial comment 'pilot studies are not usually suitable for publication' (Watson *et al.* 2007, p. 619)" (Kim 2011, p. 192). Classroom research projects by their very nature tend to be more about informing and improving practice rather than producing generalizable results, so the consideration of smaller scale pilot studies may make a lot of sense within classroom research. Pilot studies may also be useful for larger scale studies of curricula and broader scale teaching and learning projects that may be college or university-wide.

Pilot Study Examples: Shoshanna Cole (Astronomy) and Luisa Rosas (Theater)

Shoshanna Cole was interested in doing a pilot study before doing a much larger study of critical thinking that might be able to be embedded within the Astronomy curriculum at her institution. Her concerns came out of initial observations of student work and observations that showed a lack of critical thinking.

Examples of Research from the Classroom

Improving undergraduates' critical thinking skills through peer-learning workshops

Shoshanna Cole

Inspired by my frustration with the low level of discourse in American society, and particularly that of the news media, I developed and implemented a series of four "Critical Thinking Workshops" designed to explicitly teach students information literacy, critical reading, and information filtering skills in the everyday context of mainstream Internet, news, and advertisement media. The workshop materials are easily adaptable to any undergraduate, and perhaps 11th and 12th grade, classroom.

My ultimate purpose in establishing critical thinking workshops is to make the world a better place by raising the level of discourse in American society. A recent analysis by the Sunlight Foundation indicates that the complexity of Congressional speech, as measured by a Flesch-Kincaid test applied to the Congressional Record, has dropped from 11.5 in 2005 to 10.6 today (Drutman 2012). The lack of critical thinking in everyday life in current American society bothers me greatly. The news media now aim for entertainment, attention and ratings over information and education and, if reports are to be believed, the American public doesn't question the legitimacy of the information provided to them by the media. This lack of critical thinking in everyday life, this acceptance of the information provided without question, and certainly without deep questioning, leads to societal issues such as choosing a President based on "he seems like a good guy to have a beer with," and the derogation of a President for having attended superior schools for undergraduate, graduate, and professional degrees. This is not right.

Secondarily, today's young people have grown up with literally a world of information at their fingertips. Much of that information, however, is unfiltered. Young children do not have the ability to determine what is correct/legitimate/evidence-based and what is simply an uninformed person's opinion, or worse yet, deliberate misinformation, and this is to be expected. Teenagers and emerging adults are *expected* to be able to determine this, but who trains them? Their parents, many of whom are information illiterate themselves? Their schoolteachers, who are given more and more requirements with the same amount of school time?

I hoped to bridge the gap between the busy classroom teacher and the calls for educators to improve students' critical thinking and higher-order thinking and reasoning skills. My goal for designing critical thinking workshops is to create a stand-alone classroom activity that can be simply and easily incorporated into classrooms at as many institutions as possible. The teacher will need some instruction on how to conduct the workshops, but other than that, teachers should be able to incorporate the activities into their classrooms "as-is", or easily adapt them to their preferred topic(s). I hope that the workshops will ultimately be considered a standard part of introductory science curricula; one way that I will encourage this is by stressing how the workshops fit in with universities' and departments' learning outcomes.

The typical college student is of an excellent age to focus on and develop critical thinking skills. Brain development is ongoing through adolescence and young adulthood, particularly in the regions associated with higher cognitive tasks, with "synaptic pruning" progressing from the back of the brain to the front (Powell 2006). The brain matures considerably but non-uniformly during adolescence: different lobes mature at different rates, and maturation peaks at different ages for different lobes (Giedd *et al.* 1999). At the ages of 18–22, the "emerging adult" brain is still maturing: the frontal lobes of the brain, which are associated with "response inhibition, emotional regulation, planning and organization," mature considerably between adolescence and the mid- to late-twenties (Sowell *et al.* 1999). This has been observed *in vivo*: in a longitudinal MRI study, Bennett and Baird (2006) observed an increase in white matter relative to grey matter during the freshman year of college, consistent with an increase in myelination, which increases the speed and strength of processing within the brain. Teaching critical thinking skills to undergraduate emerging adults may help reinforce connections within their brains that are associated with cognitive skills.

I was a research assistant and graduate/postgraduate student in the University of Sydney's School of Physics from 2001 to 2007. Throughout this time, I was a tutor for first-year Physics workshop tutorials. The workshop tutorials were developed over several years by SUPER, the Sydney University Physics Education Research Group

(Sharma *et al.* 1999, 2005; Sharma and McShane 2008). Around 1,000 students annually enroll in first-year physics courses at the University of Sydney. In the 1990s, SUPER teacher-scholars undertook an endeavor to improve learning and exam results in these classes. The result was weekly non-compulsory peer-learning workshop-style tutorials, rather than the sage-on-a-stage tutorials typical in this field. Students work in groups of three or four, facing each other around tables covered by a sheet of butcher paper for scratch work. They complete worksheets composed of qualitative, quantitative, and demonstration questions designed to challenge the students conceptually and require them to interact and play around with the apparatus that they observe their instructors using at the front of their large lectures. Tutors circulate around the classroom, asking probing questions, guiding students through to solutions, and encouraging groups who have figured out solutions to explain their solutions when other groups have the same questions. Students receive solution sheets at the end of the workshop tutorial. Prather *et al.* (2004) employ similar workshops, termed "lecture tutorials," in introductory astronomy courses.

Having been immersed in workshop tutorials as a teaching environment for many years, it seemed natural to me to implement this teaching methodology in my own classes. As a TA in the Astronomy Department at Cornell University, I often included mini workshops, in which for half of the class meeting period I divided the class into groups of three or four students, and the students worked through one or two qualitative questions in a manner analogous to workshop tutorials.

I developed a series of four peer-learning workshops to teach students how to purposefully employ critical thinking skills in their everyday lives. The workshops' learning objectives are to enable students to:

Workshop 1: discriminate between inappropriate and potentially useful in search engine results pages;
Workshop 2: identify articles' claims, and evaluate the evidence presented in support of those claims;
Workshop 3: differentiate between causal relationships and non-causal correlations; and
Workshop 4: appraise claims made and evidence presented in advertisements.

Students sit around a table, facing each other, and complete worksheets that lead students step-by-step through

a) verbalizing their preconceptions of the workshop theme,
b) dissecting instructional materials to discover the cognitive processes they already use,
c) applying skills step-by-step in real-world situations (search engine results, news articles, ads), and
d) using metacognitive strategies of questioning and reflection.

Table 7.1 Summary of the workshops.

	Workshop 1	Workshop 2	Workshop 3	Workshop 4
Title	"Information Literacy," or, "Is it reasonable to use this website as a resource for my essay?"	"Reading Critically", or, "Understanding information and making it your own"	"Correlation is not necessarily causation"	"Putting it all together"
Learning Objective	Discriminate between inappropriate and potentially useful links in search engine results pages.	Identify articles' claims, and evaluate the evidence presented.	Differentiate between causal relationships and non-causal correlations.	Appraise claims made and evidence presented in advertisements.
Instructional Materials	Evaluating Web Pages: Techniques to Apply and Questions to Ask (UC Berkeley— Teaching Library Internet Workshops)[1]	Excerpt from Chapter 3 of *Introduction to Critical Thinking* by Bruce R. Reichenbach (2001); associated Chapter 3 Study Guide.[2]	"Did the disappearance of pirates cause global warming? Probably not . . ."[5] and Scientific Reasoning module from the Hong Kong University OpenCourseWare on critical thinking, logic, and creativity.[6]	Critical Thinking Workshops Summary: What you've learned.
Media examples	Google search results page: "What killed the dinosaurs theory."	"Global Warming Likely To Increase Stormy Weather, Especially In Certain US Locations" (ScienceDaily)[3] and "Group warms global warming promotes severe weather" (*Dover Post*).[4]	"Central Heating May Be Making Us Fat" (*New York Times*).[7]	Ace Magnetics Copper Magnetic Bracelets site[8] and *SkyMall* ads.

NOTES: All websites accessed on December 5, 2012.
1. Available at www.lib.berkeley.edu/TeachingLib/Guides/InternetEvaluate.html
2. Study guide available at www.mhhe.com/socscience/philosophy/reichenbach/m2_chap03studyguide.html
3. Available at www.sciencedaily.com/releases/2007/12/071204121949.htm#
4. Available at http://www.doverpost.com/communities/x907383491/Group-warns-global-warming-promotes-severe-weather
5. Available at www.ionpsych.com/2011/05/01/did-the-disappearance-of-pirates-cause-global-warming-probably-not . . . /
6. Available at http://philosophy.hku.hk/think/sci/
7. Available at http://well.blogs.nytimes.com/2011/01/26/central-heating-may-be-making-us-fat/
8. Available at http://www.acemagnetics.com/copper-bracelets.html

I did not develop the "instructional materials" myself. As Macdonald and Bykerk-Kauffman (1995) said, "Designing successful small group activities is an intellectually demanding and time-consuming process that occurs behind the scenes." Other practitioners have devoted time to creating these; my innovation was creating peer-learning workshops to accomplish my learning objectives in a format that I can make widely applicable. I found instructional materials suitable for each workshop and wrote worksheets that required students to actively *work through* the material, answering questions about the material itself and the students' reflections about it, rather than simply asking them to passively read the material. The workshops are easily adaptable to any college classroom; teachers can either use my material as it is, or substitute media examples that are relevant to their course content.

As an example, the first workshop was designed to help students with information literacy; specifically, how to determine if a website presents legitimate information. The everyday task was a Google search results page (off-line; I had entered the search terms and saved the resulting search page as a pdf, which was included in the handouts), and the search term was from their assignment. I wrote a worksheet to accompany "Evaluating Web Pages: Techniques to Apply and Questions to Ask," a web literacy tutorial from the UC Berkeley Library (www.lib.berkeley.edu/TeachingLib/Guides/Internet/Evaluate.html, accessed on December 5, 2012). The worksheet required the students to read the document and hand-write the steps and reasoning described by the document, and to comment on these justifications and whether they tended to follow these steps already. On the last page of the worksheet, the students applied the steps to the pdf Google search results. This pdf was the only information the students had about the websites.

Essentially, the students first learned what steps one might take to evaluate a website, and then applied those steps to the context of their essays. All the while, they were discussing the steps with each other, justifying the (stated, in the handout) reasoning behind the steps through conversation and writing, *and* answering questions regarding whether or not they already used these steps. *Then*, they individually conducted their own very similar web searches while researching their papers for their class.

The reasoning behind this limitation of available data was that it is often possible to evaluate the legitimacy of a website given the URL and a short blurb, at least to first order, and doing so can save hours of time when doing research for a college essay. I purposefully decided to have the students work with a printout of the search results rather than using a more authentic experience of an online search. I chose to do this for several reasons: (1) I wanted to ensure that the results in question contained a mixture of reasonable, questionable, and decidedly inappropriate results; (2) I wanted to make sure that all students examined the same set of search results; (3) I wanted to remove the distraction that access to the Internet inevitably is; (4) I wanted to force the students to look only at the results themselves rather than taking the easy way out of clicking on the link and accessing the site.

What I found

In their current incarnation, each workshop runs about one and a half hours. This is longer than many tutorials/sections. I am working on reducing the length of the workshops, based on student feedback about the most and least valuable questions.

To say that scheduling the workshops was difficult is quite an understatement. The three students in this pilot study had various weekly and pop-up commitments, including: athletic practice, job interviews, class meetings, class assignments, work commitments, hosting prospective students, and family visits. Despite signing up students on the first day of class and only having three students plus myself, we were not able to conduct the fourth workshop until the study period between the last day of classes and the first day of exams. The fact that the students stuck with it and completed all four workshops (one student was unable to attend the final workshop due to illness) is a testament to their perceived importance among the students. When one of the three students was suddenly unable to attend Workshop 2, he convinced a friend to participate on the following day, and one of the other students volunteered to attend it twice in order to enable that student to attend. Attempting to coordinate the schedules of myself and my three students took many hours more than I had expected. My recommendation is that the workshops be used in class during scheduled class meetings such as tutorials or recitation sections.

SUPER recommends that peer-learning groups should have three to four members. In this pilot study, conducting workshops with the three student volunteers worked well. The students worked well together, respectfully questioning each other and engaging with each other in meaningful discussion. All three students, at one time or another, questioned the others' statements. On two occasions (Workshop 2 and Workshop 4), however, only two students attended. For Workshop 2, Louis cancelled at the last minute. We decided to run the workshop with just Matthew and Cody. Louis enlisted a friend to attend the workshop the following day, and Cody volunteered to attend the workshop a second time if it would enable Louis to participate. For Workshop 4, Matthew text-messaged me a few minutes before the session began, saying that he was on his way back from the health center and would not be able to attend. On most occasions, the workshops "ran themselves": the students completed the tasks themselves, and I was primarily an observer, asking occasional questions in response to their dialogue, and querying and clarifying questions that they approached differently to how I had intended. I found myself participating more actively during the two-student workshops, as there weren't enough voices for enough views to be expressed.

Shoshanna learned quite a bit about the challenges of running a program like this from doing the pilot of a single peer-learning group of volunteers. She was also able to streamline the topics and the pedagogy of the way these sessions were run (e.g., so they could run themselves). She also realized the challenges of scheduling and organizing activities like this one outside the traditional class schedule.

147

In the next example, Luisa Rosas did not have access to her own classroom, so collaborated with one of her colleagues. She was interested in learning more about Augusto Boal's "Theater of the Oppressed" as a pedagogy that brought together notions of inequity and pedagogy and theater—all topics that Luisa was interested in examining. Boal's model is based on the earlier work of Paulo Friere's "Pedagogy of the Oppressed" in which he examines traditional notions of teaching and the ways that these may be oppressive. Intrigued, Luisa decided to attend a training workshop on "Theater of the Oppressed" and do a mini-pilot study in which she implemented a component of the model in her colleague's Anthropology classroom.

Pilot Study Example: Luisa Rosas

Examples of Research from the Classroom

Exploring the Theater of the Oppressed at the Ivy League

Luisa Rosas

As recipient of a Graduate Research and Teaching Fellowship at Cornell, I studied theater and methodologies of teaching. Through my research, I came across the work of Augusto Boal, a Brazilian dramatist, theorist, author and inventor of the Theater of the Oppressed. Boal's Theater, made popular in Brazil during the 1970s, is unique as it aims for the presentation of a play as it concurrently stages its analysis. The Joker system, a system in which the Joker or neutral facilitator is both commentator and guide in the unfolding drama, functions on two levels: first, allowing theater to develop as "fable," and second, allowing it to function as a lecture. The plays that are performed are written by a team of actors and are inspired by the real challenges they face in their daily lives. The Theater of the Oppressed thus becomes a courtroom, in which judgments are passed and the spect-actor's (active spectator participants) intervention can alter the outcome of any given scenario (Boal 1979).

Interested in identifying ways in which theater might be better adapted to a humanities or social science classroom, I decided to explore Boal's Theater of the Oppressed and see if it would facilitate student discussions on issues of privilege, class and race. Inspired by the possibilities of this work, I registered for a Joker training session in New York City. After a twenty-hour workshop, I would be certified to facilitate the Forum Theater developed by Boal. When I arrived I was surprised by the diversity of participants. Several teachers and students of theater were present, as were members of the homeless TO (Theater of the Oppressed) troupe that frequently performed in the city. To talk about oppression in this group took on a new dimension knowing the personal histories of many of the participants. The Joker who facilitated our workshop led in several trust-building activities and then we began the work of building a play; first by each sharing a story of personal oppression and then by writing a collective play that would make individual stories unrecognizable but which would have traces of all of our shared experiences. After the performance we gathered one last time and asked final questions. I asked if it were possible to take this theater to the Ivy League. The response was a resounding no. Boal's vision for this theater was that it be made by and for the people, not as a pedagogical tool, and certainly not in a space of privilege. After talking to several colleagues, they admitted to having used these techniques in their classrooms, that they were effective and students responded well to them. As we spoke, I felt that we were dealing with the clandestine transportation of knowledge. I left New York enriched by the experiences of the TO workshop, convinced that I would use this in a classroom, in spite of opposition, and aware that I would be met by a set of different challenges in my attempts to honor Boal's vision in spaces of privilege.

My project through the Center for Teaching Excellence at Cornell was simple. Because I was on a fellowship that permitted me to write my dissertation but offered a respite from teaching, I had no classroom of my own and was unable to apply Boal's theater techniques with my students. Working alongside my colleague in the Anthropology department, Inga Gruß, I conducted a small pilot study as a guest lecturer in her first-year writing seminar and helped structure a forum play in seventy minutes. Her class, entitled "Culture, Representation and Power," dealt with promoting self-reflexivity in the classroom and making students aware of their own positionality in knowing and understanding the world. Boal's objectives seemed deeply compatible given the focus of the class.

Students were given questions before and after the theater workshop and through their responses it would be assessed if they had become more empathetic readers. After some initial theater exercises they were divided into small groups and given the task of writing a play based on their shared experiences; a play in which the protagonist was met by an insurmountable obstacle. Once the scenario was developed they would proceed to stage the play for the group. After the play was performed and the scene resulted in their failure, the spect-actors would intervene and replace the protagonist, trying to perform the play differently and thus attain different outcomes by side-stepping or confronting the obstacle.

The seventy-minute time limit presented a challenge. Having a single opportunity to explain to the students the nuances of Boal's intricate Forum theater was not easy. Further, the students' did not know me and it was difficult to establish trust, nevertheless, they were, for the most part, engaged and participated well. Theater requires vulnerability and a key theme I noticed in this project was an obvious resistance from students, not to acting, but to sharing their stories. When asked to share stories in which they were denied something they needed, many of them were unwilling or unable to define the word "need" in a meaningful way. Their insurmountable obstacles (inability to dye their hair, inability to skip school on the day of the test) seemed capricious in comparison to the experiences of the New York workshop participants. With time some students opened up and were able to share something essential that they wanted yet were unable to have (an internship due to scholarly and parental pressures, for

149

example.) Acting out a situation in which a professional need was not met was undoubtedly terrifying for students' whose achievements define their sense of self.

This experience has shaped my approach to teaching in several ways. I'm convinced that bringing Boal's theater to the Ivy League is an important pedagogical tool, if only to elicit more discussions on issues of privilege, race, and gender discrimination. With their own narratives as the starting point, the activity generates a more authentic form of empathy towards others, while making students aware of mechanisms of their own oppression. Creating a space for vulnerability in as guarded an environment as an Ivy League institution also allows students to see, once they are willing to share, that there is greater diversity in their classroom than they might have known. Did we succeed in building an authentic Forum theater as Boal intended? Certainly not, and yet facing seemingly impossible obstacles with different strategies and trying to surmount them time and again seems to be in the spirit of his work and should not be excluded from any circle, regardless of how privileged it may be.

When examining both pilot studies, both researchers end up with more questions, perhaps even more than they started. They did get a better sense of some of the pedagogical and research questions going forward into a larger scale project. Luisa's provides a good example of the kind of pilot study a teaching assistant or graduate student can do without his or her own classroom—that is, start with a pedagogical research question and then work collaboratively with another teaching colleague to determine if this strategy holds water, or get more feedback on a particular question.

In Shoshanna's example, we see how going with a smaller scale implementation of a supplemental critical thinking program could be useful before going to a broader scale implementation department or schoolwide. She is confronted by challenges and begins to see some of the difficulties with implementation of a program like this.

Chapter 8

Reflective Collaborative Research Working Groups to Close the Loop and Continue the Process

In this chapter:

How can we use reflective practice in our classroom research projects?

How can we work collaboratively throughout the reflective process?

How can I organize a collaborative research working group to inform and continue the process?

How can I close the loop and/or continue the process of using research to inform and improve my teaching?

This chapter seeks to pull together the information in the previous chapters (that illustrate specific ways of doing research to inform and improve teaching) by discussing the process of working collaboratively and reflectively throughout the research process in an effort to close the loop (bridge the gap from research to practice), share findings with others, and continue the process of professional development to improve teaching and learning.

THE IMPORTANCE OF REFLECTIVE RESEARCH AND PRACTICE

Reflective practice has been a part of education and many other professions for decades. Nevertheless, settling on a concrete, working, agreed-upon definition of "reflective practice" has been surprisingly challenging. Historically, the work of John Dewey is credited at least partly with the formation of the practice within teaching:

> Reflective practice as a disposition to enquiry has at its roots, the early work of Dewey (1933), particularly in relation to the attitudes of open-mindedness, responsibility and wholeheartedness, which he argues are integral to reflective action. Open-mindedness refers to the willingness to consider more than one side of an argument and fully embrace and attend to alternative possibilities.
> (Zwozdiak-Myers in Green 2011, p. 27)

Important to our process of conducting research on teaching is an attitude of open-mindedness in particular to consider alternative strategies and possibilities.

Lyons (2010) does a nice job locating reflective practice within a historical framework, identifying the three main theorists who are often credited with pieces of this way of thinking about teaching: John Dewey from his book *How We Think*, David Schön's *The Reflective Practitioner* and Freire's *Pedagogy of the Oppressed*. She argues that it is possible to reconcile each of their contributions in this way: "it is possible to examine reflective practice simultaneously as a mode of thinking (Dewey), a way of knowing (Schön), and as critical reflection (Friere)" (Lyons 2010, p. 2). Certainly in the work of classroom research, faculty members wishing to engage in reflective practice about their research on teaching may reflect on their own thinking, what they "know" (and how they "know" it), and critically evaluate their existing notions.

Writing about reflection on teaching in medical schools, Whiting and colleagues (2012) wrote:

> A vast literature exists on teaching reflection and reflective practice to trainees in small group settings, yet, with few exceptions the medical literature does not focus on the benefits to faculty themselves. Like multiculturalism or cultural competency, the literature assumes that faculty have a propensity for reflection and that trainees are the only recipients of the benefits of such inquiry. One of the noticeable exceptions is Kumagai and colleagues' important article, "The Impact of Facilitation of Small-Group Discussions of Psychosocial Topics

REFLECTIVE COLLABORATIVE RESEARCH WORKING GROUPS

in Medicine on Faculty Growth and Development," [2008] which found that small group teaching stimulated not only students' personal and professional growth but also that of the faculty themselves.

(Whiting et al. 2012, p.2)

Much like the concerns raised by Whiting et al., we must be careful not to assume that we all have an equal understanding and grounding on what is meant by "reflective practice" as it relates to research on teaching as well. While there may not be an agreed definition, there are some consistent ideas of *open-mindedness, reflection on experience, examining biases* and what we *"know" and how we know* it, and *thoughtful reflections on research philosophies and teaching philosophies.*

David Purcell at Kent University describes the profound influence of his own reflective writing about his teaching (taking notes of observations, similar to the teaching journal proposed in the previous chapter). He found that this reflective process of taking what he calls "daily reflective notes":

> This method was developed through the analysis of nine semesters of autoethnographic data that I collected in the form of daily reflective notes. The benefits of this sociologically informed reflective practice include grounding evaluations of individual class periods and entire courses in empirical data, becoming more efficient with course preparation, providing one with a stronger sense of mastery as a teacher, and developing as a sociologist by using the classroom as a key site for engaging in praxis. This practice can help teachers refine individual courses, improve as an instructor in an overall sense and more deeply connect sociology to the Scholarship of Teaching and Learning.

(Purcell 2013, p. 5)

Even though his observations are limited to his experiences in Sociology, we can all learn from this practice—reflective practice through our own purposeful observations, a teaching journal, or even more purposeful classroom research can really improve and inform one's practice.

Building upon the work of Dewey and many others since the 1930s, Zwozdiak-Myers (2010) posits her own definition of reflective practice that may be useful in framing the discussion for faculty considering the use of research as a collaborative and reflective process: "A disposition to enquiry incorporating the process through which . . . teachers structure or restructure actions, beliefs, knowledge and theories that inform teaching for the purpose of professional development" (p. 83). She offers the following graphic framework, which I have modified from her original (Zwozdiak-Myers 2011, p. 28), to illustrate the complex dimensions of reflective practice that instructors/professors can use. As she wrote:

> Reflective practice is a disposition to enquiry incorporating the process through which student, early career and experienced teachers structure or restructure

actions, beliefs, knowledge and theories that inform teaching for the purpose of professional development.

These nine dimensions fit neatly with the key ideas described throughout this book:

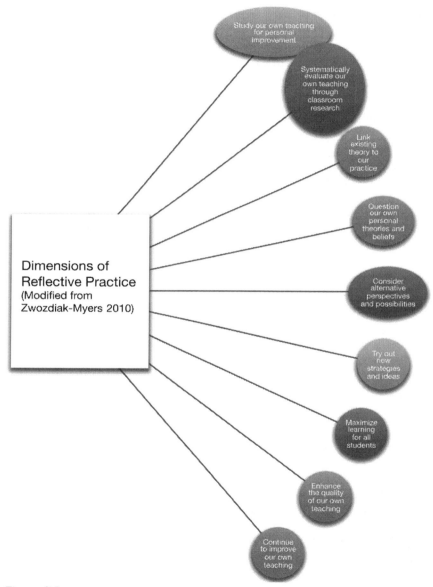

Figure 8.1

Certainly elements of this framework of reflective practice are useful for faculty wishing to engage in research on their teaching as discussed throughout this book, and use that research to improve their understanding and practice of their teaching and student learning. We have discussed each of these aspects throughout the book to varying degrees with a special emphasis on "systematically evaluating their own teaching through classroom research procedures." This chapter takes the ambitious step of taking the research and applying it to practice and pushes for ongoing work to improve one's teaching. This reflective practice and striving toward continuous improvement, those of us veteran professors know, is never finished.

Anyone who has ever taught engaged in reflective practice at some level. Some are more purposeful and some engage in it more or less consciously. We cannot help but reflect upon our teaching. It is a deeply personal and professional act. We put ourselves on the stage or serve as the guide for our students' judgment in hope that they will learn what we want them to learn. As Van Note Chism and her colleagues (2002) astutely argued:

> The foundation for the reflective practitioner model is that teaching is a complex activity requiring continual examination and refinement. This work takes place in the action context and is at the heart of thoughtful practice. Faculty are viewed as intentional actors who settle into patterns of routines, but who adapt and sometimes radically change their practice, based on both internal and external stimuli. This occurs through a process that Stevens (1988) has called professional "tinkering," and others (Chism 1994, Zuber-Skerritt 1993) have compared to models of experiential learning and action research.
>
> (p. 34)

These authors offer a framework for intervention in the process of reflection in which research is a part. As we have discussed throughout this book, research has the power to transform professors and inform and improve teaching and learning. Van Note Chism *et al.*'s framework offers points of entry into the process of transformation that they call "moments" or "stages:"

> The action research model describes cycles of change with four "moments": planning, acting, observing, and reflecting. Applied to teaching, this suggests that an instance of teaching change involves four stages:
>
> ■ selecting a new practice,
> ■ experimenting with it,
> ■ collecting information on what kind of learning the practice produced, and

155

■ reflecting on the desirability of the change as well as whether the practice should be continued, modified, or discarded under specific sets of conditions.

These cycles are usually stimulated by dissatisfaction with the results of current practice (such as, students aren't learning well), dissatisfaction with current approaches (such as, they are too time-consuming or have become boring), or unfavorable feedback (such as, poor teaching evaluations or peer review).

(Van Note Chism *et al.* 2002, p. 34)

Up to this point in the book, the discussion has focused on the first three of these stages to varying degrees. The final chapter of this book focuses more on the final parts of the reflection process—the "now what?" and "so what?" part of the process. What does all the data mean? How might it help me? How might it help others? How can I share my findings?

DOING REFLECTIVE RESEARCH PROJECTS

In my experience working with faculty and future faculty (teaching assistants) in designing and conducting research projects on teaching and learning within their own classrooms, I have been struck by a few themes. First is that those coming from a humanities background have tended to be more comfortable in doing projects that are more reflective in nature. I have found that the final products of their "teaching as research" projects have been fundamentally reflective on the process and their experiences within it. Typically, they have not felt the same compulsion that those in the natural and even social sciences have had toward more systematic qualitative and quantitative methodology and data analysis. In the peer-reviewed journals of education and teaching within the humanities, there are rich examples of reflections on experience and teaching practice.

My hope is that those engaging in this kind of research will consider their own observations of the process and their thoughtful reflections on it important and part of their projects. This may be unsettling for some who are grounded in more traditional kinds of quantitative research in which the researcher is supposed to be detached and objective. Some find it liberating to acknowledge their own role and reflections in the process as it can be quite useful in informing their practice of teaching.

To get those who are interested in being more reflective (or even those for whom it is well outside of their disciplinary comfort zones), I ask that faculty consider the following questions:

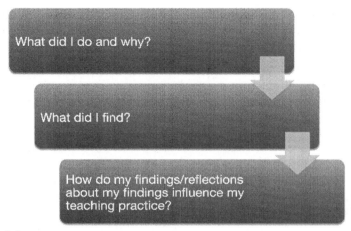

Figure 8.2

Within each of these questions above are important sub-questions such as:

What did I do and why?
Consider:

- Your own position within the research (your role, your social location, your views on particular kinds of research methodology, your views on teaching).
- What experiences specifically brought you to do this research?
- What specific methods did you use?
- What specific research questions did you have when you started out?
- How do these questions fit in with what has been done in the past?

What did I find?
Consider:

- What sources of evidence did you have?
- What claims can you make based on the evidence you have?
- What do your findings show you?
- What are some of the limitations of the evidence/findings?

How did my findings inform my thinking and/or my future practice as a teacher and researcher?
Consider:

- Will you consider changing the way you organize your course, lessons, curriculum, class sessions, learning outcomes, assessments, etc. as a result of your findings?

- Have you changed any of your underlying beliefs about teaching and learning as a result of your project?
- Have you changed any of your beliefs or ideas about research and the nature of evidence as a result of your findings?
- What are the practical implications and limitations of my findings when applied to practice?

Perhaps through this process consider: How do the faculty in your discipline tend to contribute to the creation of new knowledge? Answering this question allows people to consider their own disciplinary strengths, beliefs and biases about information, evidence and claims. Earlier in the book, we considered our biases and strengths as a researcher and philosophical underpinnings of different research methodologies, but throughout and after engaging in the process, consider the possible ways your philosophical beliefs about evidence and research may have shifted.

This reflective process can be critical to doing research on one's teaching. In many ways the reflective process is perhaps the most critical step to bridging the theory to practice gap. As knowledge producers, faculty are not always concerned with the practical applications of their findings, but in classroom research of this type, the practical applications are typically the rationale for starting this undertaking in the first place.

Creation of Collaborative Reflective Research Groups

Much of the time what we do in the classroom is private. Even the classroom research explained throughout this book was often undertaken as a solo mission by a single faculty member on his or her own class, course, curriculum, etc. Our colleagues generally have no idea what we do behind those closed doors. Occasionally we may observe our colleagues and they may observe us for promotion or review, but otherwise what happens in the classroom (for the most part) stays in the classroom. We are often left to our own devices to figure out what to do and with little to no advice (unless we actively seek it out). Even the process of research discussed in this book so far has focused on what you as the professor designing the research can do on your own.

What happens if we bring others into the mix and engage in meaningful professional development through reflective practice and sharing of classroom research projects from their inception through their conclusion? The impact goes beyond the individual classroom and stretches to the department and institution and possibly beyond.

Reflective Collaborative Research Working Groups can help in the following ways throughout the research process: during the planning process; throughout the research process; and at the conclusion of the research process. In other words, the collaborative research groups can help at all stages of the research process:

Figure 8.3

How Might We Create Reflective Collaborative Research Working Groups?

Ideally a group would work together through the research process, but perhaps you may want different groups at each stage of the process. Below are the steps within each stage of the process and possible strategies for each:

Stage 1: Reflective research groups plan research projects

1. Find a group of colleagues who are interested in informing and improving their teaching.
2. Find a time to meet.
3. Create working groups of three to four.
4. Discuss ways of using research in your classroom or elsewhere— brainstorm research questions (just brainstorm, do not judge them yet).
5. Consider the ways you might go about approaching each research question (pay particular attention to methodological biases and different philosophical views about research, and allow each person the space to consider alternatives).
6. Allow each person in the group a turn to be the focus of attention of the others as s/he explores the research questions s/he would like to explore.
7. Once research questions are identified, consider what sources of evidence might be useful for each.
8. Develop a research plan (give each person a chance to speak and share their ideas about their plan).
9. Set reasonable deadlines and times for next meeting.

Figure 8.4

Collaborative Teaching: Researching and Teaching Together

One possibility that may emerge from the Collaborative Reflective Research and Teaching Groups is a desire to collaborate throughout the entire process—including the teaching part. I had the opportunity to do this with a friend and colleague. We designed and taught a course and throughout the process engaged in critical reflection with a group of two other faculty members from different departments. Throughout the process, we discussed what we were doing, how we did it, and how we were engaging in research to determine how it was going. He and I wanted to create a "truly democratic classroom" for an Education History and Philosophy undergraduate course. Below are some of the findings from that collaborative reflective process of research and teaching together.

Examples of Research from the Classroom

Voice and choice: Can we really create democratic university classrooms?

Kimberly Williams and Khuram Hussain

The goal of education is to prepare the next generation of democratic citizens. Court cases have been battled and won based on the notion that an "adequate education" consists of preparing people to function within our democratic structures. Given this contention, how is it that most classrooms fail to operate democratically? The major constituents of our formal educational structures, from preschool through graduate school, have virtually no voice in the content or process of their learning. Students typically have a fairly prescribed curriculum, with prearranged readings and assignments and are assessed based on how the professor and state see fit. Occasionally, students do have some voice and choice—they sometimes get to choose classes and what they do projects on but, by and large, students have little to no choice over the most essential parts of their education. They have no input as to what content they are taught, what they do with the content they learn, and how to demonstrate their understanding of the content.

Our research questions we collaboratively determined were to gain a deeper understanding about:

1. How might we design a democratic classroom (the components, structure, and so on)?
2. What would some of the challenges and considerations to implementation be?
3. How might this democratic classroom impact students and our hoped-for student learning outcomes?
4. What would the implications for democracy and education be?

We approached this from the tradition of teaching as research, which has been found to inform and improve teaching practice. Information was documented and regular analytic conferences were held to examine key findings from observations. In addition, student work and reflections were analyzed to develop themes.

Data sources, evidence, objects, or materials

Data sources included notes of observations from professors, conferences with students, and reflective group meetings with other professors, course evaluations and supplemental end-of-semester surveys, ongoing results from blogs and in-class voting, and student work. Sources were analyzed using constant comparative methods and analytic memos of field notes from observations.

Theoretical framework

Dorothy Smith offered a theoretical framework within her book *The Everyday World as Problematic.* We took our classroom as the "problematic" for the purposes of this study, with the idea that we wanted to challenge traditional educational structures and practice our teaching philosophy in terms of creating a truly democratic classroom. The class took place during the 2010 spring semester, but planning started in the winter of 2009. A typical class size at this college is about twenty students. Because we were co-teaching, we allowed the class size to be raised to thirty-five students (a bargain we had to strike with the department chair to be able to co-teach).

We ended up with thirty-three students, two first year students withdrew from the course—one for academic reasons and one for medical reasons. Of the remaining students, twenty-four were first year students, five were sophomores, and we had only two juniors and two seniors. The course was not required for any major or minor and was a pure elective. There were twenty-four women and nine men (eleven prior to the two withdrawing). The college does not have a great deal of racial diversity, but this class had four women of color, two Latina and two African American, and two men of color, both African American. The remaining twenty-seven were Caucasian.

In addition, we had four people who were the top students in the class the prior year, two Caucasian males—one sophomore and one senior, and two Caucasian females—one junior and one senior. These former students served as "inquiry group leaders" (or in the vernacular of the democratic classroom, they were "representatives" of their "constituents") who each worked with a subgroup of nine student constituents and participated in weekly planning meetings, and attended and engaged in every class meeting. These students had a substantial voice in the design and execution of this course within their role of representatives as they represented the students' voices. Two of these students, both seniors, were also in the Teacher Education program to become certified elementary school teachers.

We critically examined race within educational structures—debating such issues as affirmative action, tracking, and voluntary racially segregated schooling. Many of the students who attended predominantly Caucasian K-12 schools had never examined race critically before. In fact, prior to the affirmative action debate, five students reported to their inquiry group leaders on separate occasions that they didn't know what affirmative action was.

Using constant comparative analysis of student and professor reflections on the experience of defining and creating a democratic classroom, themes were developed.

Student choice
Students were given a voice and choice in the following decisions:

1. Choosing an inquiry group. Students were told the topic selected by an inquiry group leader and they were asked to choose whether they wanted to be part of that group. Many students failed to choose and were randomly assigned to an inquiry group.
2. Whether or not they wanted to attend the weekly planning meetings, or if they felt the inquiry group leaders represented them well enough. Inquiry leaders functioned as "representatives" of their constituents in their small groups of nine students. Students voted to have more representation at the weekly planning meetings between inquiry group leaders and the professors. They were invited to attend these meetings, but they never did.
3. What philosophers were studied and what the readings were. The course is a history and philosophy of education course, and students were given the choice of which philosophers they wanted to study and the readings, with the only constraint that at least one reading had to be an original text from a philosopher. Students were given a list of possible philosophers (because they had a very difficult time coming up with possible philosophers on their own), but were told they could choose others if they could describe what made him or her a philosopher. We wanted to break students out of the notion of the traditional canon of philosophers. For example, students successfully proposed and presented Barack Obama as a philosopher and made a good case to include his education philosophy.
4. What assessment mechanisms to use. Students were given the choice to propose alternatives for weekly assessments. We settled on a weekly blog project. In addition, for the final summative project, they all worked together to create a list of options for the final culminating project.
5. How they would "teach" the class. Each inquiry group would teach the class about four philosophers of their choosing, reinforcing the reading they selected. They could do this in whatever manner they thought best, but we asked that they try to be creative and use best teaching and learning strategies. They also designed the questions for the weekly writing and blogging assignment.
6. Debates. Each group selected and engaged in three formal debates that best reflected the issues their philosophers grappled with. Students were given a list of about fifty possible debates that we created, but they were free to modify, select new ones, or propose others.

Results and/or substantiated conclusions or warrants for arguments/point of view

Results/major themes

1. *Letting go of traditionally controlled elements of the classroom is difficult.* Professors and teachers have a lot invested in making sure a learning experience is positive for all students. Relying on novices to make decisions about readings and topics for discussion can be nerve-wracking and very challenging. They lack the necessary frame of reference, but with guidance, can still make good decisions.

2. *Students grappled with the flexibility and choice initially and the notion of democracy* and what it meant for the classroom. They had very few opportunities in their lives for this kind of voice in their educational endeavors and, for many, this was difficult at first. Informed student leaders proved to be critical in serving as guides in the process of choosing readings, preparing for critical debates, and work on projects. Towards the end, many students wanted more choice and wished they had taken advantage of their choices and voice in the early stages.

   As one of the student leaders wrote in his final reflection,

   > In Mario Cuomo's famous keynote speech at the 1984 Democratic National Convention he proclaimed, "Now, we should not—we should not be embarrassed or dismayed or chagrined if the process of unifying is difficult, even wrenching at times," when speaking about unifying the Democratic Party (American Rhetoric: Mario Cuomo—Keynote Address at the 1984 Democratic National Convention). Although our own democratic experiment did not turn out exactly as we had hoped, and it was very messy at times, we are not "embarrassed or dismayed or chagrined," in our attempt to create a democratic classroom. We implemented many ideas in creating our democratic classroom, updated the structure along the way, and never veered away from the belief that students' voices should be heard and taken seriously. We also must remember due to the somewhat poor state of our own democracy outside the classroom, the idea of a true participatory democracy is foreign to many students.

   > (GP sophomore)

3. Students and professors admitted to thinking more deeply about democracy and democratic classrooms and the implications. For example, one student leader wrote:

   > "Democratic schools, like democracy itself, do not happen by chance. They result from the explicit attempts by educators to put in place arrangements and opportunities that will bring democracy in the classroom." A year ago, I would not have even thought twice about this quote from Apple and Beane's *Democratic Schools: Lessons in Powerful Education*. However, as a result of

my experience this spring and in preparation for my future as a teacher, democratic education is now always at the forefront of my mind.

(AD senior)

4. *If given enough time and support, students will do great work.* The initial adjustment period is difficult and the quality of work seemed poor, but in the end, students really raised the level of the quality of their work and learning.

Perhaps the most significant impact was on the inquiry group leaders. They all reported significant changes in their thinking as a result of their experience. An inquiry group leader explained this change saying,

> I appreciate every opportunity that I had to "go back stage" and critically think about the successes and improvements within the course. I hope in future classes the student participants will be able to glimpse just a little bit further "back stage" and take a look at the skeleton of the course. My opportunity to make suggestions about the syllabus and structure of the course increased my emotional and educational investment to an incredible degree. I sat excitedly in class during the strongest debates, and admired the intellectual thought and effort that went into many of the blogs. I hope future students are given the opportunity to participate in this course as both inquiry group leaders and class members. I trust that they will feel a strong commitment and responsibility to increasing democracy to the highest possible degree within the new classroom, as I did throughout this semester. I am grateful that I got to share this opportunity with so many brilliant and committed individuals. This was an experience that I did not think was possible at the undergraduate level and one that I am sure I will recall countless times throughout my work in education in the future.

(LF junior leader)

Components critical to the success of this project

1. Inquiry group leaders as representatives to student constituents— students chosen by the professors, who had taken the class the previous year and done well. The students functioned as members of a cabinet. They also served as representatives of the voices of their constituency groups and fellow students.
2. An initial structure to layout the program. We had students read James Loewen's *Lies My Teacher Told Me* and they all LOVED this book, and despite how uneasy it made them feel (calling into question their educational experiences), it got them to question their educational institution. It set the stage to get students to think more critically about the nature of education in preparing students as citizens, and what they are told in their American History classes. This book shook many students to the core about their educational system.

165

3. Clickers. Clickers are devices that allow student input into questions posed, a way to provide instant feedback. Our observations showed that voting using the clickers and course evaluations allowed students to vote anonymously on topics, which they enjoyed. They could also weigh in on assessing their peers' performances on formal debates.

4. Debates. Students' ability to have conflict about controversial issues within the context of the democratic classroom was critical — as was the importance of their learned ability to critique evidence and examine controversial topics from many different perspectives. Debating led to an increased understanding of key ideas for students allowing us to have profound discussions in class. In addition, the steady improvement in the quality of the debates showed their improved understanding.

5. Service learning. We both believed strongly in the importance of taking students "backstage" (as Alfie Kohn termed it). We would think through our decisions and ask students to weigh in regularly. We received feedback by asking questions like, "Are we talking too much? What aspects of the class do you find useful for your learning?" One day the discussion emerged about service as an important part of democratic structures. The students helped design a service learning project that allowed students to become engaged with fifth grade students from a high poverty local school to see first-hand some of the issues that we discussed in class. Both college students and the fifth graders participated in a blogging project using Wordpress. Students each had a "blogging buddy" and commented on each other's blogs regularly. Students posted about themselves and projects they were working on in their social studies class. College students would go to the school and work with fifth graders after school on their blogs. We worked closely with the Computer, Social Studies and English Language Arts teachers at the school. At the conclusion of the course, the fifth graders came to campus. One fifth grader said, "I was going to go into the army, but now I'm thinking I might need to look more at going to college." Teachers reported that students who hated to write and do school work stayed after school to participate in this blogging project. In addition, some of the college students volunteered their own time and gas money to go to the school to work with the students on their writing and computer skills.

One of the student leaders wrote of the service project:

> There is one aspect of the course that I felt was crucial to the creation of a truly democratic classroom, the service-learning component. On the first day of class students were asked to create a thought web of the components of democracy. I was happy, but also surprised to see service and volunteers as key components expressed by students. While majority of students treated the service-learning project as a burden at first, I think for many it became one of the most meaningful aspects of the course. For many of those students who lacked participation in the beginning of the semester, the project sparked their interest and they put themselves

whole-heartedly into the blogging project. I thought it was interesting because it taught me a little bit more about participation. For some students it may not have been that they were lazy or did not want to participate, rather it may have been more based on engagement. Regardless of how students were being engaged, this brought some much closer to the idea of participation [in] a truly democratic classroom.

(AD senior)

Scientific or scholarly significance of the study or work

Lessons learned

1. Make the class pass/fail or credit/no credit and allow students more voice in the assessment process. Grading was an issue because ultimately we as professors had to submit a letter grade for students. We still created the rubrics for the debates and the assignments. If we had more time, we would have created the rubrics as a class.

> Grades throw off the entire horizontal power structure that we were attempting to create. Although I think grades add an undemocratic element to the course I also worry about running the course credit/no credit due to the possibility that it could lower commitment.
>
> (LF junior)

2. Give more choice to students earlier in the process, for example, in the development of the class syllabus.
3. Cover less content—spend more time on the ideas of democracy in the beginning.

Two of these three ideas were eloquently analyzed by one of the inquiry group leaders:

> My greatest struggle was the lack of participation from students in the course. I believe one way to improve the course would be to emphasis the key components of a democratic classroom and focus much more in class time on Beane and Apple's *Democratic Schools*. I would recommend spending the first week developing a solid definition for democracy and central elements for this new democratic classroom. Students must be included from start to finish in order to ensure high levels of engagement. One of the major critiques expressed by students, was that the syllabus and the course itself had too much predetermined structure. Although there was choice within the structure, the actual class sessions ran in the exact same order that was developed by the professors before the start of the course. This lack of control in the overarching structure of the course may have decreased the level of participation and discouraged some students from engaging. As a way of taking students further back stage, I would recommend allowing students to spend a week developing their own thoughts and activities for the course. Students should be

asked to create their own ideas for the syllabus to be shared with their inquiry group. Then each inquiry group could create a set of suggestions for the course to be presented to the professors by the inquiry group leaders. If students are able to take part in creating one of the fundamental structures of the course, their levels of interest and participation will likely increase. Along with this notion, allowing future students to create their own service project idea may generate a greater sense of control and increase the level of interest and commitment to community service as a key aspect of democracy.

(LF Junior)

4. Make the service learning a more prominent part of the course and give students more voice in it.
5. Poll students more often to get feedback throughout. The use of anonymous electronic polling devices such as clickers worked very well for this.

Impact on our teaching and implications for others

This "democratic experiment" allowed us as professors of education to critically reexamine the ways we teach and the way college teaching is typically conducted. As is typical, we design our courses like most faculty—looking for appropriate readings, designing a course syllabus to include objectives and assignments, developing assessments to examine student performance on those objectives with a timeline of how to help students pace their learning. We had never included student voice in the choices we made. When we first sat down with our "inquiry group leaders," we asked them what they thought we should do—this was a first for both of us—that is, turning over the design ideas to students who had taken the course before. They came up with the idea of having "inquiry group leaders" working with a smaller group of students, a service-learning project, and using blogs as a way of sharing learning outside of the classroom. They also came up with the idea for the weekly structure.

We planned the first five weeks of the course content and modeled the first debate; whether we could ever create democratic classrooms. We selected the first readings, primarily Loewen and also Beane and Apple's book, *Democratic Schools*, with which we started the course.

We met every week with our inquiry group leaders to plan the following week, and to get input about how things were going in the class. Students were frustrated in the early stages—wanting more structure and more of an idea about how they would be graded. In their early blog assignments, the writing and critical thinking was minimal, so we made an "executive order" and created a take-home midterm that was challenging. Students were upset .We had a discussion in class about the importance of participating in a democracy to make it work and part of that participation was doing the reading and taking the writing, thinking, and processing assignment of the blog seriously. After the midterm, students produced higher quality work on the blog assignments.

Students learned a lot and challenged some of their ideas about education and democracy. Several students made comments such as this by a first year student for her final project:

> To me democracy means something that is carried out by the people or by means of election, and in any definition of democracy the words equality and freedom are included. These are both terms that I find very important in creating a democratic classroom. Before this class, I just thought democracy meant freedom to vote and that our country was democratic. Now I know that democracy is not everywhere, and it needs to be more present in our society such as in our education systems. Through Loewen's book, philosophers we studied, and discussions we had in class, I learned more about democratic education, styles of learning, and history itself than I ever imagined I would.

Conclusion

Despite calls to emphasize lecture less, and collaboration and discussion more in college and university classrooms, little has been done to provide students with more voice in the learning process. Typically, syllabi are created with little to no student input and classrooms rarely, if ever, are conducted democratically. What we offer here is an alternative to the business-as-usual model of teaching and learning in college classrooms. This model provides a way to conceptualize a democratic space that gives students a voice in their learning and a choice in how they learn it. Certainly, changing the structure this dramatically is difficult and can be challenging for both students and faculty, but with support and a collaborative attitude, we can go a long way. At the end of our action research project, we both concluded that investing in the creation of a more democratic classroom is worth the time and energy, because students are more engaged and learn more, not only about content, but also about the democratic structures in which they live. Ideally, through this process they will become more fully participating members of our democratic society—recognizing and challenging inequity.

Working collaboratively and reflecting on the teaching and research process can be quite enlightening. When we collaborate with others, not only in the research on our teaching process but also on the teaching aspect, we are able to see closely how our colleagues approach teaching and learning and gain new and exciting insights. We may consider new strategies. We may question our existing paradigms. We may further validate our existing beliefs and behaviors. If a true course collaboration like the one described above is not feasible, consider ways to bring others in to collaborate throughout the process—as observers, guests, or go visit others' classes. Collaboration can be challenging within the academy, but worth the effort.

Bringing in Collaborators to Observe and Collect Data

During the second stage of Collaborative Reflective Research in Teaching, groups work together to collaborate throughout the research process. This may be done in the same group as the planning group (in Stage 1), or a new group if it makes sense. We may also consider bringing in outside collaborators to help at different points in the process who may not actually be in the collaborative reflection group.

Stage 2: Collaborative reflection throughout the research process

1. Create plans to help collect data—consider observing each others' classrooms or inviting others in to observe your classroom or participate in it and ways to make careful observations of phenomenon under investigation.
2. Debrief and share data from observations through the process.
3. Critically reflect in meetings on the nature of the data being collected:
   a. themes that appear to be emerging
   b. ideas for triangulation
   c. revision of original plans (allowing each individual in the group time to be the focus of the group's attention).
4. Reconsider the viability of the established timeline.
5. Consider what additional data you might like (including how others might help with the collection if possible).

Figure 8.5

Sometimes we may like to get the perspective of outsiders who may have a more objective view of classroom or teaching and learning phenomena than we do. Bringing in outsiders to observe and collect data can be tremendously useful in the research process. Outsiders might be colleagues, peers, teaching assistants or other graduate students, or even former undergraduate students. We need to be quite clear at the outset what the objectives are—that is, what are the "outsiders" expected to do exactly? What are they to consider? How will they fit into the larger research project?

Many graduate student teaching assistants with whom I have worked have engaged in these kinds of projects with full-time more senior faculty members. Some have examined curricular issues, some have examined the utility of different

170

courses within the curriculum, and others have looked at particular classroom settings and supplemental forms of instruction to help student learning.

In this example, Carolyn Fisher, a teaching assistant in genetics, worked collaboratively with a faculty member who organized an "auto-tutorial" bio-chemistry course in which students would not engage in traditional lecture, but rather teach themselves from the textbook and series of problems and quizzes. She and the faculty member both wanted to better understand student percep-tions of that option and student reflections on the process. Carolyn worked collaboratively with this faculty member and the one teaching the "live" more traditional version of biochemistry. Here are her reflections of the process and what she did and found:

Examples of Research from the Classroom

Reactions to an auto-tutorial course in bio-chemistry

Carolyn Fisher

What brought me to this project/why was I interested

Biochemistry courses are often regarded as the most essential lynch-pin course for life science majors. However, these courses are notorious for the advanced difficulty of the material, extensive amount of knowledge that must be learned, and integration of various prerequisite subjects required for the complete understanding of the course content. For these reasons, biochemistry is often both the most feared yet interesting course that life science undergraduate majors are required to take. Thus, it is essential that biochemistry courses are effective in helping students to learn the essential material for their particular discipline or professional career path.

When I was an undergraduate chemistry major pursuing a biochemistry concen-tration, the first biochemistry course that I took in the spring of my sophomore year was the least educational course that I had ever taken in my life. While the content fascinated me, the teaching methods were less than desired. Our professor used "old school" projectors to display his ancient transparencies full of biochemistry jargon. Our grades were based on pop quizzes, a midterm, and a final. We had no homework assignments, no guidelines for what to study, and no idea what was worth knowing and what was not. We were clueless how to integrate knowledge for true understanding of the fundamentals of biological systems, so we just tried to blindly memorize everything we could in preparation for any assessment that was required of us. Despite all of these educational blockages, I truly loved the content of the course and vowed to find a way to teach the material in a better way. Ever since then, I have been in pursuit of a highly effective, enjoyable, and educational biochemistry course that I can learn from and implement as a future biochemistry professor one day.

At Cornell University, there are several choices for biochemistry courses that an undergraduate student can choose from. Specifically, if a student is ambitious enough

171

to try to complete two semesters of biochemistry in one semester of time, s/he can select from either auto-tutorial biochemistry BioMG3300 or lecture biochemistry BioMG3350. The following study was interested in determining what motivates students to select one class over another and if one specific style seemed to have better output in terms of increasing students interest in biochemistry, stimulation to take addition biochemistry courses, improvement of study habits, or altering career aspirations of students. Interestingly, more than half of the surveyed auto-tutorial students that signed up for the course because of a time-conflict they had with the lecture course or because they valued the flexible structure of the course in not having an official meeting time every week.

My objectives/outcomes for the project

The purpose of this study was to investigate the different motivations, experiences, career aspirations, behaviors, and course outcomes between students who opt to take an auto-tutorial biochemistry course or a lecture-based biochemistry course. Specifically, the following research questions were examined in this project:

- What motivated these students to take an auto-tutorial course or a lecture-based course?
- What did students feel they got out of an auto-tutorial course compared to previous lecture-based courses they have taken?
- Was the learning experience within an auto-tutorial course worth it?

I hypothesized that there are specific learning styles, behaviors, study habits, and/or extrinsic and intrinsic motivators that are specific to students who sign up for, are successful in, and have a positive experience with an auto-tutorial course versus a lecture-based course. This study will hopefully provide some insight about the specific characteristics of students who choose the auto-tutorial versus lecture-based teaching methods, and why.

Specifics of my methodology/ my role in the project

For the BioMG3300 auto-tutorial biochemistry course, ten males and sixteen females completed the paper-based survey. These twenty-six students were selected from a class of around 120 students based on the fact that they were either present at one of the two review sessions I attended to pass out the survey or self-selected in that they chose to respond to the survey I emailed the entire class. It is likely that within this small population of students, there is a bias for students that attend review sessions and perhaps are more likely to be hard-working students, as well as a bias for students that read their email and respond generously to a plea for survey responses by a desperate graduate student fellow. At the beginning of two review sessions during the same week, I read aloud the IRB approved disclaimer about my study and then distributed the survey for the students to take. I allotted approximately fifteen minutes for students to complete the survey and then collected them all back from the students. From these two review sessions, I received eleven surveys back from students. Of these eleven students, eight were female and three were male. Because the integrity of this study was at serious risk if I did not accumulate more surveys from auto-tutorial students, I then emailed the entire student body for the class asking them to fill out the survey and send it back to me. After a week and a half of responses from students, a total of fifteen responded with completed surveys. I likely would have received more responses if the survey was in the form of an online Qualtrics survey and not a Word Document. This will be something I will consider as I continue this study in the future.

Of the twenty-six auto-tutorial students that completed the survey, nine were sophomores (36 percent), eight were juniors (34 percent), six were seniors (24 percent), and two classified as graduate students or other (8 percent). The majority of these students (twenty) were some kind of biology major, though none listed a concentration in biochemistry. There were also four biological engineers, one chemical engineer, and one math major. The majority of these students (twenty-four) were 19–22 years old, with an average age of 20.3 years old. The other two students listed that they were 29 and 30 years old, and these are the same students that listed themselves as graduate student or other. The average GPA for twenty-five of these individuals (one did not report) was 3.63, within a range of 2.5 to 4.0.

For the BioMG3350 lecture-based biochemistry course, thirty males and fifty-two females completed the survey. These eighty-two students were selected from the class of around 130 students for this survey, in that they were present on the unannounced class day (for which they had a substitute professor) when I arrived and distributed the survey. It is entirely possible that there will be a bias for students that attend class on a regular basis and for students that respect attending class even when a sub is filling in for the course's professor. When the class began, I read aloud the IRB approved disclaimer about my study and then distributed the survey for students to take. I allotted approximately fifteen minutes for students to complete the survey and then collected them all back from the students.

Of the eighty-two lecture-based students, eleven were sophomores (13 percent), fifty-eight were juniors (71 percent), eleven were seniors (13 percent), and two classified as graduate students or other (3 percent). For the students that reported (two were left BLANK), the majority of these students were some kind of biology major (forty-eight). There were also nine biological engineers, seven chemical engineers, five chemistry majors, two computer science majors, two nutrition majors, two economics majors, one physics major, one French major, one human development, and one anthropology major. It should be noted that for pre-medical students, it is not required that they have a Life Sciences major, only that they take the required prerequisite courses for medical school. This rationale most likely explains the extraneous humanities majors taking a notoriously grueling life sciences course. Indeed, all of these majors also reported that their career aspiration is to be a medical doctor. The average age for this group of students was 21 years old, including one 27-year-old and one 29-year-old. The average GPA for seventy-six of these students (six did not report) was 3.50, within a range of 2.1 to 4.4.

In total from both classes, there were forty males and sixty-eight females that were surveyed. Although there is a class-specific bias for biochemistry majors to take the auto-tutorial BioMG3300 course and non-biochemistry majors to take the lecture-based BioMG3350 course, this did not appear to be a concern for this study. None of the students for either class reported that they were a biology major pursuing a concentration in biochemistry, and thus would have been required to take the auto-tutorial course in order to earn the relevant credit. It is actually very interesting that not one student reported this as a major and it begs the question of whether these students are so astute within their chosen field that they do not need to attend review sessions for the auto-tutorial course or are so smug as to not fill out un-required surveys. These wild accusations are highly skeptical and possibly grossly generalize the actual truth since the twenty-six responses I received from auto-tutorial students only reflected a little more than a fifth of the auto-tutorial student body.

How I analyzed my data

Most of the questions for this study were generated using a Likert Scale polling strategy or open-ended question format. For the majority of the Likert Scale questions, seven choices of varying degrees of responses were most often used in order reflect sufficient variance of student responses. Additionally, a "N/A" option was also available with each Likert Scale question in order for the student to abstain from answering a question that they feel does not apply to their experience. The survey used in this study is attached as an addendum at the end of this document. Data was analyzed using Microsoft Excel.

What I found

Lecture students were motivated because they preferred learning from lecture classes or from a professor. Additionally, both courses did an excellent job at stimulating interest in the course, either through self-paced study or professor enthusiasm for the material. Specifically, auto-tutorial students seemed to have more of an improvement in study habits and were more likely to take another biochemistry course compared to lecture students. These findings seem to suggest that there is not one best way to teach biochemistry as most of the students in both courses seemed genuinely content with their selection and confident they made the right choice for their own study and learning habits.

This study found that most auto-tutorial students chose the course for the flexible structure, because they had a time conflict with lecture-based course, or because they were confident in their ability to teach themselves. Most lecture students chose the course because they admitted that they lacked self-discipline to teach themselves or had a distinct preference for learning via lecture from a knowledgeable and enthusiastic professor. Auto-tutorial students seemed to generally feel that they were learning the information more thoroughly because of the design of the course. They also gained confidence in their ability to teach themselves a rigorous subject. Most of the comments (ten out of twelve) from the auto-tutorial students suggested that despite the extra effort, they did feel like they were learning and remembering more of the course content. Most of the students in the lecture course reported they would likely never take an auto-tutorial course. Compared to the lecture students, the auto-tutorial students seemed to have more of an increased interest in biochemistry, were more likely to take another biochemistry course, and saw improvements in their study habits. Several students from the lecture biochemistry course admitted that the course has altered their career aspirations to incorporate more biochemistry or scientific research.

One auto-tutorial student offers the following advice to future students of the course:

> Really pace yourself. This is not a lecture-based course, so you must stay on top of your work. However, there is a strict format and deadline schedule to adhere to and plenty of good TAs, so you're not alone. Auto-tutorial will force you to become independent and take charge of your own education—a valuable skill to have. The weekly oral and written tests will make you a mast of the material, no doubt. It's a great format to learn science in but can be difficult if not planned out correctly.

Interestingly, one student thinks that the lecture course would have been better:

> I would recommend going to the review sessions. They are very helpful. However, I wish I had known how much work was truly involved in this course before I took it. Looking back, it maybe have been worthwhile to take the lecture-based one semester course instead. That way, there was time built into my schedule for quizzes and I didn't have to plan the time on my own to go and take them.

One student offers a method to avoid over-memorizing, "Always keep up on your work. Focus on understanding the processes, not memorizing the specifics. Once you understand what's going on, the chemical names and structures fall into place." Overall, it seems as though auto-tutorial students have a better handle on how to study for biochemistry and be successful as the majority of their time is spent studying for this course since there is no class meeting time.

One lecture student offers the following advice to future students of the course, "Make sure you stay on top of the lecture material every week because the quizzes and exams come up fast, the textbook is not very helpful—focus on the lectures." Similarly, several other students commented on the need to stay on top of the material and study or review a little almost every day. Many students also commented on how future students need to be prepared to memorize. One student wrote, "It's a lot of memorization. Just memorize everything. The book doesn't help. Memorize the lectures." Another student offered some pragmatic advice, "To do well in this course, it takes more time than initially expected. It would be best to choose the course that has a learning style that works best for the individual." Students also commented on the fact that competition within the class was fierce as one student points out that "Quizzes ain't no joke. Premeds . . . premeds . . . EVERYWHERE → be ready to study your butt off." Certainly, lecture students feel the pressure from the fast-paced course, two-semesters worth of material packed into a one semester course, and competition for grades as the class is graded on a curve.

It is quite evident that this study needs to be repeated and possibly expanded to larger sample sizes. It is my intention to convert this thirty-six-question paper-based survey into a fifteen-question Qualtrics survey to send out to larger numbers of students after they have completed the BioMG3300 auto-tutorial biochemistry course and the BioMG3350 lecture biochemistry course in the upcoming semesters, in order to accumulate more data for this study. I am hoping that by expanding the sample size for both classes, more distinctive differences will emerge to statistical significance.

How these findings have informed/will inform my practice
This study has changed substantially from its original conception to this final written work. Originally, my goal was to try to ascertain which teaching style, lecture or auto-tutorial, was the best method for students to learn by in order to inform my own teaching style someday. I began this study with an inherent bias that, although I personally do not think I could be motivated and self-disciplined enough to be successful in an auto-tutorial course, I did believe that students learn more from that independent, self-paced active learning style than from a lecture-based course. Indeed, it seemed that the university supported this notion in that it is well-known that students working towards a biochemistry major can take the auto-tutorial course for credit toward their degree, but not the lecture-based course. Upon concluding this pilot study, I consider the entire situation differently. Perhaps there is not just a single effective style to teach by or to learn by but by giving students the autonomy to decide what is best for themselves, they can select a style that is best suited for them.

Personally, I am taking away the newfound respect I have for student autonomy for deciding which course is better for them to take. As for my own future teaching strategies as a biochemistry professor, I will likely employ neither of these teaching styles. Instead, I intend to teaching using an active-learning strategy known as POGIL (Problem-Oriented Guided Inquiry Learning), which is similar to auto-tutorial style in that students work through answering a series of questions to learn the material, but instead of doing so independently outside of class, students meet during a regular class time and work in groups to complete these questions. Additionally, this course structure has the flexibility for the professor to give "mini-lectures" of 10–15 minutes to help clear up confusion or address specific issues or problems. This learning style requires students to help teach each other, which is beneficial for students to learn from their peers and for students to teach their peers as it helps to solidify their own understanding of the material. This method is very team-oriented in that everyone is working together to be successful, instead of individuals competing against each other for the best class grades. Indeed, this style employs what I believe to be the best aspects of both auto-tutorial and lecture style teaching methods, and yet could still not be optimal for some students. This study has helped to open my mind and understanding of what "good teaching methods" are and that this is extremely subjective for each student. Although we may never find the one best teaching strategy for classroom use, a mixture of various strategies seems to allow all students the opportunity to find ways they might learn best.

Carolyn informed the department and the curriculum, and she also helped both professors better understand the nature of the decisions that students made about the different course options. She also found and learned new ideas that helped her as a budding young professor. Interestingly, this project was taking place at the same time that the "flipped classroom" was growing in popularity. Doing this project, those involved saw the ways students could successfully learn outside of the classroom, but others really struggled with this idea. Reconciling the notion that "good teaching methods are extremely subjective for each student," and that we should offer students options, are both important learning outcomes for Carolyn and likely her department as well.

Closing the Loop: Collaborative Reflective Research Groups to Close the Loop and Continue the Process

The process of conducting research to inform and improve classroom teaching and learning does not just end when the project ends or the semester is over, or you feel the study is finished. Or at least it shouldn't end there. The findings should inform practice—that is we should consider the "so what?" from our findings. And also consider the "now what?"

In "so what" we consider what the findings mean. What do they mean for you and your practice. The Collaborative Reflective Research Groups can help with this process—to figure out what was important from the process—what are the key takeaways and what do they mean? What are the limitations? What should we do next (the "now what")? What could this possibly mean for my teaching?

Stage 3: The conclusion of the research process to close the loop, share findings and continue the process

1. Have each group member share his/her interpretation of the results from their evidence.
2. Critically evaluate whether the findings and interpretations are aligned and justified (and not over-generalizing or over-stating)—consider collaboratively what the findings mean.
3. Consider and examine limitations.
4. Discuss the ways the findings may influence practice.

177

5. What is important to broadcast more broadly of the findings (consider venues for broadcasting findings—local and national conferences, department meetings, school and university meetings, newsletters, etc.)

6. Next steps—future research, changes to curriculum or syllabi or pedagogy.

Figure 8.6

In the following example, Jared Hale works with his department to determine the impact of optional problem solving sessions on students. Because his work was collaborative with his department, his findings were shared and the process continues as they work to build these problem-solving sessions into the curriculum earlier for students.

Examples of Research from the Classroom

Optional problem-solving sessions in genetics: All or nothing?

Jared Hale

What brought me to this project/why was I interested

I have found that many STEM (Science, Technology, Engineering and Math) courses rely heavily upon memorization of material and concepts while providing little active engagement to reinforce the concepts. I have found firsthand and believe that being given the opportunity to apply the concepts discussed in class to real-world problems in a group setting is an invaluable way to prepare students for their eventual careers. A broad survey from forty-six influential players in the private sector of biotechnology showed a repeating theme of valuing communication and teamwork, particularly within experimental design (Miller *et al.* 2011). Despite pressure from industry and the private sector, some genetics courses do not place enough emphasis on critical thinking and problem solving in a group environment. If incorporated into a course successfully this could provide a foundation in communication and teamwork in the context of experimental design.

It has become increasingly common to find promising instructional methods that incorporate group work and focus on engagement and structure to help guide the students. Methods such as POGIL or Problem-Oriented Guided Inquiry Learning have been deemed effective in STEM courses based on student and faculty response to the instructional method (Myers and Tevathan, 2012). Wherein students organize into small groups and primarily work through peer instruction and cooperation while maintaining an instructor presence that allows for feedback and guidance to facilitate the learning process. In various STEM fields ranging from information technology (Myers *et al.* 2012) to biochemistry (Bailey *et al.* 2012) the student response has been overwhelmingly positive and traditional testing methods have indicated improvement in key conceptual areas of the course. Furthermore, group learning methods such as POGIL have previously been demonstrated as feasible in small classroom settings, but recent work has shown the efficacy of such group interaction in larger classrooms at large universities where the students have little to no previous experience with such instructional methods (Bailey *et al.* 2012).

This study examined a necessary question in instructional methods for genetics courses. Assaying student attendance as well as attitudes and opinions regarding optional problem-solving sessions and correlating that data with individual student performance will likely provide insightful information towards incorporating problem solving in genetics courses. While the nature of group work is only a minor factor in this study the findings from the somewhat less-structured, problem-solving sessions can be extrapolated and used to draw inference about the potential effectiveness of the group problem-solving session. Attitudes towards individual and group problem solving as it applies to genetics will be invaluable in planning future courses and fostering the skills necessary for students to have a fundamental knowledge in genetics and be able to use that knowledge in real-world problem-solving skills as individuals, and communicate their ideas with others.

My objectives/outcomes for the project

The purpose of this study is to better understand the efficacy of optional problem-solving sessions offered during the introductory genetics course. This was divided into several main questions:

- What reason(s) motivated the students to attend or not attend the optional problem-solving sessions?
- What do the students find most beneficial about the problem-solving sessions?
- How does student performance correlate with problem-solving session attitudes and attendance?

Specifics of my methodology/ my role in the project

The participants in this study are all undergraduate students at Cornell University enrolled in the laboratory course associated with the genetics and genomics introductory course. There are seven total sections comprising the laboratory course. Paper surveys were given to students enrolled in five out of the seven course sections.

The surveys included demographic information questions, fill-in-the-blank questions, Likert scale questions and open-ended questions. The survey was given in paper form at the start of class. The student response rate was an extraordinary 100 percent for all sections surveyed (n = 103), however, students did leave occasional questions blank on occasion and, unless stated otherwise, omitted responses were removed from the data pool as applicable. The data analysis was performed by linking survey responses with student preliminary/midterm scores, while excluding any unanswered questions. Therefore, all percentages were determined from the surveys only with a response in the given category.

Demographic information was grouped according to more general terms when students listed specific details (i.e., specific ethnicity was grouped into broader categories as best as possible). Because the preliminary/midterm exams used as data were proctored as part of the associated lecture course (n = 220) the overall mean values includes students who are not necesarrily enrolled in the laboratory course (n = 150).

My role in this study was that of a teaching assistant. I taught one laboratory section out of seven offered and assisted with a second section. Because of my role as an instructor I assured the students that the survey answers would not affect their grades in the course. This was particularly necessary for the sections I was personally involved with but also for the other sections as well.

How I analyzed my data

The majority of the survey questions for this study were Likert questions or more open-ended. All of the Likert Scale questions were designed with six choices. One option was "N/A" for students who may have felt they did not have sufficient experience to comment on a particular question. There were five other choices with a central "neutral" option. In addition to the open-ended questions, all of the Likert scale questions had a section for additional comments, should the students feel the need to elaborate on why they answered a question in a particular way. All data were collected in paper format and transferred to Microsoft Excel for analysis.

What I found

In an effort to normalize the survey data students' effort in the course was evaluated using two different fill-in-the-blank questions. The first asked students to list the number of optional problem-solving sessions they had attended. The optional problem-solving sessions were offered on multiple occasions each week by the course coordinator and focused on the concepts and techniques for solving genetics problems. At the time of the survey students could have attended a maximum of ten sessions. Most students reported attending in a binomial manner trending towards the extreme ends, indicating a tendency for students to attend all (22 percent attended 7–10 sessions) or none (35 percent attended 0–1 sessions) rather than half of the sessions. When students were asked to discuss why they did or did not attend optional problem-solving sessions the consensus was that there were scheduling conflicts or the times offered where not optimal, despite having multiple sessions offered in a given week.

An alternative way to assess the effort of students was addressed by asking the students how much time they spent in an average week studying for this course. Responses varied widely, with the majority (36 percent) of students citing between 3 and 5 hours a week. A still significant portion (16 percent) listed 12 hours or more of studying for the course in an average week. This highlights the workload and difficulty of this course despite being an introductory course. Not unexpectedly, a small number of students felt it necessary to write in a footnote detailing that they study very little, if any, in a given week then study as much as possible during the week of an exam.

To better understand student self-confidence the students were asked about their own perspectives on their performance in the laboratory course, which was the focus of this survey, and also in the lecture course. In response to the statement "I feel I am doing well in the lab" the distribution of responses were in the majority (35 percent) neutral (neither agree/nor disagree) with an even spread from there leaning slightly towards disagree. Students were somewhat more positive about the lecture course with the majority (40 percent) still putting neutral, but with a spread shifted slightly towards agreeing with the statement. The respondents showed a nearly identical response curve when the question was directed towards both courses overall. Overall the students showed mixed feelings about their own confidence in their performance in both courses but were marginally more negative regarding the laboratory course. This may be the result of the portion of their grade that is known to them at the timepoint of the survey was significantly smaller in the laboratory course than in the lecture course.

Because this work is focused on understanding the effectiveness of problem solving in genetics it is reasonable to believe that student attitudes towards problem solving would be integral to its effectiveness and therefore need to be evaluated. Students were given the statement "I found the problem solving sessions to be useful for lab." The majority (39 percent) again were neutral with the remaining skewed towards agreeing. This was in stark contrast to the statement when directed at the lecture course. Students overwhelmingly (49 percent) stated that they strongly agreed with the statement while only a minority (8 percent) disagreed in any way with the statement. Interestingly, when the question was worded to address the usefulness to both courses overall the responses followed the lecture responses in a nearly identical manner. This could be interpreted as students giving more weight to the lecture course or, alternatively, since they found the problem solving helpful more for lecture than the lab then overall it was as helpful as the most helpful of those two options.

The discrepancy between student responses with the lab and lecture was revealed in the open-ended questions. Students often cited that the problem solving felt very similar to the exams given during lecture. On the other hand, students felt the problem-solving sessions were more useful to lab as additional material was covered and emphasized that aided the lab course. It is important to note that the majority of the students' grades in the lab course at the time of the survey were from laboratory reports rather than problem-based examinations. It is possible that students have a disconnect between the exam-style questions that are more classical problem solving and the more abstract problem solving of conducting an experiment and reporting on the data and conclusions.

Students' preliminary exam scores were organized according to the number of optional problem-solving sessions attended. Groups were chosen in an effort to have as even as possible n numbers in each and accordingly were assigned as students who attended 0, 1–2, 3–5, 6–8, and 9–10. The mean for each exam was known for the entire lecture course including students not surveyed and not in the laboratory course ($n = 220$). The first exam mean was 60.6. Students attending nearly all (9–10) of the problem solving sessions showed higher performance of 11.7 percent on their preliminary exams compared with the course average. Even students who did not attend any of the problem-solving sessions showed a 2.2 percent increase over the class mean. Since students surveyed were only those also enrolled in the laboratory course ($n = 103$) this may be indicative of the laboratory course reinforcing and strengthening the skills necessary for the formal exams in the lecture course. This is particularly evident when you examine the grades for all surveyed students as a whole, as they average 4.2 percent higher on the first exam and 1.4 percent higher on the second exam than the lecture average, which includes around 70 students not enrolled in the laboratory course. Taken as a whole, students attending any problem-solving sessions showed a trend towards improved performance on the exams.

Interestingly, one caveat appeared with students attending between six and eight problem-solving sessions. The average was 2.2 percent lower on the first exam than the course average and 4.6 percent lower on the second exam. The open-ended questions for these students provided little direct reason but suggested that at least a portion of these students realized they were behind after several weeks and then decided to attend the problem-solving sessions to make up for this difference.

The quantitative data from the survey and the students' recorded grades were mixed but generally positive in regards to the problem-solving sessions. However, an important component to producing an effective course is the students' own perception and attitude towards its different facets. In an effort to understand this open-ended questions were asked during the survey. Students had an overall positive attitude towards the problem-solving sessions, with responses such as "I feel the optional problem-solving sessions will help me practice and improve my genetics skills and help me to do well in the course." And ". . . I would say [the optional problem solving sessions] are 10 times more useful than the actual lecture."

Students were largely receptive and positive towards the question "Would you be interested in taking a genetics course that focused on group problem solving during lectures? Why or why not?" A typical example of student response would be ". . . problem solving helps me to master the materials the most." It is interesting to note that most students focused on this question from the lens of problem solving in general rather than the idea of group problem solving. This may be representative of the fact that the current optional problem-solving sessions are not group focused unless the students take it upon themselves to form groups.

Conversely, a number of students commented more directly on the "group" portion of the question citing "It is more realistic since no endeavor (other than college) is ever all individual . . ." and adding such personal statements as "I enjoy working with people. I also believe that teaching is the best way to understand it. You get perspectives and ways of approaching problems that you would not have attain[sic] otherwise." This demonstrates a fundamental understanding of the strong points of guided group learning, namely that trading roles within a group between student and teacher is a method of learning in both roles. Taken together the vast majority of students who responded were positive and open to the idea of incorporating group problem solving within the course.

How these findings have informed/will inform my practice

The short-term goal of this research was to try to examine the efficacy of optional problem-solving sessions in a genetics course. In the long run the goal is to address whether problem-solving sessions such as these should be more closely integrated into the genetics curriculum. Linking students' preliminary exam scores with their survey responses provided multiple ways in which to analyze the student data.

Overall, the optional problem-solving sessions were mostly viewed favorably and students were generally open to integrating them more closely into the curriculum of this course, rather than having them as an optional component. While student opinions were quite clear the actual performance associated with the optional problem-solving sessions was mixed but overall positively correlates with student performance in the course. This suggests that incorporating group problem solving into the curriculum of an introductory genetics course would likely be well received and likely to enrich and improve the learning experience for the students involved. As a result I plan to incorporate more group work and active problem solving during class and I encourage others to do so as well.

Presenting and sharing findings is central to classroom research work. Creating research questions that are designed to inform and improve practice means that others can potentially learn from our experiences. In addition, in collaborative kinds of research like Jared conducted within his department, sharing is essential to the process. In Jared's case, he was able to share his findings with the department, including the person responsible for coordinating the problem-solving supplemental course and make decisions with leaders about what to do in the future with this course—leave it optional or build it into the curriculum.

Collaborative Reflective Research Groups help share the findings with at least a small group of colleagues, but consider sharing your findings more broadly. Consider publication or presentation of your findings for a broad audience. At the end of this book are several possible organizations and journals to consider, but the list grows every day as new groups gain ground and the Scholarship of Teaching and Learning grows.

Also important to this process and "closing the loop" is the continuation of the research. Improving teaching and learning is a lifelong process that we never truly perfect. There are always ways to improve, new and innovative ideas to consider, student characteristics change, and we change as we gain more expertise. Thinking like a researcher as we approach our teaching can facilitate our career-long striving toward excellence. We collect data and analyze and use that evidence to formulate new questions and seek additional evidence.

WORDS OF CAUTION

Simone Galea (2012), drawing upon Plato and Luce Irigaray's work, argues after a critical overview of reflective practice that "reflective practice can contradict its own aims and become non-reflective, shutting off possibilities for transformations and educational differences that it has set out to achieve" (p. 245). She argues that:

> reflective practice promises an emancipation of teachers from authoritarian teaching and learning patterns that echo controlling and disciplinary schooling practices which they themselves are the subject of or have been subjected to. Teachers develop their own professional paths out of such reproductive systems through deep critical thinking about their particular experiences and contexts. This might also lead teachers toward an articulation of their own teaching philosophies. The democratization of teaching is also dependent on a representation of teachers who are emancipated enough to have their voices heard through their own narratives, reflective journals and diaries and other written texts that have become the normal accepted means of representing their teaching selves.
>
> (p. 246)

We have all been indoctrinated into a system of higher education that has accepted systems and ways of practice that have been in place for generations. Changing the status quo and challenging existing ways of teaching, and challenging our own well-established patterns that we have created as students and as teachers can be incredibly difficult. For example, if we spent most of our time in a discipline that values and rewards classic lecture-styles of teaching, it may be very difficult to challenge those structures. It may be equally difficult to defend lecture as a positive teaching/learning strategy within an environment and culture that values and rewards discussion-oriented classrooms. We must be open-minded, as Dewey suggests, when we engage in the collaborative reflective process. We must be open to what we might find.

Chapter 9

Conclusions: So What and Now What?

In this chapter:

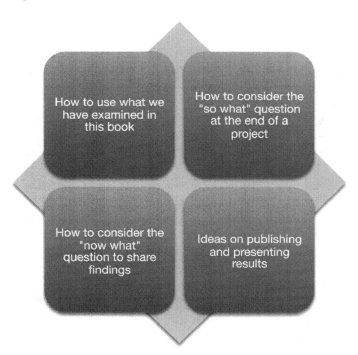

How to use what we have examined in this book

How to consider the "so what" question at the end of a project

How to consider the "now what" question to share findings

Ideas on publishing and presenting results

Hopefully after engaging with this book, the task of classroom research seems less daunting and the possibilities exciting. The truth is, it can be as simple or complex as you choose. Working with a Collaborative Reflective Research in Teaching Group might be useful. You may want to start with a little less formality than that and simply have coffee with colleagues to explore the possibilities of classroom research. Most colleges and universities now have centers or departments designed to help support faculty development and teaching. Perhaps consider reaching out to key people within those programs. This work is challenging though, and working collaboratively can certainly help.

Consider starting small with a pilot study or examining your own classroom as a case study. Try a single method—perhaps one with which you feel the most confident. If surveys seem overwhelming, try writing down notes of your observations. If you would like to try creating online surveys, try that—try a simple Likert scale and a few open-ended questions. See what you get. Ask for help from your college or university's research center (if they have one). Try strategies that feel less comfortable for you (once you get your feet wet). If you are fundamentally a qualitative researcher, try quantitative and vice versa. If you are in the humanities and have never done social science or natural science research, try to do a few different methods.

Jennifer Row (English) had never done any kind of research like teaching as research before her first project, in which she examined introducing theater activities into her first year seminar writing class. She was willing to try a lot of different strategies that she had never considered before—from her pedagogy to her research methods. Do not be afraid to go out of your research comfort zone, but be realistic and honest with yourself about what you can achieve. This is why working collaboratively in Collaborative Reflective Research in Teaching Groups can be quite useful. These groups can help with methodological considerations and support throughout the process.

Jennie, with the assistance of her peers in our class (acting like a large reflective research group), took a lot of risks—she tried qualitative and quantitative methods in her case study of her own first year writing classroom. She took risks with her pedagogy, building in acting and performance into her writing class. Below is her write-up of her experience.

Examples of Research from the Classroom

Risk, rehearsal, reading and writing: Theater techniques in the classroom

Jennifer Row

Introduction

The title of my class always elicits giggles, or at least a smirk. I never know if it's out of discomfort or because it sounds so titillating, or maybe even ridiculous to be spending a semester teaching about "The Drama of Sodomy and Incest on the Early Modern Stage." Titillating or not, I chose the first year writing seminar title largely because that was literally the subject matter I taught in the spring of 2012: thinking about transgressive sexualities and how they were represented in the sixteenth and seventeenth century in the theater. In a larger sense, however, my choice of title reflected some deeper questions and anxieties I had—How to elicit student enthusiasm for a topic that I was passionate about (does developing an edgy title work)? More importantly, how could I have students take the theme of sodomy and sexuality seriously, in two senses of "seriousness": in one sense, I needed the students not to treat it as mere kinkiness. In a second sense, however, it was important to me to elicit a type of seriousness, in the sense of respecting the term fully, by preserving the very qualities of Early Modern sodomy as a particular relation to social, hierarchical, and intimate norms, and the disruption of those norms. As Alan Bray (1994) writes in a landmark essay, "Homosexuality and the Signs of Male Friendship in Elizabethan England,"

> Elizabethan "sodomy" differed from our contemporary idea of "homosexuality" in a number of other ways also. It covered more hazily a whole range of sexual acts, of which sexual acts between people of the same sex were only a part. It was closer, rather, to an idea like debauchery. But it differed more fundamentally in that it was not only a sexual crime. It was also a political and a religious crime and it was this that explains more clearly why it was regarded with such dread.
>
> (p. 41)

In a sense, if the course was about exploring a subject that embraced exploding or blurring strict lines of social control and intimate contact, I wondered what sort of ways this might be echoed in the classroom. Sodomizing the students was probably not a good option. But the idea of destabilizing the hierarchy of power, of the top-down hegemony of pedagogy, of exploring different ways of sharing and displaying knowledge —those were things I wanted to take seriously.

It was important to me to have these terms and ideas present in the course title, even in seed form, because most Cornell undergraduates are required to take two first year writing seminars as part of their curriculum and I wanted to both "warn" and "entice" students to the explicit nature of the course material. The philosophy behind such a writing requirement is that Cornell graduates, regardless of their major or their professional career choices, need strong writing skills in order to communicate, to succeed, to exist as knowledgeable citizens of the world. Despite an extensive balloting system, the students end up choosing classes partly based on genuine interest in the course topic and partly for scheduling reasons. The courses, featuring six to nine short essay assignments to the semester and no more than seventy pages of reading per week, are often taught by graduate student instructors with varying levels of interest in pedagogy and varying levels of previous teaching training. In another sense, however, the nature of the "requirement" often means that students view the course as the chore and limit themselves in terms of their creative risks and writing explorations, viewing "essay grades" as the final and only markers of their success.

187

While I had taught language (French and English) both in Paris and at Cornell for quite a few years, this course represented the first time that I could design and develop my own syllabus and structure from the ground up. In tandem with the extensive writing program, Cornell also featured a Walk-In-Writing Service where students could drop in for individual tutoring; I had tutored with this center for so long that I had attained an Assistant Director position. All of these factors meant that I felt extra pressure to develop a truly spectacular course, or at least one that was deeply cognizant of certain types of pedagogic strategies to elicit strong writing. I believed in the importance of the writing program, and I wanted to design my course in such a way as to convince my students that they ought to explore and to engage in the study of writing, that this was a lifelong skill they could cherish, develop, and depend upon, and that they needed not approach the course with their mere teleologic view of "checking off" the requirement and snagging a good grade.

Objectives

To complicate this unilateral approach to learning about writing, I wanted my students to explore risk-taking and celebration in the classroom. Fear of making a mistake or and over-attention to "getting the *right* answer" means that students often try to "play it safe" and develop strategies of something like "teacher mind-reading" instead of allowing their own ideas to take root. For example, to my great chagrin, in one of my individual meetings with Russell (names have been changed), as I was gently pushing him to develop a stronger, more elaborate thesis, he threw down his pencil and said, "I don't know what you want me to say," as if he surmised that I had a secret "hidden" idea that I was trying to get him to guess. Another student, Corinne, would stare at me blankly while frantically typing every single word that came out of my mouth, as if she thought that by collecting all of my phrases, ideas, and questions verbatim, she could magically "see" what I was trying to have her say. These approaches to learning about writing frustrated me, obviously, and drove me to explore ways of exploding this notion that the teacher had a single set answer and that the student's job was to figure it out. I realized that half of the work of letting go of this phenomenon had to come from the students, not just from my approach to teaching. Encouraging risk-taking, in my opinion, can lead to beautiful unexpected insights, or new connections, or pushing oneself to reach a higher level of analysis or writing. To this end, offering non-traditional and creative theatre approaches to the text, showing that there are a variety of ways of engaging and responding to writing, could not only make it "come alive" for the students but also loosen their grasp on the idea that there is only "one" perfect formula for writing a strong paper.

My other objective was to complicate the notion of "celebration" or "accomplish-ment" in this project. Instead of inextricably tying together "A" with "accomplishment" I wanted to challenge each of my students to think about micro-celebrations that happen throughout the day, including small things that they accomplish and do not fully give themselves credit for. In other words, instead of having a unilateral picture of what an "accomplished" goal looks like, I want to broaden and diversify this idea: maybe celebrating speaking up in class, for a shy student, or celebrating "finally understanding why citing the text is important". Kathryn Flannery (1998) proposes that the embodiment engendered by performance techniques creates a different level of accessing textual meaning and communication:

> If all writing is in some sense disembodied, having the potential to erase the mode of its production by disconnecting itself from the hands that made it, performance restores the body to visibility. Whether composing scripts for performance or writing to make sense of what they have learned through performance, students tend to register this greater awareness of the human body in space and time, especially of the simultaneity of collective bodies in motion. Performance extends an understanding of literacy beyond the narrowly linguistic, emphasizing the extent to which the body itself serves as a signifying modality, a modality that can signify in ways that exceed the limits of print.

(pp. 44–45)

My thought was that by providing various levels of exploring the text through performance, students might have a wide range of demonstrating their textual comprehension, or interacting with the strangeness of Early Modern English, or trying to decipher confusing character choices and actions outside of the normative way of merely approaching dramatic literature as a passive, textual object.

I developed a teaching-as-research project based on using theater techniques in the classroom, incorporating a series of nine theater-based activities throughout the semester, which I will discuss in the following section. My main objectives were twofold. I surmised that the value and importance of abstract concepts that are cherished in writing instruction, such as the use of strong evidence, reading for subtext, or the concepts of editing vs revision may actually best be instructed through exercises relating to body, voice, gesture, and tone. Second, to move to a more meta-analytic plane, my project wanted to explore something I called "teaching-as-directing."

While there is a decent amount of scholarship on teaching and acting, not much has been written on the role of the teacher as "theatre director" in the classroom. A good director approaches the play and the play's text, just as a teacher approaches the classroom and the text, with some "vision" of how the performance will ultimately go; it is only through her collaboration with the actors, set designers, costumers, etc., that this vision is actually enacted. Along the way, however, in rehearsal, a director has to walk a perfect balance between over-correcting (micro-managing), giving enough space for the actors to explore and express the text, and sharing the "vision" of the performance in a constructive, productive way. Flannery writes, citing Viola Spolin (one of the founders of improvisational theater games):

> The teacher is literally to the side: "side coaching" is "an assist given by [the] teacher-director to the student-actor during the solving of a problem to help him

keep focus; a means of giving a student-actor self-identity within the theater environment."

(p. 392)

Paradoxically, in this version of lay theater, "no one teaches anyone anything," in the sense of direct or didactic instruction. This does not mean that the teacher is absent or withholding of her knowledge. Rather the teacher-director's approach is remarkably relational. She is not divested of her expertise or her authority, but she is participating in the process without holding center stage and without controlling interpretive possibilities

(p. 51)

On opening night, a good performance will seem generated almost organically from the actors' expressions, intuitions, and gestures; a heavy-handed director will seem like an unfortunate invisible puppeteer stringing along his actors. Flannery's notion of the teacher-director was something that my project endeavored to embrace.

As appealing as this "remarkably relational" approach to teaching was, however, I wanted to make sure that investigating my role as a "director" instead of a "teacher" would help me critically reflect on my position in the classroom. That is to say, instead of taking on this positive, balancing approach to power and instruction, I couldn't assume that my position as an instructor was categorically neutral, or that I had an unquestioned superior understanding of the Early Modern dramas and of writing, I wanted to be able to use the analogic metaphor of director not only to re-craft my relation to power in the classroom but also in order to develop a critical self-awareness of this power, especially in regard to these moments of celebration and risk. How did my power suppress or control risk-taking, or predetermine sorts of celebration? As Stephen Brookfield (1998) writes,

Many of us would like to believe either that we have no special power over adult learners, or that any power mistakenly attributed to us by them is an illusion that can quickly be dissolved by our own refusal to dominate the group. But it is not that easy. No matter how much we protest our desire to be at one with learners there is often a predictable flow of attention focused on us. While it is important to privilege learners' voices and to create multiple foci of attention in the classroom, it is disingenuous to pretend that as educators we are the same as students. Better to acknowledge publicly our position of power, to engage students in deconstructing that power, and to attempt to model a critical analysis of our own source of authority in front of them.

(p. 130)

Positioning myself consciously as a director would, I hypothesized, not only allow me different kinds of pathways of instruction, but also enhance my self-awareness of this position of power. It would also allow me new modes of imagining how to enact and embody this power.

Method

In order to explore these two objectives, the pedagogy of writing through theater and the notion of teaching-as-directing, I developed nine different theater activities, which focused on creative approaches to costume, music, voice, bodies, gesture, and space. These activities were of three kinds: in-class activities, take-home activities, and a final project. Overall, in response to these activities, the students reflected on the theater activities in freewrites, in-class discussion, presentations on their creative choices, and online postings to a discussion board.

In-class activities

The in-class activities included, for example, taking a phrase or one word and asking each student to say the phrase differently. The unpunctuated sentence "I did it" could be said as a proud declaration ("I did it!"), as an uncertain self-realization ("*I* did it?" — in the sense of "it was *me* who did it?") as an admission of guilt, as a euphemism ("I did . . . 'it' "), etc. From there, I was able to talk about early modern textual practices and how the standards of punctuation and spelling during Shakespeare's time were not yet concretely anchored and how one mis-transcribed word could alter the entire meaning of a line.

Other activities had students improvise scenes where absences became more powerful than presence, or to dramatize the relationship between seduction and knowledge.

Take-home activities

The take-home activities gave students a greater amount of time to prepare their presentations, and I enjoyed devising activities that mimicked situations real-life theater professionals might be faced with. Students were challenged to come up with a costume for a modern-day production of Christopher Marlowe's *Edward II,* or to figure out what type of music would be playing during key moments during Jean Racine's *Phaedra* or Pierre Corneille's *Polyeucte*. For these, I asked students to read the text carefully and be able to justify their choices with textual evidence. My intention was to make sure that they knew how to refer back to the text constantly to support their choices, just as they would need to rely on textual citations and evidence to support their thesis statements and arguments in their writing. Additionally, I wanted them to explore not just the obviously thematic, or what was said, but also the unspoken and subtextual in their writing, as well as in their performance choices.

Other than the visual and aural responses, however, I designed the activities to make sure that there was a good mix of group and solo performance responses. I also made sure that students had access to recordings, good YouTube clips of performances, and more.

Final project

Students were divided into small groups and each group was assigned one of the five plays that we had read this semester. They were asked to choose a scene from the play and interpret it as they liked.

Results

By and large, I found that seeing the theater activities in class helped me as a teacher-director. When students' activities really demonstrated a concept clearly, I would be able to take that presentation as a jumping-off point for discussion. For example, I could have lectured on the doubleness of Othello's character: that at times he feels equally torn between uncontrolled rage and irritation as well as his feelings of insecurity and neurosis. Having the students stage Othello two different ways, and precisely demonstrate this character split, not only illuminated it for the other students but also allowed me to confirm that they understood the text. Often, these exercises allowed me a way to gauge their level of textual comprehension and amend my lessons accordingly.

One aspect I did not anticipate was the development of interdependent learning. One student wrote in a freewrite: "I think the partner projects that require reading scenes in different tones and rhythms was my favorite, because I was able to understand the reading of the scene better and saw how other groups approached the scenes in different ways." This sentiment was echoed through many of the freewrites, and, in the write-up of their final project, I could tell that the students had put a good deal of work explaining the scene to each other, making sure all group members were on the same page, etc. In my over-haste to analyze the power dynamics of the top-down teacher-director structure, I had completely forgotten about the fact that theater was an entirely collaborative, joint experience. In the future, I would make sure to stress the interdependent learning aspect and see if there were certain activities I could design to make sure that they were able to take turns clearly teaching each other.

Of the fourteen enrolled in the course, thirteen provided freewrite responses. Five students (38 percent) thought the activities were both enjoyable *and* useful for their writing and reading comprehension. One student, Laura, summarized her favorite activities and described in detail the ways that opening up polyvalent avenues of analysis enriched her understanding of the text:

> The use of drama in this course was integral to the analytic aspect of the writing seminar, as I found myself forgetting the performance of the works and focusing solely on the plays as text at times. It opened new doors to textual interpretation when truly thinking of the range of tone, emotion and wordplay possible in any given scene and what that could mean for a student's analysis. The "*Othello* Two-Ways" and "Pauses" exercises were especially telling for me, as I tended to pigeonhole some of the scenes into my own primary reading of it rather than explore the text as read aloud. They also reminded me how important it was to read said

texts aloud when completing reading assignments, as well as occasionally seek out a YouTube clip or two when confused about how certain lines might be portrayed classically. The *Edward the Second* costume exercise gave way to thoughts about the extent of performance and adaptation, bringing to light the extensive thought and attention to detail the playwrights must have had when exporting their text to stage and what those details can mean to a production now, especially when adapted to modern-day contexts.

Three students (23 percent) thought it provided a creative outlet for textual exploration, but the value of the activities seemed to be ambiguously "useful." In these cases, I'm not sure if the students were just unable to articulate the ways that the activities were beneficial to them, or if they mostly appreciated the distraction. For example, one student wrote: "it makes the writing seminar more unique and enjoyable because we are doing more than just writing. Plus we learn material in a more direct method, which I really enjoy." Two (15 percent) thought it was enjoyable but not useful; one student, for example, said "I don't have a problem with them, nor without them". Two (15 percent) found the activiites to be not at all useful: "It may be that I'm too close minded and when I don't like something I don't pay attention or try to learn as much."

Discussion

The students seemed to enjoy the final project the most. Randy wrote,

> Because the play [*The Duchess of Malfi*] has so many themes and is so long, by focusing only on one scene, you really begin to understand in depth that one theme or issue you are focusing on. I better understand the rest of the play by exploring one theme, like filth and immoral characters. Having looked at one scene closely, iterations of that theme become clear throughout the rest of the play.

Clearly the fact that I required the students to spend a great deal of time with the text, reading one scene closely and imagining how it would be staged, meant that they would naturally "get more" out of the text, because they had paid a certain kind of closely attentive and interpretive time with the text in preparation for their projects.

On the other hand, while the students appreciated the final project, I realized that they didn't quite understand its placement in the sequence of theater activities and its relation to the other written work that they were being graded on. As one student noted in an anonymous freewrite response:

> I think that the final project was the most helpful because we had more time to prepare our thoughts and focus. The rest of the theater exercises in class were very last second type of exercises and thus didn't allow you to fully develop your ideas, which caused them to be less helpful.

193

At the same time, however, I specifically designed the other theater activities (playing with pauses, extremes of voice, highs and lows, costuming, etc.) so that they would be prepared or somewhat familiar with the different avenues of creative expression, in anticipation of this final project. I would, in the future, make it clear that all of the in-class activities, while they feel "last second," also engender a certain type of spontaneous engagement with the text, certain kinds of insights and inspirations. Furthermore, while the assignments that required more at-home preparation had clearer, more direct "payoff" in terms of their comprehension, the other in-class assignments fed into the larger structure.

Students were also confused about being evaluated for a different form of response to the text other than writing. Another student, Paul, said,

> One of the most helpful activities, in my opinion, was the latest theatre activity. The modern adaptation of the different groups allowed me to relate to some of the plays. This assignment should be done as the class goes on rather than at the end, when being able to relate to the assignment does not really help.

Interestingly enough, for Paul, the "helpfulness" of the theater assignment is gauged by how it can help clarify a text in order to write about it. Since the final projects presenting the plays came at the end of the semester, after students had already written essays on those texts, Paul felt that the assignment was not useful. He read the use-value of the exercise in terms of its ability to help him produce a written assignment, without considering that the performance itself, and his reflection on the performance was also still a response and a demonstration of his mastery of the text in some way. In the future, if I were to do the course again, I would definitely make it clear that all of the smaller theater assignments, including improvisation, help textual comprehension, and that the final assignment *is* still a type of performance-based assessment of his engagement with the text.

Another aspect I hope to work on in the future for the class is the nature of inclusion. One student, Rina, wrote:

> Having done four years of children's community theater, four years of high school drama club, and four years of high school musical theater, I intentionally chose writing seminars both semesters that involved theater. [. . .] I really enjoyed the assignment where we had to present the same scene in two different ways, with different emotions, personalities, reactions, etc. I thought that really highlighted the importance of an actor's interpretation of a character. When you're reading the lines, your mind usually jumps to one way of interpreting them, and one way of imagining what a character is feeling at that moment, and how they are acting. But when you have to take a scene and decide what meaning you want to put behind every single word, it becomes much more clear just how open to interpretation plays and characters can be. I really enjoyed all the theater assignments we did

194

for this class; I felt that the plays we read necessitated a little acting and a little creativity, in order to truly comprehend and grasp all of the potential meanings and messages to be found.

I felt that students who were naturally extroverted or who felt comfortable and enjoyed performing got the most out of these activities. Another student, Lily, said that the projects "require a bold sense of self to perform; thus, it can be a little embarrassing."

In the future, I believe I need to make sure that students don't feel "pushed" into performing or to make them uncomfortable. Risk-taking does require a certain level of discomfort, but I wonder if it is within the bounds of my prerogative as an instructor to push students to a certain kind of risk or self-exposure. While on the one hand, "theater activities" can seem like an unambiguously positive way of rendering the classroom more dynamic, engaging, or enriching, sometimes such activities also need to be critically analyzed as well. In a parallel privileged classroom structure, the "circle" of chairs (as opposed to rows of desks), Brookfield (1998) complicates the notion of the circle as "unsullied democratic purity" by arguing that

> beneath the circle's democrative veneer there may exist a much more troubling and ambivalent reality. For learners who are confident, loquacious and used to academic culture, the circle holds relatively few terrors. But for students who are shy, aware of their different skin colour, physical appearance or form of dress, unused to intellectual discourse, intimidated by disciplinary jargon and the culture of academe, or conscious of their lack of education, the circle can be a painful and humiliating experience. These learners have been stripped of their right to privacy.
>
> (p. 134)

In the future, as I try to explore and extend these theater activity projects, I would want to ensure that there are mechanisms of "opting out" available to students who do experience those "painful and humiliating" experiences. Halfway through the course, I decided to change the nature of the theater assignments and ask for volunteers who wanted and did not want to perform—the non-performers shared their musical choices for a character's imaginary iPod, for example, and many of the other students enjoyed these non-performing activities because they were still able to think about the text in a very enriched, dynamic way without putting someone on the spot. I think that I would re-structure the activities in such a way in the future.

A final point is to consider the classroom as "rehearsal" time. I had some thoughts about the nature of direction before I started teaching—about the ways that a director had to come with a "plan" or a vision for the script, etc. After reading Robert Gross's (1978) article on "Rehearsal as Interpretive Technique," I think that I would reformat my approach to classroom time. This technique that he proposes is to not go into rehearsal (or classroom time) completely ignorant of some themes, nor to approach it with an overly fixed vision of how the play "should be," nor to be overly weighted down by literary-tropic analysis. Rather, one should approach classroom time (or rehearsal time) with a type of radical openness to an ever-evolving appreciation of the text:

> Making rehearsals interpretively productive requires prerehearsal interpretations that ask "why" over and over again until every perceivable moment of the script has been fully rationalized and reconciled with every other moment into a coherent "action to be communicated," not merely an action to be executed before an audience. The most useful way for the director to formulate this action is in terms of final cause; that is, as a web of understandings of the communicative job to be done, of the impact performance that they should have on the audience moment by moment. During rehearsal, this sketchy cognitive structure of how the play should be communicated should be tested, revised, and fleshed out.
>
> (p. 1)

I really appreciated the last line of "tested, revised, and fleshed out"—and I would restructure my class in such a way to make sure that students are all on board with being cooperators in this explorative endeavor—to be testing, revising, and fleshing out with me (as the director?) through activities, through writing, and through interdependent learning.

While this project was a first exploration and a first attempt at sketching out an approach to teaching writing through the theater, I feel I gained infinitely much, even through some flubbed activities or some mis-organized structures. Although the theme of my project was encouraging my students to take risks, I ended up taking risks myself in teaching this first course in such a way that defied the "safe" structure of merely having students read and write. I feel there is so much that has been explored—but still so much to perfect and hone as I continue to develop this project.

Jennie explored the "so what" questions and considered what her findings meant to her and her teaching—particularly this notion of risk-taking and asking students to engage in activities that are challenging.

What might be the next steps for a study like this one (the "now what?")? First, Jennie might consider publishing in a journal like *College English* that, according to its website, "is the professional journal for the college scholar-teacher." Other discipline-specific journals include "College Composition and Communication" and "Journal of Intensive English Studies," or "Journal of Teaching Writing," and "Research in the Teaching of English." We see here that Jennie is quite reflective in her write up of her project. She steps outside of her methodological comfort zone and engaged in some qualitative and quantitative evidence gathering within her case study. She also used student assessments. She admitted to using Excel to analyze some statistics for the first time in her life. She reflects on what she learned—her struggles and successes. She takes risks as she asked her students to do the same with their performances. As a new faculty member, she has learned a lot from her project.

Baidura Ray, after completing his case study of his engineering class with his colleague Rajesh Bhaskaran, decided upon an engineering-specific education journal and submitted to the *International Journal of Mechanical Engineering Education* (Ray and Bhaskaran 2013). The title of his article is "Integrating Simulation into the Engineering Curriculum: A case study." It is published in the July 2013 issue of the journal. For a direct link to the publication visit http://manchester.meta press.com/content/w603n67751488h20/fulltext.pdf?page=1. The abstract gives a better idea of their study:

Examples of Research from the Classroom

Integrating simulation into the engineering curriculum: A case study

Baidura Ray and Rajesh Bhaskaran

Abstract

In this paper, we describe improved strategies for teaching computational fluid dynamics (CFD) using the commercial software ANSYS Fluent to upper-level undergraduates and graduate students. We consider a case study from an upper-level elective fluid dynamics course and evaluate various out-of-class learning materials and in-class active learning techniques. We show that, in agreement with previous research, most student learning happens out of class. We show a direct correlation between the materials developed in a reference hand-out and the students' expertise in the area. We introduced i-clickers as a means of promoting active learning in the classroom to emphasize the "expert approach" in simulation. Their use received a mixed response from the students and we discuss the reasons and a possible remedy. We demonstrate that carefully designed out-of-class learning materials are crucial to students' learning of CFD, and that i-clickers have to be used with care if they are to be effective in engaging students during the lectures. All of these findings inform not only future renditions of this course, but also instruction of CFD in general.

Ray, like Jennie, explored methods outside of his disciplinary comfort zone. He conducted a case study examining the use of a simulation software package to determine its effectiveness as a pedagogical strategy. He also examined how students interacted with the written materials and active learning activities and use of technology with the clickers.

This example is compelling because it too uses a variety of components discussed in this book and ultimately is published in a journal that is specific to mechanical engineering education. It shows how much the field is growing. More and more journals are created within the disciplines that value research on teaching and substantive articles to inform learning and pedagogy. We want our students to learn. We want to determine the most effective and efficient ways to have that happen.

At the conclusion of our projects, we should, as researchers, ask ourselves, "so what?" Specifically we should ponder: what does this all mean and what is compelling, interesting, and/or useful to me? And then, we should consider "now what?" That is, now what should we do with the results. Some of the faculty with whom I have worked chose to share their work with their colleagues. Some have chosen to publish in peer-reviewed journals. Most have presented at University-wide symposia created to share projects such as these. Some have presented nationally. They all use the information to inform and improve their practice and hope to inform the practice of others.

Engaging in this kind of scholarship may require a philosophical shift for some faculty, but not necessarily. However, this shift is not necessarily fundamental. And it is possible for faculty to stay within their research and philosophical "comfort zones" and still engage in meaningful and useful research that informs and improves their teaching. The hope is that faculty, instructors, teaching assistants, and others working and teaching in higher-education settings continue to do more and more research on teaching and learning, using the variety of strategies discussed in this book: qualitative, quantitative, mixed-methods, using assessment data, case studies, and pilot studies. Hopefully they will continue to build upon existing work, work collaboratively and share their findings through reflective practice groups, conference presentations (local and global), and publications. As the trend continues, teaching, learning and research will continue to be informed by thoughtful and systematic research, and ultimately improved.

I recognize that opportunities for true interdisciplinary collaboration in academe are rare. Despite our best efforts, the academy is not set up to reward this kind of reflective practice and collaborative effort. It will take effort to share our research on our pedagogy across disciplines. It will also require patience and understanding as those in different disciplines come to appreciate the beauty in each others' methods, and philosophical underpinnings of those methods. The academy is comprised of brilliant learners eager to expand their horizons, broaden their knowledge base, and hone their craft. We can learn a great deal from our colleagues across campus. We need to create opportunities to engage with one another in meaningful and purposeful ways.

College and university faculty, as they earn their doctoral degrees to become faculty members, learn research strategies that allow them to contribute to the academic conversation and become more astute consumers of information, while simultaneously becoming generators and producers of new information and ideas.

198

They are taught ways to contribute to the academy. Using research strategies described in this book, and perhaps new strategies they create on their own, college and university faculty can contribute even more to the knowledge base of the academy—not only within their disciplines, but in teaching the next generation of knowledge producers as well.

Additional Resources: Possible Publication Venues and Organizations Supporting Scholarship of Teaching and Learning

RESOURCE AGGREGATES

- Center for the Integration of Research, Teaching and Learning (CIRTL)
  www.cirtl.net
- Carnegie Foundation for the Advancement of Teaching
  www.carnegiefoundation.org
- Center for Teaching Learning and Scholarship (CTLS), Georgia Southern University
  http://academics.georgiasouthern.edu/ctls/
- International Society for the Scholarship of Teaching and Learning (issotl)
  www.issotl.org/SOTL.html
- The Scholarship of Teaching and Learning (SoTL), Illinois State University
  http://sotl.illinoisstate.edu/
- Center for Teaching, Vanderbilt University
  http://cft.vanderbilt.edu/teaching-guides/reflecting/sotl/

TUTORIALS, SUBSTANTIAL INTRODUCTIONS

- The Scholarship of Teaching and Learning (SoTL) by Derek Bruff, Assistant Director, Vanderbilt Center for Teaching
  http://cft.vanderbilt.edu/teaching-guides/reflecting/sotl/
- International Society for the Scholarship of Teaching and Learning (issotl) tutorial, three sections:
  (1) essential definitions, concepts, rationale and other background

(2) administrative "how to" examples of campus programs and faculty projects

(3) research essentials to launch own projects.

www.issotl.org/tutorial/

- CIRTL College Classroom Course

  Designed especially for graduate students in STEM disciplines, the College Classroom course provides a forum in which to discuss learning, teaching, and assessment. Cognizant of issues of diversity and equity throughout, participants create a learning community within the class in which to engage in discovery and analysis of the interconnected components of teaching through the lens of teaching-as-research (TAR). After completing this course, participants will be active participants in the interdisciplinary learning community that develops within the course and outside of it, know how to create an inclusive classroom environment that engages all learners, and use TAR in future classrooms of their own.

  www.cirtl.net/files/guidebook_collegeclassroomcourse_0.pdf

PROJECT EXAMPLES

- Examples of previous CTE GRTF projects/posters

  http://blogs.cornell.edu/kimberwilliams/

- The Scholarship of Teaching and Learning: Strengthening Education Through Research and Collaboration

- Buffalo State—State University of New York, T. Mills Kelly—History

  In this course portfolio, George Mason University history professor T. Mills Kelly addresses the question, "How does the introduction of hypermedia into a history course influence student learning in that course?" He describes his experience teaching two sections of the same Western Civilization course. In one section, he made primary source documents available on the course website. In the other section, primary source documents were only available in print form. By surveying students on their use of primary source documents and by analyzing student essays and papers, Mills was able to draw several conclusions about the use of hypermedia in his course.

  www.historians.org/teaching/aahe/Kelly/Pew/Portfolio/welcome.htm

- James Sandefur Mathematics

  In this article, Georgetown University mathematics professor James Sandefur describes his investigations into his students' problem-solving strategies. He conducted "think alouds" with his students, in which a student is asked to solve a problem and say aloud everything that they think as they do. Sandefur videotaped a number of these think alouds and learned much about the strategies (good and bad) his students often use

to solve mathematics problems. He also describes how what he has learned has impacted his teaching.
www.cfkeep.org/html/snapshot.php?id=709

BIBLIOGRAPHIES

- SoTL Bibliography
  http://sotl.illinoisstate.edu/resources/castl/bibliography.shtml
- CASTL Annotated Bibliography—revised 2002
- elibrary—Carnegie Foundation for the Advancement of Teaching
  www.carnegiefoundation.org
- CIRTL—Network Bibliography of Publications, Presentations, Posters
  and Teaching-as-Research Projects
  www.cirtl.net/bibliography/keyword/CIRTL%20Publication&sort
  =author&order=asc
- SoTL Publications —ISSOTL
  www.issotl.org/SOTL.html#publications
- "Navigating the Web of discourse on the Scholarship of Teaching and
  Learning: An annotated Webliography", by Musa Abdul Hakim. *College
  and Research Libraries News*, July/August 2002
  www.ala.org/ala/mgrps/divs/acrl/publications/crlnews/2002/
  jul/scholarshipteaching.cfm

INSTITUTIONS/PROGRAMS

- Peer Review of Teaching Project
- Carnegie Academy for the Scholarship of Teaching and Learning
  (CASTL)
- International Society for the Scholarship of Teaching and Learning
  (ISSOTL)
- SoTL at Indiana University—Bloomington
- SoTL at Illinois State University
- SoTL at SUNY—Buffalo State
- SoTL at the University of Washington
- The Delta Program at the University of Wisconsin-Madison
- CASTL Annotated Bibliography, Revised 2002
- College Classroom Course: A guidebook, CIRTL (Center for the
  Integration of Research, Teaching, and Learning)
- The Formation of Scholars: Rethinking doctoral education for the
  twenty-first century, George E. Walker, Chris M. Golde, Laura Jones,
  Andrea Conklin Bueschel and Pat Hutchings, The Carnegie Foundation
  for the Advancement of Teaching

- Gauisus: Selected Scholarship of Teaching and Learning at Illinois State University 2004–09. Kathleen McKinney and Patrcia Javis (eds), Illinois State University.
- The Scholarship of Teaching and Learning: Strengthening education through research and collaboration, Buffalo State—State University of New York
- SoTL Bibliography—Summer 2010 Complied by K. McKinney, Illinois State University.

Syllabus for Teaching as Research Course

ALS 6016 TEACHING AS RESEARCH IN HIGHER EDUCATION

Spring Semester 2014 (2 credits)

Cornell University

Instructor: Dr. Kimberly Williams
Office hours: Mondays 8:30–11:30am
Telephone: 607–255–3990
Email: kw299@cornell.edu
Office: CTE—CCC 4th floor
Class meetings time: Mondays 1:30–4pm in Caldwell 282

COURSE INFORMATION

This course will expose students to the literature on the Scholarship of Teaching and Learning (SoTL) and facilitate their engagement in teaching as research within their disciplines. Within this academic conversation about the Scholarship of Teaching and Learning and teaching as research, students will design and complete their own original research project to inform teaching in their discipline. This course culminates in the creation of a completed teaching as research project to include: an in-depth literature review incorporating SoTL resources from one's discipline; a methodology designed to address a particular need in one's teaching and/or within teaching in one's discipline; a critical analysis of the results and conclusions in a final, formal research report. Throughout the process students will give and receive critical feedback on their progress during key developmental stages of the research process. Students will present their reports in at least three different venues (i.e., in class, for one's department, and for the CTE in a final

SoTL Symposium). Students will be encouraged to write their papers for publication and/or to present at an academic conference. In addition, students will reflect on the broader implications of their findings within the body of research on teaching and present these ideas in a workshop to their departments.

REQUIRED TEXTS

Bishop-Clark, C. and Dietz-Uhler, B. (2012). *Engaging in the Scholarship of Teaching and Learning: A guide to the process, and how to develop a project from start to finish*. Sterling, VA: Stylus Publishing.

Huber, M.T. *et al.* (2002). *Disciplinary Styles in the Scholarship of Teaching and Learning: Exploring common ground*. AAHE/Carnegie Foundation available as download on Blackboard.

Additional articles available on Blackboard

LEARNING OUTCOMES

As a result of taking this course, students will be able to:

1. Evaluate the scholarship of teaching literature within their disciplines in a literature review.
2. Critique various research methodologies used in teaching as research (e.g., qualitative, quantitative, mixed-methods, teacher-action research methods) to select the most appropriate methodology for their own projects.
3. Describe the all ethical implications of their study as evidenced within the "risks" portion of their IRB applications.
4. Develop all parts of a research on teaching report (i.e., abstract, introduction, literature review, methods, results, conclusions, discussion, references, appendix) to include all critical elements defined in the final project rubric.
5. Present their research findings in three different settings using presentation strategies discussed in class (i.e., poster, discussion, lecture, etc.) to meet the criteria stated in the presentation rubric.
6. Students will help create a working paper series on Teaching as Research.
7. Identify ways to continue their own teaching as research.

LEARNING PROCESS, FORMAT AND EXPECTATIONS

This class is highly interactive and will seek to meet each individual's needs to develop the best research project possible. Together we will work toward the creation of a democratic and inclusive learning climate and community that

205

allows for freedom of expression, critical reflection, active listening, constructive dialogue, meaningful participation and enhanced understanding. In this democratic classroom, I urge you all to share ideas and materials to make sure that it meets the needs of all. Please let the instructor know if you have special needs or accommodations needed to participate and fully engage in course activities.

The course is "blended" to include a combination of web-based and face-to-face format. The seminars include small and large group discussion, a variety of audio-visual media, reflection activities, and opportunities for students to lead class discussion in their research areas of expertise.

It is expected that you will actively participate in all class and web-based activities, conversations and assignments. Active participation includes raising thoughtful questions, making useful observations about the course content and process, engaging in critical reflection on your own and others' assumptions in a respectful manner, sharing ideas, providing useful feedback and undertaking ongoing evaluation of different aspects of the course and your own learning.

Students will engage in meaningful self-assessment and peer assessment. Ongoing self-directed and collaborative evaluation is essential to the effectiveness of the course. Everyone will provide constructive feedback on the quality of the course content, methods of instruction and learning processes. Efforts will be made to accommodate suggestions and resolve concerns. Changes may be negotiated provided that they do not compromise the core elements of the goals, and objectives of the course.

You are expected to complete the assigned readings and post weekly reflections on Blackboard prior to class and hand in written assignments on time. If you are unable to attend class, please notify the instructor AND another person attending class in advance so that the appropriate course adjustments can be made. In the event that you must miss class, **it is your responsibility** to make arrangements with your colleagues to review the session.

All academic work must meet the standards contained in the "Cornell University Code of Academic Integrity." Students are responsible for informing themselves about those standards before completing any academic work.

Academic Integrity

Each student in this course is expected to abide by the Cornell University Code of Academic Integrity. Any work submitted by a student in this course for academic credit will be the student's own work.

Accommodations for students with disabilities

In compliance with the Cornell University policy and equal access laws, appropriate academic accommodations will be made for students with disabilities.

Except for in unusual circumstances, requests for academic accommodations are to be made during the first three weeks of the semester.

Requirements

This is a two-credit course for which you will receive a grade of S (satisfactory) or U (unsatisfactory). To complete this course satisfactorily, you must do the following:

Course activities and assignments/assessments

Weekly readings and participation in class discussion (20 points): Participation is critical to the success of this course. This course will be collaborative and involve regular self-assessment as well as peer-assessment of work. Attendance at all class sessions is expected.

Workshop on Teaching as Research (10 points): Students will help facilitate a workshop for others about "Teaching as Research" at the end of the semester as part of the May Symposium.

Drafts of Literature Review, Methods, Results, Conclusions, Discussions (25 points—5 points each)

Final project poster and presentations (45 points): There will be assignments that will ultimately all culminate in the final research project. Students will have an opportunity to practice presenting their final research project for the class. Students will also present their research three other times for three different audiences including their departments, the Center for Teaching Excellence and a broader university audience. Students will assess themselves and each other using the rubric provided.

The course syllabus may be adjusted during the semester with insights and input of participants. We may choose to alter the nature of the final assignment based on class discussion and agreement.

WHAT IS "TEACHING AS RESEARCH?"

According to the Center for the Integration of Research, Teaching and Learning

Teaching-as-Research involves the deliberate, systematic, and reflective use of research methods to develop and implement teaching practices that advance the learning experiences and outcomes of students and teachers. Participants in Teaching-as-Research apply a variety of research approaches to their teaching practice.

They outline the following steps as important in the teaching-as-research process. Students will reflect upon these steps throughout the course as they engage in the creation of their "teaching as research" projects:

1. Learning foundational knowledge. (What is known about the teaching practice? What research has been conducted?)
2. Creating objectives for student learning. (What do we want students to learn?)
3. Developing hypotheses and objectives for practices to achieve the learning objectives. (How can we help students succeed with the learning objectives? What do we observe throughout the process?)
4. Defining measures of success. (What qualitative and quantitative evidence will we need to determine whether students have achieved learning objectives?)
5. Developing and implementing teaching practices within a research design. (What will we do in and out of the classroom to enable students to achieve learning objectives?)
6. Collecting and analyzing data. (How will we collect and analyze information to determine what students have learned?)
7. Reflecting, evaluating, and iterating. (How will we use what we have learned to improve our teaching?)

(Adapted from the Center for the Integration of Research, Teaching and Learning—CIRTL's "College Classroom Course: A Guidebook" available at www.cirtl.net/files/Guidebook_College ClassroomCourse_0.pdf)

Weekly Schedule, Assignments and Readings: This is a Draft and will be Revised and Adapted to Best Meet your Needs

Week	What is due	What we will cover in class
Week 1 January 27	Bring a copy of what you have completed so far. If you are just starting this project bring ideas for your project. Start reading through the Bishop-Clark, C. and Dietz-Uhler, B (also known as "SoTL book").	Pre-test What is research on teaching? What is the Scholarship of Teaching and Learning (SoTL)? What is Teaching as Research (setting measurable objectives, creating and testing hypotheses and qualitative examination of the culture using a variety of research methods, critical examination of evidence and drawing conclusions and informing future practice)? How to get started. Discussion of the final project—book chapter versus journal article?

Week 2 Feb 3	Find an article on the Scholarship of Teaching and Learning within your discipline. Look at the resources provided. Bring a copy of the article to class and a one-page synopsis and be prepared to discuss it and post on Blackboard discussion board. Read 1–4 in Bishop-Clark and Dietz-Uhler—use and complete table on p. 19 (table 3.1 Steps in SoTL study, and pay particular attention to examples on pp 22, 24, 25). Also read Huber *et al.* on Blackboard to inform the studies that you find. Look at the Preface (particularly the section "The Project" in Learning Limits—link on blackboard.	Discussion of SoTL in the disciplines. Critiquing SoTL resources and databases. Library sheet. Discussion of annotated bibliography and literature review. Planning to lead discussions in areas of methodological expertise.
Week 3 Feb 10	Take IRB course online and read the material on the IRB website. IRB COURSE COMPLETED. Read Ch 5 in SoTL text. Scan through CIRTL "College Classroom Course: A Guidebook" (on CIRTL—be sure to register there) to define and critique "Teaching as Research."	IRB and ethics in research (make sure you have completed the online course). Designing assessment part I: Assessment objectives.
Week 4 Feb 17 No class	February break.	
Week 5 Feb 24	Bring in a qualitative (preferably teacher/action research project example to share)—you may also share your own if you have results. Chapter 6 and 7 in SoTL text (focus on "qualitative parts").	Qualitative research: Conducting to inform teaching and learning. Those with qualitative backgrounds and expertise will facilitate discussion.
Week 6 March 3	Guest Facilitator: Survey Development and quantitative research. Read Chs 6 and 7 in SoTL book (focusing on quantitative methods—use table on p. 55). Bring in a quantitative article on research in teaching to share (or you can share your own research if you have results). ANNOTATED BIBLIOGRAPHY DUE emailed to me at kw299.	Mini-Teaching as Research "Experiment". Quantitative research: Conducting to inform teaching and learning. Those with quantitative expertise will facilitate discussion. Design and implement a questionnaire strategy to determine if this class has been successful. Share annotated bibliography observations.

Week 7: March 10	Read on Blackboard: Angelo article on Classroom Assessment Techniques.	How can we use classroom assessment techniques to inform research in teaching? Formative/Summative assessment. Assessment objectives. Building upon what was covered in 6015
Week 8 March 17	Bring in a "model" methods section from one of your articles used in your literature review that is similar to your project design. LITERATURE REVIEW DRAFT DUE.	Essential components of methodology sections in research on teaching.
Week 9 March 24	Interpreting evidence and reporting. METHODS SECTION DUE.	Analysis, Results, Writing Results in research on teaching.
March 31	No class—Spring break.	
Week 10 April 7	Bring in "model" article from your literature review with an analysis of the conclusions/discussions/implications.	Writing conclusions/discussions.
Week 11 April 14	RESULTS SECTION DUE (If you need more time to collect end-of-term data, gather what you have so far and submit an analytic memo of findings so far).	Putting everything together. Writing compelling research papers. APA style.
Week 12 April 21	Presenting research (readings on blackboard). DRAFT OF COMPLETE PROJECT DUE. Read Ch 8 in SoTL text. PLAN FOR DEPARTMENT WORKSHOP ON RESEARCH IN TEACHING.	How to present research—different strategies/audiences. Improving public speaking.
Week 13 April 28	Sharing/presenting final projects—post projects on blackboard and read ones that are being presented today and provide feedback.	Be prepared to use rubric to provide feedback to presenters based on written and presented projects.
Week 14 May 5	Sharing/presenting final projects—post projects on blackboard and read ones that are being presented today and provide feedback. PEER REVIEW FEEDBACK ON PARTNER'S POSTER DUE. FINAL COMPLETED POSTER DUE FOR PRINTING!	Be prepared to use rubric to provide feedback to presenters based on written and presented projects.

Week 15	FINAL TEACHING AS	Poster Presentation.
May 16	RESEARCH SYMPOSIUM.	Panel discussion.
NOTE:		Guest speakers.
This is		Plan on all day attendance.
a Friday		
By May 16	CRITICAL SELF-ASSESSMENT DUE. FINAL WRITTEN PROJECT DUE.	Post-test and course evaluations.

SPECIFIC GUIDELINES FOR YOUR FINAL PAPER, PRESENTATIONS, POSTER AND FINAL REPORT

Research on Teaching in Higher Education Assignment Guidelines

Conducting and presenting your research

Participants will have the spring semester to conduct, analyze, and present the findings from their research projects on undergraduate teaching and learning. Participants will enroll in the spring Research on Teaching course that will provide further guidance and feedback on the design and implementation of research proposals and presentations. Building on the lessons learned about teaching and teaching as research from the fall semester, participants will conduct and finish the research paper by including their findings and analyses. These findings will be presented in at least three venues; the home department, as part of the spring CTE Teaching Excellence series and in the end-of-the-year *Graduate Teaching Symposium*, hosted by the Center for Teaching Excellence (via a poster presentation). The spring course will provide a forum for GRTF participants to share their research and receive feedback on posters, final papers, presentations and reports. The goals of this stage of the assignment are to: (1) finalize the research design and conduct the research you propose; (2) share your work with the Cornell community (i.e., GRTF colleagues, department, CTE, and final SoTL Symposium) and broader academic community; and (3) provide you with tangible representations (i.e., poster, final paper and report) of your work that you may turn into a publication and/or present at an academic conference.

Research implementation

- Research is conducted according to the proposed research plan (or, if research design/methods changed, a rational for the changes is provided in the final research paper).

- Research meets IRB standards of ethical research and upholds IRB rules and guidelines.

Final Research Paper

- Twenty pages (including all of the sections described in the rubric and include your IRB application).
- Conveys engagement with the current literature on the topic.
- Contributes to knowledge of undergraduate teaching and learning.
- Applies theories/methods in a relevant and meaningful way to the analysis.
- Includes your findings and an analysis thereof.
- Includes a critical reflection of the research process (What about this process was most surprising? Difficult? Enlightening? Briefly discuss the research experience and what you found to be the most important aspects of the research, both in terms of the knowledge gained and the process itself).
- Develops content logically and systematically.
- Writes in a style that is easy to read.
- Communicates ideas clearly.
- Uses adequate resources.
- Cites them properly using APA style.
- Uses grammar, spelling, punctuation correctly.

References

Abu-Lughod, L. (1991). Writing against culture. In R. Fox (ed.) *Recapturing Anthropology: Working in the present*, pp. 137–62. Santa Fe, NM: School of American Research.

Abu-Lughod, L. (2002). Do Muslim Women Really Need Saving? Anthropological reflections on cultural relativism and its others. *American Anthropologist, 104*(3), 783–90.

Altrichter, H., Feldman, A., Posch, P. and Somekh, B. (2006). *Teachers Investigate Their Work: An introduction to action research across the professions* (second edn). London: Routledge.

Angelo, T. A. and Cross, K. P. (1993). *Classroom Assessment Techniques: A handbook for college teachers* (second edn). San Francisco, CA: Jossey-Bass Publishers.

Apple, M. W. and Beane, J. A. (2007). *Democratic Schools: Lessons in powerful education* (second edn). Portsmouth, NH: Heinemann.

Bailey, C. P., Minderhout, V. and Loertscher, J. (2012). Learning Transferable Skills in Large Lecture Halls: Implementing a Pogil approach in biochemistry. *Biochemistry and Molecular Biology Education, 40*, 1–7.

Baker, T. I. (1994). *Doing Social Research* (second edn). New York: McGraw-Hill.

Bennett, C. M. and Baird, A. A. (2006). Anatomical Changes in the Emerging Adult Brain: A voxel-based morphometry study. *Human Brain Mapping, 27*(9), 766–77.

Bernard, H. R. and Ryan, G. W. (2010). *Analyzing Qualitative Data: Systematic approaches*. Los Angeles, CA: Sage.

Boal, A. (1979). *Theater of the Oppressed*. New York: Urizen Books.

Bogdan, R. C. and Biklen, S. K. (2006). *Qualitative Research in Education: An introduction to theory and methods*. Boston, MA: Allyn and Bacon.

Boyer, E. (1990). *Scholarship Reconsidered: Priorities of the professoriate*. Stanford, CA: Carnegie Foundation.

Bray, A. (1994). Homosexuality and the Signs of Male Friendship in Elizabethan England. In J. Goldberg (ed.), *Queering the Renaissance*. Durham, NC: Duke University Press.

Bromley, D. B. (1986). *The Case-study Method in Psychology and Related Disciplines*. Chichester: Wiley.

Bronowski, J. (1973). *The Ascent of Man* (first American edn). Boston, MA: Little Brown.

Brookfield, S. (1998) Against Naïve Romanticism: From celebration to the critical analysis of experience. *Studies in Continuing Education, 20*(2).

Bykerk-Kauffman, A. (1995). Using Cooperative Learning in College Geology Classes. *Journal of Geoscience Education, 43,* 306–16.

Center for the Integration of Research, Teaching and Learning (CIRTL) (2005) *College Classroom Course: A guidebook*. Retrieved from www.cirtl.net/files/Guidebook_CollegeClassroomCourse_0.pdf. Accessed on January 5, 2014.

Chism, N. (1994). How Faculty Develop Teaching Expertise. In M. Weimer (ed.) *Faculty as Teachers Taking Stock of What We Know*. State College, PA: Pennsylvania State University Press.

Cohen, L., Manion, L. and Morrison, K. (2000). *Research Methods in Education* (fifth edn). New York: RoutledgeFalmer.

Dartmouth College (2006, February 6). Brain Changes Significantly After Age 18, Says Dartmouth Research. *ScienceDaily*. Retrieved from www.sciencedaily.com/releases/2006/02/060206105011.htm. Accessed on June 17, 2014.

Denzin, N. (2006). *Sociological Methods: A sourcebook* (fifth edn). Piscataway, NJ: Aldine Transaction.

Dewey, J. (1933). *How We Think: A restatement of the relation of reflective thinking to the educative process*. Boston, MA: D. C. Heath and Co.

Drutman, L. (2012). The Changing Complexity of Congressional Speech. Retrieved from http://sunlightfoundation.com/blog/2012/05/21/congressional-speech/. Accessed on June 17, 2014.

Escobar, A. (1992). Imagining a Post-development Era? Critical thought, development and social movements. *Social Text, 31/32,* 20–56.

Flannery, K. (1998). Performance and the Limits of Writing. *The Journal of Teaching Writing, 16*(1).

Freire, P. (2000). *Pedagogy of the Oppressed* (30th anniversary edn). New York: Continuum.

Galea, S. (2012). Reflecting Reflective Practice. *Educational Philosophy and Theory, 44*(3), 245–58.

Gay, L., Mills, G. and Airasian. P. (2006). *Education Research: Competencies for analysis and application* (eighth edn). New York: Prentice Hall.

Giedd, J. (2008). The Teen Brain: Insights from neuroimaging. *Journal of Adolescent Health, 42,* 325–43.

Giedd, J. N., Blumenthal, J., Jeffries, N. O., Castellanos, F. X., Liu, H., Zijdenbos, A., Paus, T., Evans, A. and Rapoport, J. (1999). Brain Development during Childhood and Adolescence: A longitudinal MRI study. *Nature Neuroscience, 10,* 861–3.

Glasser, B. (2008, January 1). Grounded Theory Institute. In *The Grounded Theory Methodology of Barney G. Glaser, Ph.D.* Retrieved from www.groundedtheory.com/what-is-gt.aspx. Accessed on February 25, 2014.

Green, A. (2011). *Becoming a Reflective English Teacher*. Maidenhead: Open University Press, McGraw-Hill.

Gross, R. (1978). *Rehearsal as an Interpretive Technique*. Washington, DC: US Department of Health, Education & Welfare National Institute of Education.

Guion, L., Diehl, D. and McDonald, D. (2011). Triangulation: Establishing the validity of qualitative studies. *Department of Family, Youth and Community Sciences, Florida Cooperative Extension Service, Institute of Food and Agricultural Sciences, University of Florida*, *1*, 1–3.

Haraway, D. (1988). Situated Knowledges: The science question in feminism and the privilege of partial perspective. *Feminist Studies*, *14*(3), 575–99.

Howell, S. and Shryock, A. (2003). Cracking Down on Diaspora: Arab Detroit and America's "War on Terror". *Anthropological Quarterly*, *76*(3), 443–62. George Washington University Institute for Ethnographic Research. Retrieved on June 17, 2014, from Project MUSE database.

Huber, M. T. and Morreale, S. (2002, April 4). Situating the Scholarship of Teaching and Learning: A cross-disciplinary conversation. In *Disciplinary Styles in the Scholarship of Teaching and Learning: Exploring common ground*. Carnegie Foundation for the Advancement of Teaching. Retrieved from www.carnegiefoundation.org/elibrary/situating-scholarship-teaching-and-learning-cross-disciplinary-conversation-disciplinary-st. Accessed on June 10, 2014.

Hutchings, P., Huber, M. T. and Ciccone, A. (2011). *The Scholarship of Teaching and Learning Reconsidered: Institutional integration and impact*. San Francisco, CA: Jossey-Bass.

Jensen, R. (2010). The (Perceived) Returns to Education and the Demand for Schooling. *The Quarterly Journal of Economics*, *125*(2), 515–48. doi:10.1162/qjec.2010.125.2.515.

Johnson, R. B., Onwuegbuzie, A. J. and Turner, L. A. (2007). Toward a Definition of Mixed Methods Research. *Journal of Mixed Methods Research*, *1*(2), 112–33.

Kim, Y. (2011) The Pilot Study in Qualitative Inquiry: Identifying issues and learning lessons for culturally competent research. *Qualitative Social Work*, *10*, 190–206 (first published on May 18, 2010. doi:10.1177/1473325010362001).

Krathwohl, D. R. (2002). A Revision Of Bloom's Taxonomy: An overview. *Theory Into Practice*, *41*(4), 212–18.

Kuh, G. (2008). *High-impact Educational Practices: What they are, who has access to them, and why they matter*. Association of American Colleges and Universities. Retrieved from www.aacu.org/leap/hip.cfm. Accessed on February 24, 2014.

Kumagai, A. K., White, C. B., Ross, P. T., Perlman, R. L. and Fantone, J. C. (2008). The Impact of Facilitation of Small-group Discussions of Psychosocial Topics in Medicine on Faculty Growth and Development. *Academic Medicine*, *83*(10), 976–81.

Lattuca, L. R. (2001). *Creating Interdisciplinarity: Interdisciplinary research and teaching among college and university faculty*. Nashville, TN: Vanderbilt University Press.

Loewen, J. W. (1995). *Lies My Teacher Told Me: Everything your American history textbook got wrong*. New York: New Press.

Lyons, N. (2010). *Handbook of Reflection and Reflective Inquiry*. New York: Springer.

Macdonald, R. H. and Korinek, L. (1995). Cooperative-learning Activities in Large Entry-level Geology Courses. *Journal of Geoscience Education, 43*, 341–5.

McIntosh, P. (1997). *White Privilege: Unpacking the invisible knapsack*. Wellesley, MA: Wellesley College Center for Research on Women.

Marzano, R. (2009). Setting the Record Straight on "High Yield" Strategies. *Phi Delta Kappan, 91*(1), 30–7.

Marzano, R. J., Pickering, D. and Pollock, J. E. (2001). *Classroom Instruction That Works: Research-based strategies for increasing student achievement*. Alexandria, VA: Association for Supervision and Curriculum Development.

Mathison, S. (1988). Why Triangulate? *Educational Researcher, 17*(2), 13.

Maykut, P. S. and Morehouse, R. (1994). *Beginning Qualitative Research: A philosophic and practical guide*. London: Falmer Press.

Maykut, P. S. and Morehouse, R. (2002). *Beginning Qualitative Research: A philosophic and practical guide*. London: Falmer Press.

Mies, M. (1983). Towards a Methodolology for Feminist Research. In G. Bowles and R. D. Klein (eds), *Theories for Women's Studies* (pp.117–39). London: Routledge & Kegan Paul.

Miller, J. K., Repinski, S. L., Hayes, K. N., Bliss, F. A. and Trexler, C. J. (2011). Designing Graduate-level Plant Breeding Curriculum: A Delphi study of private sector stakeholder opinions. *Natural Sciences Education, 40*(1), 82–90.

Miner, H. (1956). Body Ritual Among the Nacirema. American Anthropological Association. *American Anthropologist, 58*(3). Retrieved from www.msu.edu/~jdowell/miner.html. Accessed on June 16, 2014.

Myers, T., Monypenny, R. and Trevathan, J. (2012). Overcoming the Glassy-eyed Nod: An application of process-oriented guided inquiry learning techniques in Information Technology. *Journal of Learning Design, 5*(1), 12–22.

O'Donoghue, T. and Punch K. (2003). *Qualitative Educational Research in Action: Doing and reflecting*. London: RoutledgeFalmer.

Patton, M. Q. (2002). *Qualitative Research and Evaluation Methods*. Thousand Oaks, CA: Sage Publications.

Polit, D. F., Beck, C. T. and Hungler, B. P. (2001). *Essentials of Nursing Research: Methods, appraisal and utilization* (fifth edn). Philadelphia, PA: Lippincott, Williams & Wilkins.

Powell, K. (2006). Neurodevelopment: How does the teenage brain work? *Nature, 442*, 865–7.

Prather, E. E., Slater, T. F., Bailey, J. M., Adams, J. P., Dostal, J. A. and Jones, L. V. (2004). Research on a Lecture–Tutorial Approach to Teaching Introductory Astronomy for Non-science Majors. *Astronomy Education Review*, *3*(2), 122.

Purcell, D. (2013). Teaching, and Reflective Practice: Using writing to improve. *Teaching Sociology*, *41*(1), 5–19.

Ray, B. and Bhaskaran, R. (2013). Integrating Simulation Into the Engineering Curriculum: A case study. *International Journal of Mechanical Engineering Education*, *41*(3), 269–80.

Rodrigues, S. (2010). *Using Analytical Frameworks for Classroom Research: Collecting data and analysing narrative*. London: Routledge.

Rosaldo, R. (1989). Imperialist Nostalgia. *Representations*, *26*, 107–22.

Schnabel, L. V., Maza, P. S., Williams, K. M., Irby, N. L., McDaniel, C. M. and Collins, B. G. (2013). Use of a Formal Assessment Instrument for Evaluation of Veterinary Student Surgical Skills. *Veterinary Surgery*, *42*, 488–96. doi: 10.1111/j.1532–950X.2013.12006.

Schön, D. A. (1983). *The Reflective Practitioner: How professionals think in action*. New York: Basic Books.

Sharma, M. D. and McShane, K. (2008). A Methodological Framework for Understanding and Describing Discipline-based Scholarship of Teaching in Higher Education Through Design-based Research. *Higher Education Research and Development*, *27*(3), 257–70.

Sharma, M. D., Millar, R. and Seth, S. (1999). Workshop Tutorials: Accommodating student centred learning in large first year university physics classes. *International Journal of Science Education*, *21*, 839–53.

Sharma, M. D., Mills, D., Mendez, A. and Pollard, J. (eds) (2005). *Learning Outcomes and Curriculum Development in Physics: A report on tertiary physics teaching and learning in Australia*. Victoria, Australia: School of Physics, Monash University.

Smith, D. E. (1987). *The Everyday World as Problematic: A feminist sociology*. Boston, MA: Northeastern University Press.

Sommers, N. I. (1980). Revision Strategies of Student Writers and Experienced Writers. *College Composition and Communication*, *31*, 378–87.

Sowell, E. R., Thompson, P. M., Holmes, C. J., Jernigan, T. L. and Toga, A. W. (1999). In Vivo Evidence for Post-adolescent Brain Maturation in Frontal and Striatal Regions. *Natural Neuroscience*, *2*, 859–61.

Stevens, E. (1988). *Tinkering with Teaching*. Review of Higher Education, *2*(1), 63–78.

Van Note Chism, N., Lees, N. D. and Evenbeck, S. (2002). Faculty Development for Teaching Innovation. *Liberal Education*, *88*(3), 34–41. Retrieved from http://search.proquest.com/docview/209811852?accountid=10267. Accessed on January 14, 2014.

van Teijlingen, E. and Hundley, V. (2002). The Importance of Pilot Studies. *Nursing Standard*, *16*(40), 33–6.

Watson, R., Atkinson, I. and Rose, K. (2007) Pilot Studies: To publish or not? *Journal of Clinical Nursing*, *16*(4), 619–20.

Whiting, E., Wear, D., Aultman, J. M. and Zupp, L. (2012). Teaching Softly in Hard Environments: Meanings of small-group reflective teaching to clinical faculty. *Journal of Learning Through the Arts*, *8*(1), 15.

Williams, K. M. (1998). *Learning Limits: College women, drugs, and relationships*. Westport, CT: Bergin & Garvey.

Yin, R. K. (2004, January 20). Case Study Methods. *Complementary Methods for Research in Education*. American Educational Research Association. Retrieved from www.cosmoscorp.com/Docs/AERAdraft.pdf. Accessed on January 18, 2014.

Yin, R. K. (2011). *Applications of Case Study Research* (third edn). Thousand Oaks, CA: Sage Publications.

Zwozdiak-Myers, P. (2010). *An Analysis of the Concept Reflective Practice and An Investigation Into the Development of Student Teachers' Reflective Practice Within the Context of Action Research*. Retrieved from http://search.proquest.com/docview/899747614?accountid=10267. (899747614). Accessed on June 14, 2014.

Zwozdiak-Myers, P. (2011). Reflective Practice for Professional Development. In A. Green (ed.), *Becoming a Reflective English Teacher*. Maidenhead: Open University Press.

Zuber-Skerritt, O. (1993). Action Research for Change and Development. *Journal of International Development*, *5*(5), 561–62.

Contributors

Joel Anderson is a PhD candidate in the Medieval Studies Program at Cornell University. After his graduation from Bates College, he studied at the University of Oslo as a Fulbright grantee and then earned an MA in Medieval Icelandic Studies from the University of Iceland. A religious and cultural historian, Joel's research focuses principally on the global networks and administrative apparatuses of the later medieval Church. At Cornell, he has been privileged to teach first-year writing seminars on topics such as heresy, sanctity, and the history of reading. His experiences in his history of reading seminars formed the basis for his project, "Teaching Medieval Books in a Digital Age," which he completed as a 2012–13 Graduate Research and Teaching Fellow and Teagle Fellow at the Center for Teaching Excellence.

Adem Birson is a PhD candidate/teaching assistant at the Cornell University Department of Music. His research is focused on theory and analysis of eighteenth-century European Classical music, with a secondary specialization on the relationship between musical taste and national identity in the modern Republic of Turkey. As a teacher, Adem tries to incorporate music making in the theory classroom, and is himself an active performer and composer of music for the piano, violin and the Middle Eastern lute ('ud). His classroom research project entitled "Engaging with Mozart: Using composition to teach music theory" was conducted when he was a Graduate Research in Teaching Fellow.

Kevin Carrico is a postdoctoral fellow at Stanford University's Center for East Asian Studies, having completed his PhD in Anthropology at Cornell University in 2013. Kevin was a GRTF fellow from 2011 to 2012, and his project for this fellowship is entitled "The Pedagogy of Controversy: Teaching the Cultural Revolution." His full project is published in the June 2014 issue of the journal *Learning and Teaching in the Social Sciences*.

Shoshanna Cole is a lecturer in the Department of Physics and Astronomy at Ithaca College, and a PhD Candidate in the Department of Astronomy at Cornell University. Her thesis research examines the geologic history of the Columbia Hills of Mars using data from the Mars Exploration Rover Spirit. She is a Graduate Research and Teaching Fellow in Cornell University's Center for Teaching Excellence (2011–12) and a NASA Harriett G. Jenkins Predoctoral Fellow (2010–13).

Adhaar Noor Desai is a PhD candidate in the Department of English at Cornell University. He was a Graduate Research in Teaching Fellow 2012–13. He has taught writing seminars on Shakespeare, interactive media, and the literature of the scientific revolution, and has served as a teaching assistant for a survey course of English literature. He was a Graduate Research and Teaching Fellow at Cornell's Center for Teaching Excellence from 2012–13, during which he conducted a research project concerned with student perspectives on close reading entitled " 'I See it as a Crime Scene': Taking close reading outside the literature classroom."

Lorenzo Fabbri, PhD is an Assistant Professor of French and Italian at the University of Minnesota, Twin Cities. He has published in critical theory and film studies, with his work appearing in *Diacritics*, *California Italian Studies Journal*, *Res Publica*, *Radical Philosophy Review*, *Journal of Italian Cinema and Media Studies*, and *Critical Inquiry*. His first book, *The Domestication of Derrida. Rorty, Pragmatism and Deconstruction*, was released by Continuum in 2008. His classroom research project is entitled "Maximum Security, Zero Technology: Teaching in a maximum security prison."

Carolyn Fisher is finishing her doctorate in the Department of Molecular Biology and Genetics, field of Biochemistry, Molecular, and Cell Biology. She was a Graduate Research in Teaching Fellow and Teagle fellow with the Center for Teaching Excellence at Cornell University from 2012–13. Other fellowships include: NSF Graduate Research Fellowship 2010–13, Graduate Teaching Assistant Fellowship 2013–14. The title of her project was "Investigating the Differential Learning Experiences for Students in an Auto-tutorial and Lecture-based Biochemistry."

John Foo is a doctoral student in the Biomedical Engineering program at Cornell University. He was a Teagle Fellow in 2012–13 academic year and a Graduate Teaching Assistant Fellow for the Center for Teaching Excellence from 2012–14. His project examined the impact of the "think-pair-share" pedagogical strategy on a biomedical engineering classroom. The title of his project is "Does Think-Pair-Share Help Students Retain Information Better?"

220

Diana Garvin is a teaching assistant and doctoral candidate in the Department of Romance Studies at Cornell University. She was a Graduate Research and Teaching Fellow during the 2012–13 academic year and her project was entitled "Communicative Blogging for Student Engagement and Blended Literacy." She is also an Oxford Cherwell Scholar. Her dissertation is entitled "All-Consuming: Food, women, and power in Fascist Italy."

Inga Gruß is a PhD candidate in the Department of Anthropology at Cornell University. In 2012–13 she participated in the graduate research and fellowship program. Her teaching as research project focused on assessing students' progress mostly through their writing and is entitled "Writing My Opinion or Masking it as Fact? Learning/teaching (the implications of) positionality." She is currently completing her dissertation that is based on fieldwork with migrants from Myanmar in Thailand.

Jared Hale is a fifth-year doctoral student and teaching assistant in the department of Molecular Biology and Genetics at Cornell University. In addition to being a fellow for the Graduate Research and Teaching Fellowship and a Teagle Fellow he is also a Graduate Teaching Assistant Fellow, where he aides other instructors in improving their teaching methods and their students' learning. His project is entitled "All or Nothing? The impact of optional problem-solving sessions on a genetics course."

Khuram Hussain, PhD is an Assistant Professor in the Education Department at Hobart and William Smith Colleges in Geneva, NY. He teaches a variety of history of education courses with a focus on Civil Rights education and equity and access. His scholarly interests include Black Press History, Religion and Schooling and Culturally relevant pedagogies. He co-authored and facilitated the classroom research project entitled "Voice and Choice: Can we create truly democratic classrooms?"

Emily Pollina, PhD is a Visiting Assistant Professor at North Central College in Naperville, Illinois in the Department of Botany and Ecology. She teaches in the area of ecology, botany, plant physiology and biology. She studies the effects of elevated CO_2 and ozone on the spread and severity of an insect-transmitted plant virus. Her classroom research project is called "Explicit Instruction in Primary Literature to Enhance Student Writing and Scientific Understanding."

Baidura Ray, PhD is a Senior Technical Professional in Advanced Computational Sciences with Halliburton doing research and development. A published version of his classroom research project, co-authored with Rajesh Bhaskaran entitled "Integrating Simulation into the Engineering Curriculum: A case study" is published in the July 2013 *International Journal of Mechanical Engineering Education*, *41*(3), 269–80. He was a Graduate Research in Teaching Fellow during the 2011–12 academic year.

Luisa Rosas is a doctoral candidate in French in the Romance Studies Department at Cornell University. Her dissertation, entitled "Genealogies of Cruelty: Alternative theaters in an Early Modern World", looks at the intersection of travel narratives and Artaudian drama in the sixteenth and seventeenth centuries. Her Graduate Research and Teaching Fellowship project focused on the work of Brazilian dramatist Augusto Boal, and by her collaboration with Inga Gruß, she tried to see how through the use of drama students might better engage in discussions on race and power. Her research project is entitled "Exploring the Theater of the Oppressed in the Ivy League."

Jennifer Row, PhD is an Assistant Professor of French at Boston University. Her research focuses on seventeenth-century French and English literature with a special interest in queer theory, theater studies, critical theory, and rhetoric. She is completing a book manuscript entitled *Ephemeral Velocity*: *Inarticulate Erotics on the Early Modern Stage,* exploring the ways that early modern temporal norms govern the field of sexual expression in the theater. Her classroom research project was entitled *Risk, Rehearsal, Reading and Writing: Theater techniques in the classroom.* She teaches courses in seventeenth-century French studies, dramatic literature, sexuality/queer studies (historiography and the archive), and critical theory.

Lauren Schnabel, DVM, PhD, Diplomate American College of Veterinary Surgeons, is a tenure track Assistant Professor of Equine Orthopedic Surgery at North Carolina State University. She spends 25 percent of her time in the hospital performing surgery and training residents, interns, and students. The remaining 75 percent of her time is spent in her NIH-funded research laboratory where she investigates regenerative therapies for the treatment of equine musculoskeletal disorders. In particular, Dr. Schnabel is focused on understanding the immunologic and immunomodulatory properties of both mesenchymal and induced pluripotent stem cells. In the laboratory, she mentors and teaches undergraduate, veterinary and graduate students. Her classroom research project is published in *Veterinary Surgery* and is called "Use of a Formal Assessment Instrument for Evaluation of Veterinary Student Surgical Skills."

Index